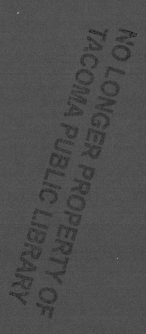

Floyd Cardoz
FLAVORWALLA

Floyd Cardoz
FLAVORWALLA

Big Flavor. Bold Spices.
A New Way to Cook the Foods You Love.

with **MARAH STETS**
PHOTOGRAPHS BY LAUREN VOLO

ARTISAN
NEW YORK

Library of Congress Cataloging-in-Publication Data

Cardoz, Floyd, author.
  Floyd Cardoz : flavorwalla / Floyd Cardoz with Marah Stets.
  pages cm
  Includes bibliographical references and index.
  ISBN 978-1-57965-621-8
  1. Cooking (Spices) 2. Cooking, American. I. Stets, Marah. II. Title. III.
Title: Flavorwalla.
  TX819.A1C36 2016
  641.6'383—dc23   2015034240

Design by **Michelle Ishay-Cohen**

Artisan books are available at special discounts when purchased in bulk for
premiums and sales promotions as well as for fund-raising or educational
use. Special editions or book excerpts also can be created to specification. For
details, contact the Special Sales Director at the address below, or send an
e-mail to specialmarkets@workman.com.

Published by Artisan
A division of Workman Publishing Company, Inc.
225 Varick Street
New York, NY 10014-4381
artisanbooks.com
Published simultaneously in Canada by Thomas Allen & Son, Limited

Printed in Malaysia

First printing, March 2016

10 9 8 7 6 5 4 3 2 1

This book is dedicated to my mother, Beryl, and my late father, Peter, who encouraged my love for food.

Good food and good cooking are about more than how food tastes or looks on a plate; they are about how good the food makes the person cooking it and the person eating it feel.

Contents

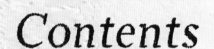

Introduction

When I immigrated to the United States from my native India in 1988, I couldn't know exactly where I'd be or what I'd be doing twenty-five years later, but I was certain that my life would involve equal measures of food and family. It has been this way since I was a kid. Back then, we caught and ate mullet and zebra fish from the Arabian Sea and held barbecues with our neighborhood friends, and our cook chased down the best produce from the *wallas,* or vendors, who walked our neighborhood peddling their delicious wares every day. These days, I catch striped bass and fluke off the New York coast with my sons, Peter and Justin, and host backyard cookouts with my wife, Barkha, as often as I can; and if I'm not in the kitchen or with my family, you'll find me working in my garden or at the farmers' market. For as long as I can remember, my days have been focused on what I can look forward to eating or cooking for my next meal. I actually get mad if I have to miss a meal! When I am working I miss at least one meal a day, so I strive to ensure that every weekend day at home includes three complete meals.

My love for food and cooking guided me on my path to becoming a chef. When I started out in the hospitality business, I didn't realize the direction it would take me in. I became a cook before the era of "celebrity chefs," back when it was not at all cool to be in the kitchen. I have worked for many years in professional kitchens in New York City, including some very good and some not-so-good Indian restaurants. My first serious break came when I was hired as a line cook at Lespinasse. There my cooking style blossomed. When I manned the stoves at the much-acclaimed and beloved Tabla, we earned a prestigious three stars from *The New York Times.* During that period, I also had the opportunity to develop a taco stand called El Verano at the Mets' Citi Field and the Washington Nationals' Nationals Park. El Verano was one of the first taquerias ever to be located in a baseball stadium. I went on to open North End Grill and then White Street, both in Lower Manhattan, where I cooked modern American food with international influences. But as the years went by and I got further away from the kind of cooking I had done at Lespinasse and, especially, Tabla, I realized that my guests at the newer restaurants craved my bold style of flavoring food, and I missed letting loose as I once had. Since then I've refocused on my spice roots, opening the Bombay Canteen in my native Bombay and Paowalla in New York City, two restaurants that celebrate the wonderful flavors of India.

Between my time at Tabla and at North End Grill, I was offered the chance to participate in season 3 of *Top Chef Masters* on Bravo, an opportunity that I almost declined because I had planned to go on a food tour of Europe. I'm sincerely glad that I ended up skipping the trip and accepting the offer to go on the show, since I eventually won the whole darn thing, including a $110,000 donation for my charity, the Young Scientist Foundation. If you've eaten in one of my restaurants or seen me on TV, you know that I cook bold, flavorful food.

My professional life is extremely important to me, but that's not what this book is about. When I cook in restaurants, I am free to use as many ingredients and components as I feel a dish needs. This book, on the other hand, is about how and what I cook when I'm eating at home with my wife and kids, entertaining our friends and family, or, especially, when preparing food for tailgating before or watching on television any Mets or New York Giants game. Furthermore, this is not a book of "Indian food." Yes, I was born and raised in India, and my culinary origins are there. But I have now lived and worked in the United States for more than twenty-five years, and I've traveled the world. My food (like my life) is a fusion of many different cuisines and cultures, with subtle Indian accents. Beyond geographic influences, though, what really marks the food I cook is the unique and complex flavor profile of every dish. Because of the way I seasoned food when I worked with him at Lespinasse, chef Gray Kunz called me Spicy Man. Another colleague christened me Spice King. I like both terms just fine, but the narrow focus on spices is a little misleading. My cooking is about all the flavors I use, not just the spices. That's why I prefer the nickname Flavorwalla. In India, a *walla* is a merchant of a specific item or someone who is knowledgeable about a trade. For instance, a *chawiwalla* is a locksmith, a *machiwalla* is a fishmonger, and a *paowalla* is a bread seller.

I'm the *flavorwalla* because I have made my mark as a creator of bold, exciting food with balanced layers of flavors and textures that play off each other. The cooking I do at home is different from what I do in my restaurants primarily in that I use fewer components. However, the layers and balance of flavor and texture are the same. I crave bold flavors in everything I cook and eat. That said, I am certainly an equal-opportunity diner, which means that I love all kinds of food and almost every ingredient. My craving for exciting food sometimes leads me far from home. When Barkha and I travel, I often plan our trips around the food—from specialty markets to carts and restaurants—that will be at or close to our destinations. We do have slightly different definitions of "close," though. This is sometimes the cause of dissension between us, as Barkha doesn't always agree that a two-hour drive to and from a meal is entirely rational.

We did agree, however, when our kids were young that one of the most frustrating aspects of parenthood was figuring out what to feed them. Like most kids, Peter and Justin preferred simple food. But to Barkha and me, making only very simple dishes with no variation was not palatable. Plus, considering how much we both love food, it was important to us that the boys learned to really like it, especially because I believe that food is not just about nourishment. It is a vehicle for connecting with your family through your culture. Food is about sharing. I like to say that breaking bread is the best way to break down borders. We knew we had to keep our sons engaged in the process rather than risk alienating them with foods they weren't yet ready to enjoy. I figured that actually asking them what they wanted to eat as opposed to making them something that we wanted was a good way to go about it. Often we would leave the main protein very plain, and then we'd expand the flavor profile of the side dishes, adding a little bit of spice and more flavor to them to introduce the kids to new tastes. Even today, when I make a roast chicken or a steak at home, I often keep that fairly straightforward and make the starch and vegetables more complex. Our boys have grown into very adventurous eaters. And even though they love Indian food now, they, like Barkha and me, don't want to have it at every meal. On the other hand, if I ever cook food that is as bland as the food they once craved, they are disappointed that they are missing the excitement of the spices and the layers of flavor.

THE KEYS TO GOOD COOKING

Over a lifetime of cooking and eating near and far, I've learned the key to creating the most exciting and flavorful food: achieving a good balance of spice, salt, acid-sour, bitter, sweet, and heat. These elements of flavor are the building blocks of every one of my dishes, from a plate of scrambled eggs to a whole leg of lamb that is marinated for a day and then roasted for many hours. When you strike the correct balance, the food will resonate beautifully with your diners. You'll know you've gotten it just right when they can't quite put their finger on what the combination of flavors is or why they feel that they must take another bite . . . and another. That's the sign of perfectly balanced elements, and it's definitely something you can learn how to do in your own kitchen. Begin by cooking the recipes in this book as they are written so that you can get a feel (and taste!) for how I do it. Then you can riff on the recipes or borrow the spice and flavor combinations I use here for other dishes you already know. In time, you'll find yourself looking for this balance in everything you cook and eat.

Following are the primary ingredients I rely on to bring each element of balance to my food. Some of these ingredients can be added in two or three different ways with really nice results. For instance, if I'm using apples, I might add apple cider and apple cider vinegar as well. Ingredients from the same source are naturally complementary, and pairing them can provide complexity without toppling the balance in a dish.

You may notice that there is no mention of a creamy or buttery element. I do use both cream and butter in moderation. Either can be part of an exciting, boldly flavored dish, but neither will bring that excitement or flavor; in fact, butter and cream can sometimes have a deadening effect on a dish. Here are the elements and ingredients that *do* enliven everything I cook.

Spice

There is spice in everything I cook, and sometimes several different spices, but I don't believe in adding spice for spice's sake. Each one is included for a reason, and each dish calls for its own particular spice profile, depending on the other ingredients or the season of the year. That said, generally speaking there are natural affinities between certain spices and main ingredients, as you will see in the following list. Although many factors go into determining how much spice to add and whether a particular dish needs every spice listed, this "affinity cheat sheet" is a good general road map to how I flavor with spices. (For more on specific spices, see "What's in My Spice Cabinet," page 21.)

- **Red meat:** coriander and black cardamom
- **Poultry:** cumin and coriander
- **Pork:** cloves, cinnamon, and mustard seeds
- **Fish:** coriander and fennel
- **Vegetables:** cumin and mustard seeds

Salt
The most obvious source of saltiness in my cooking is salt, naturally (for more information on salt, see page 24). But I also use soy sauce, dried salted fish, anchovies, and capers to add a bit of saltiness to various dishes.

Acid-Sour and Acid-Sweet
Good sources of straight acid-sour are tamarind, vinegar, tart citrus (such as lemons and limes), kokum (see page 28), and yogurt. For acid-sweet, I like mango, pineapple, tomato, apple, and sweet citrus (such as oranges). Which of these ingredients I use sometimes depends on the season. For example, I only use fresh tomatoes when they are fully ripe during the summer; during other times of the year, I use good-quality fire-roasted canned tomatoes for that crucial hit of acid.

Bitter
Ginger, citrus zest, and mustard seeds bring a bit of bitterness to food, as does the act of caramelizing ingredients, such as onions, carrots, and meat.

Sweet
My go-to sources for sweet are citrus fruits, sugar, palm sugar, maple syrup, honey, and fruit juice, as well as the natural sugars in vegetables and fruits.

Heat
My friend David once observed that I use heat as a flavor. Until he said it to me, I hadn't ever thought of my food in that way, but he is absolutely correct. Most of my cooking does contain some heat, whether it's from fresh or dried chiles, peppercorns, mustard, or horseradish. But it's never gratuitous heat (added just for "the burn"), and that's why it works. To keep the heat in a dish safely in the realm of a flavor and away from the broader, less discriminating "just hot" effect, make sure that it is complementary to, never overpowering, the other ingredients in the dish.

MY GUIDING PHILOSOPHIES

Good methodology in the kitchen goes hand in hand with good, well-balanced ingredients. And for that, I owe my grandmother so much. Every time I cook, I send her silent thanks for teaching me to embrace the habit of not wasting *anything*. I wouldn't be the chef I am today had I not learned this priceless lesson from her. Its application goes far beyond the narrow confines of making sure we eat everything on our plates and save (and use!) any leftovers. It's an all-encompassing philosophy that gets you a higher yield from your precious resources of food, time, and energy, with less effort.

Make Your Food Stretch

Although we have meat or fish at almost every meal at home, we almost never eat big amounts of it. I'll prepare a one-pound steak for four people. Four ounces is a healthy portion of meat, and it is wise not to spend too much money on expensive proteins when you don't really need that much. Instead use a more modest amount, season and prepare it well, and serve it with a variety of vegetables and starches to add texture and interest to the meal. The Flank Steak with Thai Salad (page 58) is a great example of this far more satisfying way to eat meat.

Don't Throw Anything Away!

I have an aversion to wasting anything when I cook. When I'm in the restaurant, this might mean that when we trim big rib-eye steaks, we reserve the trimmed end pieces for burger meat. In a home kitchen, where meat has usually come fully trimmed and ready to go, this kind of economy isn't usually practical, but there are many other areas where it does make sense. When shelling shrimp, for instance, reserve the shells and heads in the freezer for making stock another time. Or, when roasting a chicken, freeze the neck, trimmed skin, wing tips, and gizzards that come with it, and then, after roasting, add the carcass to the freezer and use them all to make delicious stock later. In this book, you'll learn many ways I preserve the bits and pieces from the preparation of one dish to form the base of another dish down the line.

Save Time and Energy

In my kitchen, economizing goes beyond using ingredients efficiently; it extends to using resources of time and energy to their maximum potential as well. For example, I always try to use the oven or grill for cooking multiple items at the same time. If the oven is on to cook a main dish, then I'll also make a braise or roast a couple of different kinds of vegetables. This both frees up space on the stovetop and saves energy. If I'm preparing a braise for one meal, I very often do two at once. And I put these in the center of the oven so that I can roast something else, such as vegetables or a couple of chickens, on the bottom rack. Similarly, when I'm grilling meat or fish, I also grill a bunch of vegetables, either before or after the main course is cooked.

I don't do any of this additional preparation with the intention of serving all the food at once; instead, the other dishes and components go into the fridge for a future meal. Using a single piece of equipment for a few different preparations is one of a chef's very best habits, and it is certainly applicable to a home kitchen, where time and energy are often the most precious resources you have. This is especially true when there are kids in the house.

I have talked a lot about flavor, and balance, and preserving resources. But when all is said and done, we are the most successful cooks when the food we prepare captures a lovely feeling or recollection, and perhaps even transports someone else to their own happy memory. Flavor and balance may be the most important technical factors in cooking, but great food is not only about look and taste. It's also about how good it makes the person or people cooking *and* eating it feel. I have enjoyed countless meals in my life, and I've encountered a few I did not care for. The common denominator of every one of the meals I enjoyed is that the cook who prepared it put his or her heart into it. Without love, cooking has no soul. For me, cooking is a way to bring love to the table.

That's how everyday food becomes something unexpected, and that may be the real secret of me, the flavorwalla. And, with the advice and recipes in this book, I hope to show you how to become a flavorwalla in your own kitchen. Please consider this book your guide to adding an element of bold flavor and spice to everything you cook. I don't want you to think of it as a rigid map that must be strictly followed, but I do urge you to prepare each recipe as it's written the first time you cook it so that you can experience cooking and seasoning the food the way I do. After that, treat the recipe as a jumping-off point from which you can improvise and substitute ingredients according to what you and your family love to eat. What matters more than anything is what *you* put into the dish. When the person cooking and the person eating a dish feel great, it is a great dish.

Cooking with Me
My Go-To Ingredients, Tools, and Techniques

Here is a list of the spices, aromatics, and other ingredients; tools and gadgets; and techniques and habits I use most frequently at home. Most of them will be familiar to you. The few unusual ingredients can be found in well-stocked grocery stores or ethnic supermarkets. Any that can't be easily purchased nearby can be bought online (see Sources, page 345).

SPICES

With very few exceptions (primarily turmeric, cayenne, and paprika), I always buy fresh whole spices and grind just what I'll use for a recipe or meal when I need it. Similarly, I don't generally use store-bought spice mixes, with one exception: MDH chaat masala. I always buy my spices from an ethnic store or a reputable online spice company (see Sources, page 345) where there is a lot of traffic so the inventory turns over frequently and the spices are relatively fresh. One thing you'll never see in any of my kitchens or my recipes is curry powder. The term "curry" just means a sauce with spice. Curry doesn't have to contain a lot of spice—it can be as little as one type of spice and as many as ten or more—and it definitely doesn't have to include anything called curry powder. No self-respecting cook of real Indian food will ever have anything labeled that in his or her kitchen.

Storing Spices

Store spices in tightly sealed containers and away from heat and light. Keep them for no longer than one year.

Grinding Spices

The most efficient tool for grinding spices is an electric coffee grinder. In fact, the type of blade coffee grinder I've used for years is now sold as a combination "coffee and spice" grinder; there is even a company, GIR, that is making a burr grinder for spice. Use a mortar and pestle to crack hard spices such as cinnamon sticks, dried ginger, and cardamom pods before grinding them in a spice/coffee grinder or when it's important that the spice not be ground too fine. If you don't have a mortar and pestle, place the spices in a ziplock bag, seal it, pressing all of the air out of it, put it on a hard surface, and pound the spices with a wooden rolling pin until they are crushed to the desired coarseness.

Whichever tool you use, when you are coarsely grinding more than one spice for a dish, you should grind them separately, since spices of different densities grind at different rates. You don't want your softest spices to become powder while the harder ones are still in large pieces. If you're finely grinding everything, however, it's usually acceptable to grind a combination of spices together.

I never add the ground spices to the blender when I am making a rub, paste, or sauce. If you add the dry ingredients to the blender, you'll need to add extra liquid to help keep everything moving, and more often than not, this will throw off the balance of the recipe. You also risk burning out the blender's motor. Instead, transfer the blended mixture to a bowl or other container and stir in the ground spices.

Cleaning an Electric Spice/Coffee Grinder

Grinding spices can leave behind lots of fine powder and oils, so it's a good idea to clean the grinder after each use to prevent the flavors of whatever you have ground from flavoring whatever you grind next. To clean the grinder, wipe it out with a dry paper towel, then add a handful of raw rice or several pieces of dry bread and grind it for ten to twenty seconds. Dump out the rice or bread and wipe the grinder and the inside of the lid once more with a paper towel.

Cooking Spices

The beauty and complexity of spices lie in their aromatic oils, and the best way to get at them is to heat the spices. Cooking extracts the flavor as well as the health benefits of the aromatic oils. Toasting is one way to do this, *but it is not the only way.* Spices can also be sautéed in oil—I call this "blooming."

Only toast whole spices, never ground spices. It is almost always best to toast each whole spice separately. The density of each spice is different, and some cook faster than others. Toast whole spices in a small heavy-bottomed skillet over medium heat, shaking the pan frequently, until fragrant and several shades darker, usually about 3 minutes. Remove the spice from the pan and let cool completely before grinding.

Whole spices are also often bloomed, or cooked in hot oil, at the beginning of the preparation of a dish to extract maximum flavor. Add harder, denser, larger spices, such as cinnamon sticks and cloves, to the hot oil before softer spices like cumin, because they take longer to cook.

To bloom most whole spices, heat the oil in a pan over medium heat until it shimmers. Add the spices and cook, stirring, until they are fragrant and little bubbles form around them, about 1 minute.

When blooming mustard seeds, it's important that the pan be sufficiently hot when the seeds are added so that they pop. So, first heat the dry pan until it's hot, then add the oil and heat until it is very hot and shimmery. Only then should the mustard seeds go in. They'll start popping in several seconds, and then you can add the remaining spices.

Ground spices can burn quickly if bloomed in hot oil, so I always mix ground spices with some liquid to make a paste. The paste is typically added further along in the preparation, so that the spices don't scorch.

What's in My Spice Cabinet

The following are the spices I use most often to build flavor.

Allspice

This warm spice is an important ingredient in West Indian cooking. Its flavor, as its name indicates, is like a combination of nutmeg, cinnamon, and cloves, with peppery overtones. Used frequently in baking, allspice is also good in pickling spice mixes and in marinades for fish, meat, game, and poultry.

Cardamom

Green and black cardamom are heat-generating spices (in India, their use is limited during summer). Both are integral to garam masala (see page 23). Green cardamom has a fresh, lemony flavor. Sweeter and more delicate than the black, it is versatile enough to be used in desserts. Black cardamom is strong and musky; it works very well with meats like lamb and beef.

Chaat Masala

This popular Indian spice blend has a spicy, sweet, hot, bitter, and sour flavor profile. Dried mango, dried pomegranate seeds, mint, black pepper, and cumin are the predominant ingredients. This is the only commercial spice blend I use, because unlike most spice blends, for some reason, commercial chaat masala blends tend to be pretty good. The one made by MDH is excellent.

Chiles, Dried

Ask me which of the spices in my cabinet most define my cooking, and I'll say chiles. This is not because my food is particularly spicy, although chiles can of course be a source of heat—to a greater or lesser degree, depending on what kind and how much you use. But to me, the most important attribute of chiles is their flavor. Once you start to look at them this way, and consider each variety's specific fruitiness, earthiness, depth, smoke, muskiness, *and* heat, you'll see a whole world of flavor notes open up to you. I included heat in the list of flavor notes because that is exactly how I think of it. Heat is a flavor, and it shouldn't be taken for granted or overused any more than any other flavor.

I often call for whole or broken-up dried chiles in dishes. Although I sometimes take the whole chiles out, chop them up, and stir them back into the pot before serving, usually I just leave them whole and try to make sure that I get to them before anyone else does. I leave the seeds in most chiles when I want the extra heat, but I always seed anchos and guajillos because their seeds tend to be bitter. Remove the stems from chiles before using; even with long cooking, the stems never soften into anything that anyone would want to eat.

To add an extra layer of roasted flavor, toast dried chiles in a heavy skillet over medium heat, turning once, until fragrant and, in some cases, slightly colored on both sides; this usually takes about 5 minutes.

Chile flakes are good for adding straight-up heat to a dish. You can always add more or less than what is called for in the recipe, according to your preference. I use Aleppo pepper when I want both fiery heat and smokiness.

There are dozens of dried chiles available and I've probably used most of them, but here are the ones you'd find if you looked in my kitchen spice cabinet right now:

- The ancho is a dried ripe poblano. It is fruity, almost pruney, with a slight bitterness that makes it great in sauces as well as marinades. It is best when lightly toasted.

- The chipotle is a smoked dried jalapeño with really nice complexity. I love to cut chipotles into thin strips and add them to stews and vegetables. Note that I only use dried chipotles; I never use canned chipotles in adobo.

- The guajillo chile is fruity with mild to medium heat.

- Kashmiri chiles can be hard to get in the United States, so if you ever see them, snatch some up. The Kashmir has a great color, and its flavor is of delicate heat with sweet notes.

- The New Mexico chile possesses an earthy, sweet flavor with hints of acidity, weediness, and dried cherry. The heat is often described as crisp and clear. It's a great chile to use if you want to add color to a dish.

- The pasilla de Oaxaca is a smoky, raisiny chile from Mexico that has a great complex heat and a deep smokiness. It also has a slight flavor of bacon or ham that I like.

- The peri peri chile, also called African bird chile, was introduced to India and Brazil by the Portuguese. It has a remarkable heat that seems strong at first and then dissipates, leaving only a lingering tingle and a nice flavor.

Cinnamon

A sweet, warm, aromatic spice, cinnamon is widely used in both sweet and savory cooking. It's just as good with meat and vegetables as it is with fruits or in baked goods—it's excellent in meat and game stews and curries. I never buy ground cinnamon because once ground, it loses its potency rapidly and tends to get a bit muddy tasting.

Cloves

Great with meat, this hot, sweet spice is widely used in stocks.

Coriander

Coriander is one of the spices I use most frequently, because of its versatility. Its citrusy notes work well with most proteins, and it works extremely well in marinades for grilled foods because it is soft and cooks quickly. For fresh coriander, see Cilantro (page 26).

Cumin

Common in many Middle Eastern cuisines, earthy, musty cumin works well with seafood and vegetables. When cumin is toasted and added at the end of cooking, it gives a nice complexity to the finished dish.

Fennel Seeds and Fennel Pollen

Fennel is an amazing spice that adds a distinctive sweetness to foods from fresh salads to grilled meat and fish to pork stews. Lucknow fennel, also called sweet fennel, is my favorite type. The seeds are smaller and more aromatic than ordinary fennel seeds. Lucknow fennel is what is in the colored sweetened balls that are served in most Indian restaurants, usually set out in a self-serve dish by the door. Lucknow fennel works very well with seafood. Fennel pollen is more intense than the seeds; it's a little like tasting regular or Lucknow fennel through an amplifier, so use it sparingly.

Garam Masala

Garam masala, meaning "hot spices," is a warm—and warming—spice blend that is usually added toward the end of preparing a dish to finish it. I do not like commercial garam masalas, as they have too many fillers, so I make my own in small quantities so that I will use it up fairly quickly. (I like to use Indian bay leaves for this. They come from the cassia tree, whose bark is dried to make cinnamon.) To make your own, individually toast (see page 20) the following ingredients:

10 green cardamom pods

4 black cardamom pods

6 whole cloves

Two 2-inch pieces cinnamon stick

3 whole dried mace flower arils
  (see Nutmeg and Mace, below)

3 star anise

3 Indian (cassia) bay leaves

When all the ingredients are cool, finely grind in a spice/coffee grinder. Store in an airtight container in a cool, dark place and use within 1 to 2 weeks.

Ginger, Dried

Dried ginger is more potent than fresh (see page 27), which is desirable for some dishes and especially for baking. Rather than buying preground ginger, which loses its pungency quickly, I prefer to buy packaged pieces of dried ginger and grind it as I need it. It's worth seeking out dried ginger (not the same thing as preserved or candied ginger) at Indian and Asian grocery stores; its flavor is superior and a little goes a long way.

Mustard Seeds

Mustard seeds are aromatic, slightly bitter, and hot. Whether to use yellow or brown mustard seeds depends on how they are being used. For ground spices, most times I use yellow. If using the seeds whole, I usually choose brown. I always use brown mustard seeds if I'm blooming them, because yellow mustard seeds get a very dirty color if cooked whole in oil.

Nutmeg and Mace

Nutmeg is a wonderfully warm spice with notes of cinnamon and pepper. It is the seed of a tropical evergreen tree, and mace is the lacy red aril that grows

around it. Mace's flavor is similar to that of nutmeg, albeit a little sweeter and mellower and with a deeper color. These highly aromatic spices really lose their punch once ground, so it's preferable to buy whole nutmeg and grate it on a fine grater as needed. Similarly, buy whole mace arils, or "flowers," or broken-up arils, which are called "blades," and grind them in a spice/coffee grinder as needed.

Paprika

Sweet paprika comes from dried mild red chiles and it's one of the few ground spices I keep on hand. I like it for its subtle but distinctive flavor. I only use sweet paprika or smoked sweet paprika. I never use hot paprika, because when I want heat in a dish, I rely on fresh or dried chiles instead.

Peppercorns

No spice adds more to a dish than freshly ground black pepper, which is why pepper always gets its own line in the ingredients lists in my recipes. So integral is this spice to the success of a dish that you'll never see a recipe from me that says "salt and pepper" on a single line. Black pepper is as important an ingredient as any other in a recipe. (Or in the world, for that matter; black pepper was one of the main reasons for the colonization of Southeast Asia.) Always grind black pepper fresh; so fleeting are its flavor and pungency that I don't use pepper that has been ground even twenty-four hours in advance. I want to reemphasize this: The beauty of pepper lies in its aroma too, so please do not pregrind it.

One of the reasons that peppercorns are called for in many of my recipes in the same way as other spices—i.e., "1 tablespoon black peppercorns, finely ground"—is so that no one is tempted to reach for preground pepper. In addition to grinding pepper into almost every dish I prepare, I sometimes add a spoonful of whole black peppercorns and then leave them in the cooked dish. It's a trick I learned years ago from my wife, and I love the burst of heat (tempered by cooking) and flavor that biting into a peppercorn gives you. I only use black because I find white pepper (which is black peppercorns shorn of their outer layer) flat and one-dimensional.

Salt

Generally I use fine sea salt for fish or seafood dishes and kosher salt everywhere else, including in desserts. In addition, many dishes profit enormously from a sprinkle of finishing salt just before serving, and by that I mean anything from a plate of sliced garden tomatoes to grilled steak. My favorites at home to sprinkle on many dishes to finish them are Hawaiian red salt, Maldon flaked sea salt, Amagansett salt, and Goan salt.

Star Anise

Star anise is a star-shaped pod with eight points, each of which contains a small seed. The whole spice, including pod and seeds, is used. The flavor is licorice-like and slightly bitter. Native to China, star anise comes from a small evergreen tree. It is used in Chinese five-spice powder and works well with poultry and pork. It is potent, though, so use a light hand; a little goes a long way.

Turmeric

Here is the secret to the ubiquitous yellow color of curries. That color is the reason turmeric is sometimes called poor man's saffron in India. From a health perspective, turmeric has wonderful antibiotic and antibacterial properties. From a cooking perspective, it is lovely when used judiciously, but it can be overpowering; when you use it in excess, you risk making a dish very bitter.

Warming and Cooling Spices

As critical as spices are to building flavor in a dish, flavor is actually only part of why we use them. Many spices have powerful healing properties. Some can even help the body modulate its internal temperature. Warming spices help to warm the body and are typically used more liberally during the colder months. Cooling spices are good during hotter weather. Many of them make you perspire and so help to cool your body down. This is the reason countries in hotter climates generally have spicier foods. Whether a spice is warming or cooling generally, although not strictly, determines when and how I use them. Following are the warming and cooling spices.

Warming Spices	Cooling Spices
Allspice	Chiles
Cardamom	Coriander
Cinnamon	Fennel seeds
Cloves	Peppercorns
Garam masala	
Ginger	
Mustard	
Nutmeg and mace	
Star anise	

MORE FLAVOR BUILDERS

A well-stocked spice cabinet is clearly crucial to building great flavor, but so are a few other important ingredients. Just adding a little of one of the ingredients below will enhance the complexity and tastiness of a dish.

Anchovies and Fish Sauce

These pungent, salty ingredients add what I call great "funk," a deep umami flavor that makes dishes more interesting and delicious. Fish sauce in particular lends an almost indistinguishable flavor that causes people to ask, sometimes out loud, "Wait, what is that taste?" and follow that up with, "I don't know what it is, but I love it." So do I.

Chiles, Fresh

Fresh chiles bring heat and brightness to dishes. I consider seeding fresh chiles a matter of preference, rather than a necessary step. Most of the heat is contained in the seeds of chiles, and you can control how much or little heat to add by seeding them or not. For my part, I almost always leave the seeds in the chiles. I like to thinly slice chiles crosswise so that they become little rings of bursting heat and flavor. If you want less of either element, you can seed the chiles and/or mince them so that their heat is more evenly dispersed throughout the dish. Chiles become much spicier during the summer when it's really hot, while chiles grown during cooler months are generally milder. The amount you use should therefore change as well: During the summer, use somewhat less than you would in, say, February.

- Anaheim chiles can be used interchangeably with finger hots and serranos (see below). They have some heat and will usually be hotter during the summer.

- Finger hots, or Calistans, as they are called in some places, are long, moderately hot chiles that I use when I want a little less heat and pungency.

- The serrano is one of my favorite fresh chiles. When green, which is how I use it most often, it has nice grassy flavor and a good amount of heat. When fully ripe and red, it has more sweetness, but also a lot more heat, so use it judiciously. I never remove the seeds when cooking with green serranos at home, but I do seed them when using them in my restaurants, to accommodate many people's low tolerance for heat.

- Fresh Thai chiles give a ton of heat and should be used sparingly. If less heat is desired or if cooking for guests not used to spicy food, it's better to use serranos or finger hots instead.

Cilantro, or Fresh Coriander

Cilantro, the plant from which coriander seeds come, is probably the herb I use most often. I especially love the grassy, earthy flavor of cilantro stems. If they are thin and in good shape, I always use them along with the leaves. Cilantro is usually very sandy, so it's important to thoroughly wash and dry it (see page 39).

Citrus and Citrus Zest

Limes, lemons, and oranges are probably the most common ways I add acid to a dish, one of the crucial layers of flavor in my cooking. I use a lot of citrus juice so a juicer is essential; my favorite is the electric juicer made by Breville. Always juice citrus just before you need the juice (it does not store well) and bring citrus fruits to room temperature first so that they give up their juice more easily.

As for citrus zest, I don't generally recommend using the very fine Microplane grater, as many cooks do. It is so sharp that it's dangerously easy to get right down to the bitter white pith. Plus, I find that the strands end up so fine that they just disappear into the dish they're destined for, meaning that both their texture and, to some extent, their flavor are lost. It's important to feel and taste the zest in a dish, so I always remove it using a vegetable peeler or a citrus zester, which has five holes, to pull off long strips or threads of zest. Pull the peeler or zester from tip to stem to cut off long strips, making sure to avoid the bitter white pith. In some recipes, the zest is left in large pieces, which add great texture and bite to the finished dish. In recipes where grated zest might typically be called for, use a five-holed zester or a peeler to remove the zest, and then finely mince it.

Coconut Milk

Because it's wonderful in curries, delicious in rice, and an ingredient in one special cake (see page 331), it's fair to say that I've gone through a good amount of coconut milk in my life. By far the best brand I've used is Chaokoh, so it's all I ever recommend.

Curry Leaves

Despite their name, curry leaves are not present in all curries. But they have an unmistakable aroma and flavor that work very well with spicy foods.

Garlic

Never buy prechopped or pureed garlic, or even already peeled garlic, even if it seems like a great shortcut. It's not just that prechopped or pureed aromatic ingredients like these don't taste as good as fresh, it's that they usually *add* unpleasant aromas and flavors. I don't know whether this is because of the preservatives necessary to keep their color attractive or because the ingredients aren't as ripe or of good quality when they are processed, but I do know that fresh is so far superior that it's well worth the few extra minutes to do the chopping yourself.

When smashed garlic is called for, place the whole clove on a cutting board, lay the side of the blade of a chef's knife against it, and hit the blade with your fist to crush the clove. Discard the papery skin.

Ginger, Fresh

I love fresh ginger for its pungency and flavor and the bit of warmth that it adds. Sometimes I cut it crosswise into thin coins, which mellow during cooking and provide interesting texture as well as lovely taste to the finished dish. Another nice way to use ginger is to cut it into thin strips. This technique, known as *julienne* in professional kitchens, gives you very thin strips that add both visual and textural interest. When vegetables and aromatics are cut this way, they are delicate enough to not be overwhelming but not so small that they disappear entirely. To julienne ginger, very thinly slice a peeled knob lengthwise. Stack the slices on top of each other and then gently push the stack sideways to fan the slices so that they overlap one another slightly. Slice into thin strips, slicing with the grain if the knob was small and tender or against the grain if the knob was larger and more fibrous.

As with garlic (preceding page), please don't be tempted to buy pureed ginger. It gets bitter if it sits, so it's always best to use fresh and puree or chop it yourself. Peel fresh ginger before using it.

Horseradish

I prefer to buy fresh horseradish—you can find it in the produce section of good markets year-round (not just during Passover)—and peel and grate it as I need it. Fresh horseradish has significantly more kick and flavor than the jarred prepared version (although an equal amount of the latter can be used in place of freshly grated if necessary). To store fresh horseradish, wrap it in dry paper towels and seal in a ziplock bag. It will keep in the crisper drawer for several weeks.

Kokum

This sour fruit from the west coast of India adds a nice acidity to dishes. It is sold salted and dried. Kokum is milder than tamarind and imparts a deeper red color to dishes. It works especially well in sauces and vegetable dishes. Always use wet kokum, which is moist and has a nicer flavor and is easier to use than dry kokum. Be sure to remove any pits before using.

Tamarind

With a deep, fruity, acidic flavor, tamarind is essential in the Indian kitchen. The fibrous fruit is pressed into rectangular blocks that must be softened in warm water and then pressed through a sieve to remove all the seeds and fibers. It's easiest to use when it's been turned into a paste so that it can simply be spooned out; see page 340. Jarred tamarind paste and concentrate are less flavorful, less complex, and a waste of money.

MY FAVORITE TOOLS

As for any chef, my good knives are probably my most trusted partners in the kitchen, but that's not all it takes to make great food (and telling you which knives I like won't help you decide what knives you will like). Following are other key tools that most help me determine the way my food looks and tastes.

Food Processor and Blender

I use one or both of these indispensable tools very often, and while they're generally interchangeable, there are a couple of important differences between them. The blender (I love the Breville) will make things smoother, but it often needs added liquid to keep the contents moving, which can throw off the balance of a recipe. The food processor may not give you perfectly smooth results, but it rarely requires extra liquid, so it preserves the balance of liquid.

Mandoline

Nothing beats a vegetable slicer for slicing vegetables very thinly and uniformly. My preference is a professional-quality stainless steel mandoline, even

at home, but there are lots of less-expensive versions, including the popular plastic Japanese Benriner. This gadget consists of a rectangular surface with a blade positioned about halfway down. You slice food by running it up and down the surface across the blade. One of my favorite tricks is to wear two regular tight-fitting surgical gloves on whatever hand you use to slice—then you will almost never cut yourself while slicing. Or use a guard, if included, which protects your hands and allows you to simultaneously slice several smaller ingredients, like Brussels sprouts, radishes, or garlic cloves, at a time.

Pots and Pans

A few particular types of pots and pans that I prefer are listed below, but they all have one thing in common: They are all double-core stainless steel pans. This means that the base (and sometimes the whole pan) consists of an inner layer of aluminum or copper that is sandwiched by stainless steel. These sorts of pans heat most evenly and retain heat best. Stainless steel doesn't react with spices or acids, and the pans are really easy to clean (but never in the dishwasher!). My advice is to invest in a few nice pots and pans, and then you'll be good for years. The pots and pans in our home kitchen are the ones Barkha and I bought at Macy's when we got married more than twenty years ago, and they're still in fantastic shape. I don't usually use nonstick except for making omelets. If you do use nonstick, it's definitely worth investing in All-Clad, which makes the best nonstick pans I've used.

I recommend particular pots and pans for specific reasons. For instance, I like to use wide pans when simmering soups and making sauces. Tall or narrow pans don't allow enough surface area for these to reduce properly. On the other hand, a tall stockpot is perfect when you don't want the liquid to reduce too much—when you're making stock, for instance. The most frequently used pans in my kitchen are a 12-inch chicken fryer and a rondeau, both of which have ovenproof lids. The fryer is a wide moderately shallow pan—kind of like a deep skillet—that I use for almost everything. It's good for stir-fries, soups, and curries. In some instances, you can use a shallow Dutch oven instead. A rondeau is a wide heavy-bottomed pot with straight sides, great for braises and stews. I most often use a medium-sized one, bigger than a saucepan and smaller than a stockpot. A stew pot or deep Dutch oven is an acceptable alternative, and I rarely call for a rondeau in these recipes, because most people have those alternatives instead.

My favorite pot of all is probably my pressure cooker. I think pressure cookers have gotten a bad reputation among today's home cooks (not to mention more than a few professional chefs) because of antiquated stories about older models that exploded. Today there are excellent—and extremely safe and affordable—pressure cookers available. You can toast and bloom spices, cook aromatics, and sear meat directly in a pressure cooker, unlike in a slow cooker (where if you want to brown any ingredients, they must be done in a separate

pan and then transferred to the slow cooker). A braise that takes up to 3 hours on the stovetop can be done in 25 minutes in a pressure cooker. *That's* what I call an energy-saving device: finished in a fraction of the time and only one pot to clean! And all this efficiency comes without any sacrifice of flavor. Indeed, there are certain dishes (like the mung beans on page 107) that I only prepare in the pressure cooker. It is also extremely handy for quickly preparing big batches of staples like beans and potatoes.

For best results, keep a couple of things in mind when using a pressure cooker. First, don't fill it past the "fill to" line. Usually that's about halfway, but sometimes there's a second, higher line that you can go to when cooking certain things. Read your cooker's manual to learn what the lines mean; if you don't have the manual, I advise just sticking to the no-more-than-halfway rule. Finally, when a recipe instructs you to let the pressure cooker cool, just turn off the heat and walk away for 15 to 20 minutes until the pressure has released naturally.

Silicone Spatulas

Good-quality silicone spatulas are real workhorses in my kitchen. Heat-resistant at high temperatures, they are great for making eggs, stirring sauces, scraping bowls, and just about everything. I recommend the GIR brand; these are very well made and I respect the business philosophy of the company.

TECHNIQUES AND METHODS

You'll see a few specific techniques and key terms used throughout this book. Knowing the philosophy and methodology behind them will help you better understand them and effectively implement them in your own kitchen.

Temping and Resting Meat

It's almost never a good idea to cook meat straight from the refrigerator, because when it's cold, it often won't cook evenly or will take much longer to cook properly. Therefore, it's important to let the seasoned meat (and sometimes fish) sit at room temperature—by which I mean around 70°F—to warm up a bit before cooking. Chefs call this *temping*. Most meat needs to sit for 20 to 30 minutes, or about the time it takes to heat the grill or oven. Bone-in chicken and large roasts should sit out for up to about 45 minutes, since it takes longer for them to lose their chill. Remember that if you put insufficiently temped meat into the oven, it may take longer to cook.

After roasting or grilling, it's important to rest meat, poultry, and some fish, which means to let it sit on a cooling rack at room temperature for a few minutes or so before you slice and serve it. During cooking, meat tightens up and most of its moisture moves to its outer edges. When allowed to rest, untouched and uncovered, for several minutes after cooking, the meat relaxes. This allows those juices to flow back toward the center and become evenly distributed throughout so that the meat is moist rather than dry and stringy. Don't cover the meat or fish with foil or place it on a solid surface, or it will steam, overcook, and become soggy, and any lovely seared outer crust will turn unpleasantly soft.

Cooking and Inactive Times

I give a Cooking Time for every recipe, and I often give an Inactive Time, but please don't consider these times hard-and-fast. Rather, they're meant to be a way to give you a general idea of how long the recipe will take. Cooking Time is the time it takes to transform the ingredients as called for into something you can eat or drink; whether heat is applied to ingredients or not, it's still "cooking." (Therefore, cooking times are given in recipes for dishes like salads and for cocktails.) Note that the Cooking Time does not include whatever peeling, chopping, or other preparation is listed in the ingredients.

The Inactive Time includes time for marinating, steeping, and/or temping ingredients before cooking, as well as for resting cooked meat or poultry before slicing and serving it. In the case of temping (which can take as long as 45 minutes), I count it only if nothing else is happening during the same time. For example, if a recipe instructs you to let a steak sit out at room temperature for about 30 minutes and no other preparation is done during this time, the Inactive Time will include that 30 minutes. But if you're instructed to do something else, such as make a salad, while the meat is sitting out, then I do not count the steak temping time at all, because the salad preparation time is counted as part of the Cooking Time. This prevents that time being counted twice and making the recipe appear to take longer to prepare than it does.

Chopping and Cutting Ingredients

When very coarsely chopped herbs are called for, it means no more than one or two distinct cuts with a very sharp knife. Don't ever run your knife multiple times over your herbs as if you are crushing them, or you will lose a lot of the juices (which means flavor) on the cutting board.

When I call for herbs to be stacked and thinly sliced, I mean to slice very thinly and very cleanly (again, with a sharp knife). This is *chiffonade* in chefspeak.

When a recipe says to cut an ingredient into thin strips, it means to slice it into very thin strips, like matchsticks. This is *julienne* in chefspeak.

Seasoning with Salt

When you are cooking a dish, it's most often a good idea to season with salt as you go, adding a small pinch of salt along with each new addition to the pan, rather than waiting until the end. This way, you build flavor as you cook.

There are some caveats to this. First, don't overdo it if you'll be adding salty ingredients later, such as fish sauce, anchovies, soy sauce, or even a well-seasoned stock. And be aware that adding salt to onions at the beginning of their cooking will cause them to release more liquid; sometimes this is desirable, and sometimes it is not. Once the onions have cooked a little and are softened or browned, adding salt will not affect how much liquid they give off.

As for marinades, whether I add salt depends on a couple of factors. When marinating chicken, I do add salt. When marinating beef, pork, or lamb for more than an hour or two, though, I won't add salt to the marinade; however, if marinating these meats for less than 2 hours, I do add salt (about 1½ teaspoons per serving).

Blanching and Shocking Vegetables

When you blanch vegetables in boiling, salted water and then shock them in ice water, it keeps their bright color and crisp texture intact and preserves their fresh flavor. If blanching large vegetables, cut them into equally sized pieces so they cook evenly. Don't add more than a few cups of vegetables at a time to the pot or the temperature of the water will drop too much.

To blanch and shock vegetables, bring a large pot of water to a boil. Set a large bowl of ice water next to the stove. Add a few generous pinches of salt to the boiling water, then add the vegetable and cook until its color is very bright, 1 to 4 minutes. Use a spider, skimmer, or slotted spoon to immediately transfer the vegetable to the bowl of ice water to stop the cooking.

If you are blanching more than one vegetable, bring the pot of water back to a boil and prepare another bowl of ice water. Continue as directed above.

When the vegetables are completely cool, drain them thoroughly.

Proper Cooling for Safe Storage

I often cook big batches of stews or braises for eating in the days ahead. This is a great time-saver during busy weeks—and these sorts of dishes usually taste better a day or more after they're cooked—but it's important to cool them properly. When cooling big pots of stew or braises, although you don't want to put a hot pot directly into the refrigerator, it's not a good idea to let a big pot of food sit at room temperature until it is cool enough to refrigerate. Bacteria can grow quickly and cut down on the length of time the food will keep without spoiling. So, to maintain the quality of food you will store, you want to cool it quickly and then get it into the refrigerator or freezer. To do that, prepare an ice bath: Fill a large bowl with ice and water (about half and half is good). As soon as the food is cooked, transfer it to a bowl that is smaller than the ice-bath bowl and nestle the bowl in the ice water. Let it stand, stirring frequently, until the food has cooled to room temperature. Then transfer it to a container with a tight-fitting lid and refrigerate or freeze.

CHAPTER ONE

Weeknight Meals

FLAVORFUL COOKING WHEN TIME IS SHORT

We all lead busy lives, and it's painfully easy to get so overwhelmed and distracted by the minutiae of each day that we ignore how important good food and nourishment are to our overall well-being. We forget that making time for the simple (it can be simple!) act of preparing and sharing a meal is the best antidote there is to the stressed, anxious, overbooked feeling that can dominate our day-to-day life.

Back when my sons, Peter and Justin, were younger, they had schoolwork, of course, along with baseball, football, soccer, and fencing practice, not to mention friends, after-school jobs, and church activities. My wife, Barkha, spent many years juggling the demands of their schedules with her own work and life schedule, all while being married to a chef—which meant she was flying solo on most nights. Those were not easy days for her! In addition to all of that, she also wanted very much to find time to regularly prepare meals for three hungry guys who are pretty discerning eaters, as is she. I count myself among the hungry guys she wanted to feed, because no matter how late it is, I always eat dinner at home after work. And even if I'm the one who generally plans the weekend menus in our house, on weeknights, Barkha does all the heavy lifting.

Life has become such that we all have to compromise somewhere, and food is often where that compromise happens. For some, perhaps, it's that dinner is "just food," but I suspect that you're like me, and that this is not the case in your house. Over the years, I learned that if we wanted our family to eat good, flavorful food, we had to find dishes that could be prepared with the least possible time and effort. For me, though, for whom cooking is both a profession and a passion, there's more to it. There have been days when I am free to run rampant in the kitchen at home for as long as I like. The results of those happy days spent cooking fill most of this book. But then there are days when

Barkha insists I take it easy and not spend my entire day off cooking for the family. The results of *those* happy days, mostly spent with the people I love in a place other than the kitchen, are in this chapter.

Cooking a good dinner in less than an hour takes some planning—there's no way around it. You also need a good arsenal of raw materials and tools at your disposal. For us, this means certain staples are always in our pantry or freezer: raw and cooked beans; rice; canned fire-roasted tomatoes; quick-cooking meats such as thinly cut steaks and ground beef or lamb; quick-cooking seafood that freezes well, like crab, shrimp, and squid; eggs; homemade stocks; frozen vegetables such as peas, beans, and corn; seasonings like anchovies, fish sauce, chiles, and dried mushrooms; and some kind of flavorful pork product, such as linguiça, chorizo, or bacon.

For cooking these delicious ingredients, two pieces of equipment in particular are time-savers in our house: the pressure cooker and the gas grill. I talked about the pressure cooker in more detail at the beginning of the book (see page 29), so I won't say more here except that there is no better tool for quickly cooking delicious meals. Except maybe the gas grill, which is a very close second. Yes, when it comes to grilling the perfect steak, or slowly grill-roasting a pork roast, or smoking ribs, nothing compares to the charcoal grill. But when you're trying to feed hungry people in very little time and you don't want to smoke up the house or clean a lot of pots, the gas grill is without peer.

So there we are: A well-stocked pantry, a couple of tools, and a little bit of planning are all you need to put together quickly prepared meals that are healthy and delicious!

ROMAINE-CUCUMBER SALAD with LIME and THAI CHILE

Years ago, when I was at Lespinasse, one of the Thai cooks often made a delicious Thai salad for the staff's family meal. This recipe is based on that salad, and over the years it has become a family favorite. It has wonderful sweet and tangy Thai flavors and a nice kick from the chiles. And all that great taste comes in a dish that is ridiculously easy to make, a major plus for family dinners. Some nights I'll slice some leftover steak, chicken, or fish and arrange it on top of the salad to turn it into a very quick and tasty main course. I add lots of onions, because I love them, but you can use the smaller amount here if you think your crowd will be less keen on them. I never buy the regular supermarket cucumbers, because they usually have unpleasantly thick skin and too many seeds, and they often don't taste very good. I prefer the long English hothouse or smaller Persian cucumbers, which generally have lovely thin skins that don't require peeling, good crunch, and a nice sweetness. **SERVES 4**

2 tablespoons canola oil

Juice of 1 large lime

1½ tablespoons fish sauce or minced anchovies

1 tablespoon minced peeled fresh ginger

½ fresh Thai chile, finely minced

¼ teaspoon sugar

½ to 1 cup thinly sliced red onion

1 English hothouse or 3 Persian cucumbers, cut lengthwise in half and sliced into thin half-moons (3 cups)

4 radishes, trimmed and thinly sliced

2 romaine hearts, cut crosswise into strips

1 cup washed and dried cilantro leaves (see below) with tender stems

½ cup mint leaves

Kosher salt

Freshly ground black pepper

In a medium bowl, combine the oil, lime juice, fish sauce, ginger, chile, and sugar and whisk until well mixed. Add the onion, cucumbers, and radishes and toss to coat. Let stand at room temperature for 10 to 20 minutes.

Add the romaine, cilantro, and mint to the salad and toss gently to coat with the dressing. Add salt and pepper to taste. Serve.

COOKING TIME: ABOUT 10 MINUTES / INACTIVE TIME: 10 TO 20 MINUTES FOR MARINATING

WASHING AND DRYING CILANTRO

You may notice that I use a lot of cilantro in my cooking. I know there are some who don't care for it—it's really one of the few love-it-or-hate-it ingredients in the world—but I am definitely a fan. What I am not a fan of, however, is the grit that can come with fresh cilantro. It requires assiduous rinsing and drying, which can be done efficiently with a large salad spinner.

Trim away the coarse, thicker stems from the cilantro; I always use the tender stems along with the leaves. Fill the base of the spinner (or a large bowl) with cold water. Add the trimmed cilantro and swish around gently several times (like you do when rinsing rice; see page 136). Lift the cilantro from the water and transfer it to the spinner basket. Don't just pour the water and cilantro into the basket, or you'll end up keeping all the grit you just spent all that time getting rid of. Spin the cilantro until thoroughly dry.

As long as it is very well dried, cleaned cilantro can be stored in a tightly sealed container in the refrigerator for several days.

FREEZER-STOCK RAMEN

This is one of my favorite quick dinners, made entirely from our kitchen staples. It's super easy and endlessly adaptable. You can use any homemade stock you have on hand: anything from pork or chicken to lobster or shrimp stock. It's entirely up to you and what's in your freezer, but since the stock is a major player here, I do suggest that you use homemade, not store-bought.

Dried squid and stockfish, long, thin strands of unsalted dried fish, add really nice flavor to the broth. Adding either is entirely optional, but if you find yourself in a Korean or other Asian grocery store, I urge you to pick some up. Both are inexpensive and will last for a very long time in a cabinet or in the freezer.

I suggest poaching the eggs here, because that's a nice way to enrich the broth and I like it best this way, but you can instead add a halved hard-cooked egg to each bowl or beat the eggs and stir them into the simmering broth just before serving. Any method works, and the added protein makes this a full meal. **SERVES 4**

FOR THE BROTH

2 quarts Chicken Stock (page 337) or other homemade stock

1 cup dried squid or dried stockfish (optional)

2 whole cloves

1 star anise

One 2-inch piece fresh ginger, peeled and sliced into thin coins

3 garlic cloves

12 dried shiitake mushrooms

Kosher salt

FOR SERVING

6 cups baby spinach

8 ounces/227 grams ramen noodles

2 cups thin strips carrots

4 teaspoons thin strips peeled fresh ginger

Freshly ground black pepper

1 cup sliced scallions (white and green parts; cut on the bias)

4 extra-large eggs

4 cups bean sprouts

1 packed cup washed and dried cilantro leaves (see page 39) with tender stems

To make the broth, in a stew pot, combine the stock, dried squid if using, cloves, star anise, ginger, garlic, shiitakes, and salt to taste. Slowly bring to a boil over medium heat, then reduce the heat and simmer for 20 minutes.

Strain the broth into a clean pot. Discard all of the solid ingredients except the shiitake mushrooms. Cut the stems from the shiitakes and discard them. Slice the caps into strips and set aside. Keep the broth warm over low heat.

Divide the spinach and the reserved shiitakes evenly among four large soup bowls. Set aside.

Bring a large pot of water to a boil and add several generous pinches of salt. Add the noodles and cook until al dente, 4 to 5 minutes.

Continued

Meanwhile, add the carrots and ginger to the broth and bring to a boil. Taste and season with salt and freshly ground pepper.

Use a spider or strainer to remove the noodles from the pot and divide them among the bowls. Sprinkle the scallions on top of the noodles.

Return the noodle cooking water to a simmer. Working quickly, crack each of the eggs into a cup and drop them one by one into the water. Do not stir, and make sure that the water does not come to a boil. Cook gently until the whites are set but the yolks are still soft, about 2 minutes.

Use a slotted spoon to transfer one egg at a time to the bowls. Top with the bean sprouts. Pour the hot broth into the bowls. Top each serving with ¼ cup of the cilantro and serve.

COOKING TIME: ABOUT 50 MINUTES

BRAISED BABY KALE with WHITE BEANS and BACON

Any time I prepare a dish that includes beans and bacon, it reminds me of my grandmother Esme, and this dish in particular takes me back to her kitchen. When I was growing up, she lived in a very small apartment, which turned out to be a kind of blessing, because it meant that when she had any of her grandchildren visit her, she could only take one of us at a time. It's hard to express what sweet respite a couple of days spent with Nana were for a boy who had five brothers and sisters. I don't know what special dishes she made for the rest of the kids, but for me it was always beans and bacon served on toast. And it was always delicious. This recipe uses more or less the same ingredients that she did, and though I'm sure she'd quickly point out the differences between my version and hers, this dish is enough to remind me of those lovely days when Nana gave me the gift of a little time spent alone with her.

I first began using chickpea flour to accommodate an increasing number of requests from restaurant diners who were managing wheat allergies. As I used it more frequently, I found that I often actually prefer it to regular all-purpose flour. Chickpea flour has a pleasing nutty flavor, it's a great thickening agent, and it's very high in protein, a nutritional bonus. **SERVES 4**

¼ cup (1 ounce/28 grams) chickpea flour

2 ounces/57 grams thick-cut bacon, sliced crosswise into ½-inch pieces (½ cup)

Salted butter or extra-virgin olive oil as needed

4 garlic cloves, sliced

¼ cup minced shallots

1 teaspoon minced peeled fresh ginger

1 pound/454 grams baby kale

1 cup Chicken Stock (page 337) or high-quality store-bought stock

2 cups cooked white beans or chickpeas (see page 341) or canned beans or chickpeas, rinsed and drained

1 tablespoon whole-grain mustard

Leaves from one 6-inch rosemary sprig, minced

½ teaspoon chile flakes

Kosher salt

Freshly ground black pepper

In a large skillet, toast the chickpea flour over medium heat, stirring frequently, until lightly browned, 4 to 6 minutes. Immediately transfer to a bowl to cool. Set aside.

Wipe the skillet clean, add the bacon, and cook over medium-low heat until the fat is rendered and the bacon is cooked but not crispy. Remove the bacon to a dish with a slotted spoon. Pour the fat into a glass measuring cup and add enough butter or olive oil to bring the total to 2 tablespoons. Set aside to cool. (If you will be using the same skillet to finish the dish, let it cool completely, or the garlic will burn.)

Place a large skillet over low heat, add the garlic and the reserved cooled fat, and cook slowly until the garlic starts to color, 5 to 8 minutes. Increase the heat to medium, add the shallots, ginger, and bacon, and cook until the shallots are translucent, 3 to 5 minutes.

Add the kale and stock, increase the heat to high, and bring to a boil. Reduce the heat and simmer, stirring occasionally, until the kale is just tender, about 5 minutes.

Meanwhile, in a large bowl, combine the white beans, mustard, rosemary, chile flakes, and reserved chickpea flour. Stir to mix and to break up any lumps.

Stir the mixture into the kale and cook until the beans are warmed through and the mixture has thickened, 3 to 5 minutes. Taste and season with salt and pepper. Serve.

COOKING TIME: ABOUT 40 MINUTES

SHRIMP with SPICY TOMATO SAUCE

One Sunday night years ago, all four of us were hit with a mean craving for Thai flavors, and this dish was the result. For a little while it was one of my Sunday-night specials, but once Barkha realized how easy it is to make, she added it to her repertoire of weeknight dinners. She likes cooking a big batch because it makes great lunch leftovers, as Justin can attest—since he's usually the one taking it to school with him the next day. It is also an especially good dish for our lives because she can just put aside some sauce and leave a portion of shrimp uncooked. Then when I get home from work, I can simmer the shrimp in the sauce and have my dinner ready in just a few minutes. Its amazing flavor belies its ease.

I've always used palm sugar in this dish because the original inspiration was our Thai food craving, and it's a very common ingredient in that cuisine. I like it better than granulated sugar because it has a finer, less sweet effect and it adds a nice glazed look. You can pick it up at Asian grocery stores or order it online (see Sources, page 345); then grate it to use. If desired, instead of using chicken stock or water, buy head-on shrimp in the shell and use them to prepare shrimp stock as directed on page 311. **SERVES 8 TO 10**

1 lemongrass stalk

¼ cup canola oil

1 tablespoon brown mustard seeds

1½ teaspoons cumin seeds

2 whole cloves

1 to 2 dried chiles, such as pasilla de Oaxaca or chipotle

1 bay leaf

⅔ cup sliced shallots

4 garlic cloves, sliced

One 2-inch piece fresh ginger, peeled and sliced into thin strips

4 cups canned diced fire-roasted tomatoes, preferably Muir Glen brand, with their juice (from three 14.5-ounce/411-gram cans)

2 cups Chicken Stock (page 337), high-quality store-bought stock, or water

One 13.5-fluid-ounce can Chaokoh-brand coconut milk (stir well before using)

2 tablespoons Tamarind Paste (page 340)

2 tablespoons grated palm sugar

3 Kaffir lime leaves

1 tablespoon chile flakes, or to taste

Sea salt

2 pounds/907 grams (21–25 count) peeled and deveined shrimp

Freshly ground black pepper

1½ loosely packed cups Thai basil leaves

¾ loosely packed cup mint leaves

2 pounds/907 grams short pasta, cooked until al dente, for serving

Peel off and discard the outer leaves of the lemongrass stalk. Thinly slice it on the bias and transfer to a blender. Add a little water and blend until pureed, adding a little more water if necessary. Set aside.

Continued

Heat a large stew pot over medium heat. Add 2 tablespoons of the oil, and when it starts to shimmer, add the mustard seeds and cook until they begin to pop. Add the cumin, cloves, chiles, and bay leaf and cook, stirring, until fragrant and little bubbles have formed around the spices.

Add the shallots, garlic, and ginger and cook until the shallots are translucent, 2 to 3 minutes. Add the reserved lemongrass puree and cook, stirring, until aromatic, 2 to 3 minutes.

Add the tomatoes and bring to a simmer. Add the stock, coconut milk, tamarind paste, palm sugar, lime leaves, and chile flakes. Season to taste with salt and cook until all the flavors come together, 10 to 15 minutes.

Remove and discard the cloves, bay leaf, and lime leaves and set the sauce aside, covered to keep warm. (The sauce can be made up to 2 days in advance. Store in a covered container in the refrigerator. Reheat in a medium saucepan before continuing with the recipe.)

Heat a large chicken fryer or shallow Dutch oven over medium heat. Meanwhile, season the shrimp with salt and pepper. Add the remaining 2 tablespoons oil to the pan and heat until it shimmers. Add the shrimp and sauté until it is just firm, 3 to 4 minutes. Stir in the basil and mint leaves.

Add the sauce to the shrimp and stir to combine. Serve over the pasta.

COOKING TIME: ABOUT 45 MINUTES

CHANGING IT UP

To add more fiber and green color, stir in fresh spinach or pea tendrils along with the basil and mint leaves.

UNDERSTANDING SHRIMP SIZES

The numbers you often see associated with shrimp—usually expressed as either a range, such as "21–25 count," or a single number following the letter U, as in "U10"—refer to roughly how many shrimp are in 1 pound, and this is the best indication of their size. In the examples above, the count would be 21 to 25 individual shrimp per pound, or medium-sized shrimp; U10 means under 10 per pound, so these are big. I try to get head-on shrimp if I'm using 16–20 count or larger. Anything smaller than that can be tiresome to peel and devein. So just buy slightly smaller shelled shrimp, remembering that 16–20 count shrimp in the shell are more like 21–25 shelled.

STIR-FRIED CRABMEAT and SWEET CORN

This quick stir-fry doesn't need any accompaniment—it stands on its own beautifully. It can be served hot from the skillet (no wok required), or you can chill the corn base and then fold in the crab and tarragon to serve as a satisfying salad. Spoon it into baked mini tart shells for a really lovely hors d'oeuvre.

To prepare the roasted corn, you can fire-roast it right on your gas stove. Or, if you have the grill going a day or two ahead, throw the corn on and grill it until marked in spots, then just cut the kernels off and refrigerate or freeze until needed. Alternatively, if you live near a Trader Joe's or Whole Foods, pick up a bag or two of frozen roasted corn. Be sure to let frozen corn sit out at room temperature to defrost before using it; adding frozen corn to the hot pan will quickly lower the temperature of the skillet and cause you to steam, rather than stir-fry, the corn. **SERVES 4**

3 tablespoons canola oil

3 cups diced onions

¼ cup salted peanuts, lightly chopped

1 tablespoon minced peeled fresh ginger

1 tablespoon minced garlic

1½ teaspoons thinly sliced seeded wet kokum

1 serrano chile, finely minced

3 cups fire-roasted corn (see following page) or defrosted frozen fire-roasted corn

¼ teaspoon ground star anise

3 cups fresh or high-quality canned lump or jumbo lump crabmeat, picked over to remove shells

Leaves from 3 tarragon sprigs, coarsely but gently chopped

Sea salt

Freshly ground black pepper

In a large sauté pan or chicken fryer, heat the oil over high heat until shimmering. Add the onions and stir-fry until lightly colored but still firm, 8 to 12 minutes. Push the onions to one side of the pan and add the peanuts, ginger, garlic, kokum, and chile to the other side. Cook, stirring occasionally, for 3 minutes. Stir the onions into the peanut mixture. (The recipe can be made through this step up to 1 day in advance, cooled, and refrigerated. Return the mixture to the pan and heat over medium-low heat until hot, then turn the heat to high for the next step.)

Add the corn and star anise and cook, stirring, until the corn is heated through.

To serve hot, fold in the crab and tarragon and cook just until heated through. Season to taste with salt and pepper and serve.

To serve cold, remove the pan from the heat and let cool. Refrigerate the corn until well chilled, or for up to 1 day. Stir in the crab and tarragon just before serving.

COOKING TIME: ABOUT 30 MINUTES

Continued

FIRE-ROASTING CORN

The toasty sweet flavor of fire-roasted corn can't be beat, and the process takes only a few minutes on a gas stove. If you don't have a gas stove, you can use a gas or charcoal grill.

To fire-roast corn, turn on two gas burners to medium-high and place two shucked ears of corn directly over each flame. Use tongs to turn the cobs occasionally until they are marked in spots; this will take about 10 minutes. Set the ears aside until completely cool, then use a sharp knife to cut the kernels from each one. You'll get about 3 cups roasted kernels from 4 medium-large ears of corn.

SHELLFISH and LINGUIÇA STEW

The list of ingredients here may look long, but the dish comes together quite quickly once cooking is under way. It always makes an impression when you bring an abundant potful of steaming stew to the table.

If you're not familiar with it, linguiça is a Portuguese sausage sold both smoked and fresh. In spite of the fact that when I was growing up I spent one month every year in the heavily Portuguese-influenced state of Goa in India, I didn't actually discover linguiça until I came to the United States. I loved it at first blush for its smoky goodness, and I became a true devotee when I discovered its Portuguese pedigree. If you can't find linguiça—it's common in areas with a large Portuguese or Brazilian community—just use whatever other smoked sausage you can find easily.

For a quick preparation, use already shelled shrimp, as called for here. If you get shrimp with their heads and shells on, though, and you have a few extra minutes, after you remove the shells and heads, simmer them in the fish stock for deeper flavor. **SERVES 4**

¼ cup extra-virgin olive oil
2 ounces/57 grams linguiça, sliced
1 tablespoon fennel seeds, pounded in a mortar with a pestle or rolling pin
1½ teaspoons coriander seeds, pounded in a mortar with a pestle or rolling pin
One ¼-inch piece dried chipotle chile, thinly sliced
4 garlic cloves, thinly sliced
½ cup thinly sliced onion
1 fennel bulb, trimmed and diced into ¼-inch pieces
One 6-inch rosemary sprig
1 teaspoon turmeric
½ cup white wine
2 cups White Fish Stock (page 338)

One 14.5-ounce/411-gram can diced fire-roasted tomatoes, preferably Muir Glen brand, with their juice
16 clams, rinsed (see following page)
20 mussels, rinsed and debearded (see following page)
8 peeled and deveined large (12–15 count) shrimp
1 pound/454 grams cleaned squid, with tentacles, bodies sliced ½ inch thick
Sea salt
Freshly ground black pepper
Leaves from 2 tarragon sprigs
Crusty bread or steamed potatoes for serving (optional)

In a large stew pot or Dutch oven, heat the olive oil over medium heat. Add the linguiça and cook for 2 minutes. Add the fennel seeds, coriander, chipotle, and garlic and cook until lightly colored and very fragrant, 2 to 3 minutes.

Stir in the onion and fennel and cook, stirring occasionally, until translucent, 5 to 8 minutes. Add the rosemary, turmeric, and wine, bring to a boil, and cook until reduced by half.

Add the stock to the pot, then stir in the tomatoes. Cover the pot and cook for 4 minutes.

Continued

Add the clams, cover the pot, and cook for about 4 minutes.

Add the mussels and shrimp, stir, cover, and cook until the shellfish are open, about 3 minutes.

Season the squid with salt and pepper. Stir the squid and tarragon into the pot, cover, and cook for 1 minute. Discard any clams or mussels that have not opened.

Serve in warmed shallow bowls, with bread if desired.

COOKING TIME: ABOUT 30 MINUTES

PREPARING CLAMS AND MUSSELS FOR COOKING

It's important to scrub clams and to scrub and debeard mussels before cooking them to remove grit, but I always do a simple test to make sure that the shellfish are still alive before I go to the trouble of cleaning them. You never want to eat a clam or mussel that was not alive before being cooked, as that may be a sign that it's gone bad. It takes only one bad clam or mussel to ruin the entire pot.

So, before cleaning clams or mussels, put them in a bowl of cold water. Discard any that stay open in the water—this means that they're bad. Also discard any that have cracked or broken shells. Once you have confirmed that every clam or mussel is intact and closed, scrub the grit off the shells with a stiff brush. Use a paring knife to pull off the tough black beards from the mussels. Then set aside in the water until ready to use. Just before cooking, lift the shellfish out of the water and transfer to a colander to drain thoroughly.

PORK NECK with ONIONS, GARLIC, and KOKUM

The neck is another cut of meat that belongs in the underappreciated hall of fame. Pork, beef, lamb—you name it—the neck of anything is delicious and typically really inexpensive. Because it's a part of the body that moves a lot, the neck usually doesn't have a lot of fat, but it does have lots of flavor. It needs some time to cook in order to become properly tender, but it's really forgiving, which is nice. You can actually roast it and even if it gets well-done, it's still very tasty. But my favorite way to prepare neck meat is in the pressure cooker, where it'll become falling-apart tender in literally minutes. If your local grocery store doesn't carry pork neck (sometimes labeled "pork neck bones"), you can ask the meat department to order it for you, or head to an Asian grocery store. This is good served with crusty bread or steamed rice. **SERVES 4**

2 pounds/907 grams pork neck
　(roughly 2-inch pieces)
Kosher salt
Freshly ground black pepper
2 tablespoons canola oil
1 tablespoon brown mustard seeds
4 whole cloves
One 2-inch piece cinnamon stick
3 cups sliced onions
One 2-inch piece fresh ginger, peeled and
　finely minced

6 garlic cloves, smashed
1 dried chipotle chile, broken into ¼-inch
　pieces
2 bay leaves
1 tablespoon black peppercorns
2 teaspoons cumin seeds
8 quarter-sized pieces wet kokum,
　seeded and sliced
2 tablespoons Tamarind Paste
　(page 340)

Season the pork neck with salt and pepper. Set aside at room temperature for about 20 minutes.

Heat the oil in a pressure cooker over medium heat until it shimmers. Add the mustard seeds, cloves, and cinnamon stick and cook until the mustard seeds pop. Stir in the onions, ginger, garlic, chipotle, and bay leaves and cook until the onions are translucent, 5 to 8 minutes.

Meanwhile, in a spice/coffee grinder, finely grind the peppercorns and cumin seeds.

Add the ground spices to the pot and cook for 3 minutes. Add the pork neck and enough water to cover the meat halfway, then add the wet kokum, tamarind paste, and salt to taste and bring to a boil over medium-high heat.

Continued

Reduce the heat to a simmer, cover the pressure cooker, and seal. Follow the manufacturer's instructions to bring it up to pressure (it will begin to steam), then cook for 10 minutes, adjusting the heat as necessary to keep steady pressure. Remove the pressure cooker from the heat and let stand, covered, until the pressure releases. Open the pressure cooker. Remove and discard the cloves, cinnamon stick, and bay leaves.

COOKING TIME: ABOUT 30 MINUTES / INACTIVE TIME: ABOUT 20 MINUTES FOR TEMPING THE MEAT

Note: Alternatively, to cook in a covered Dutch oven, proceed as directed above, except add more water, enough to just cover the meat. Once the mixture comes to a boil, reduce the heat to medium-low, cover, and cook until the meat is fork tender, about 1 hour and 45 minutes.

FLANK STEAK with THAI SALAD

Peter's and Justin's eyes light up every time I make this dish; it's one of their favorites. For my part, I especially like it during the summer because the steak doesn't have to be served hot to be delicious. I love beef, but I believe that for reasons of both health and the environment, it's important to keep our beef consumption in balance. One pound of beef is plenty for four when it's served with this generous herb and green onion salad. When I want to make dinner even more substantial, though, I add whatever looks good in the garden or at the farmers' market. Romaine, cucumbers, or radishes—just about anything would be great in this salad. Except green bell peppers. I hate raw green bell peppers. But you can certainly add them if you feel differently. **SERVES 4**

FOR THE STEAK

3 tablespoons canola oil

6 garlic cloves, smashed

Kosher salt

Freshly ground black pepper

One 1-pound/454-gram flank steak

FOR THE SALAD

⅓ cup fish sauce

3 tablespoons canola oil

Juice of 3 limes

1½ tablespoons sugar

1 tablespoon minced peeled fresh ginger

½ teaspoon minced fresh Thai chile, or more to taste

1 bunch scallions, thinly sliced on the bias (white and green parts)

1 cup thinly sliced Thai basil leaves, with tender stems

1 cup thinly sliced washed and dried cilantro leaves (see page 39) with tender stems

1 cup mint leaves

½ cup thinly sliced red onion

In a large ziplock bag, combine the oil, garlic, and a generous pinch each of salt and pepper. Seal the bag and rub the mixture around a bit to blend it together. Add the steak and massage the bag to coat the steak with the marinade. Seal the bag and refrigerate for 4 hours. (If you leave the salt out, you can marinate the steak for up to 24 hours.)

In a large bowl, combine the fish sauce, oil, lime juice, sugar, ginger, and Thai chile; stir. Cover and set aside at room temperature for 15 minutes to 2 hours.

Prepare a high-heat grill. Remove the bag with the steak from the refrigerator and let stand at room temperature while the grill heats.

Remove the steak from the marinade and salt it on both sides if you did not add salt to the marinade. Grill for about 6 minutes per side for rare, or to the desired doneness. Transfer the steak to a cooling rack to rest for 6 minutes.

Meanwhile, add the scallions, Thai basil, cilantro, mint, and red onion to the bowl with the vinaigrette. Toss gently to combine.

Slice the steak against the grain and arrange on a serving platter. Spoon the salad over the steak and serve.

COOKING TIME: ABOUT 30 MINUTES / INACTIVE TIME: 4 TO 24 HOURS FOR MARINATING THE STEAK

STIR-FRIED GROUND LAMB and EGGS

This dish comes almost directly from the streets of Bombay. When I was a student, during long nights of studying, my friends and I would buy this stir-fry from food carts—the *original* food trucks—before we went home. The combination of toothsome lamb, creamy eggs, ripe tomatoes, ginger, onion, and a host of aromatic spices was just the thing to smooth the way to another few hours of studying before sleep. Nowadays this is an anytime meal in my house. Take note, though, that the tomatoes must be ripe. Please don't top this with hard, unripe winter tomatoes. It's better to just skip them when tomatoes aren't in season. The stir-fry is still delicious without them.

Serve this with a soft bread, such as Portuguese rolls, or roll up in warm tortillas or roti. **SERVES 4**

12 ounces/340 grams ground lamb

Kosher salt

Freshly ground black pepper for seasoning the meat, plus 2¼ teaspoons black peppercorns, finely ground

¼ cup plus 1½ teaspoons canola oil

2¼ teaspoons coriander seeds, finely ground

1½ cups minced onions

1½ tablespoons minced peeled fresh ginger

1½ teaspoons turmeric

¼ teaspoon cayenne

6 extra-large eggs, beaten

3 tablespoons minced mint leaves

3 tablespoons minced washed and dried cilantro (see page 39) or parsley

About 6 tablespoons diced ripe tomatoes for garnish (optional)

Lightly season the ground lamb with salt and pepper.

In a large sauté pan, combine the 1½ teaspoons oil, coriander, and ground peppercorns and cook over medium heat until fragrant, about 2 minutes. Add the lamb, increase the heat to high, and cook, stirring and breaking up the meat, until browned, about 5 minutes. Transfer the lamb to a bowl.

Add the remaining ¼ cup oil to the sauté pan, along with the onions, ginger, turmeric, and cayenne. Cook, stirring constantly and scraping up any stuck bits from the bottom of the pan, until the onions are translucent, 4 to 5 minutes.

Return the lamb to the pan and cook for 2 minutes. Reduce the heat to medium-low, add the beaten eggs, and cook, stirring with a silicone spatula, until the eggs are creamy and moist. Stir in the herbs and salt to taste.

Divide the lamb and eggs among four warmed plates. Garnish each serving with diced tomatoes, if desired. Serve.

COOKING TIME: ABOUT 30 MINUTES

GRILLED CHICKEN SKEWERS

I like to prepare this easy marinade on Sunday nights and pop the chicken in the fridge. Then the next day, when Barkha returns from work, she can turn on the gas grill, quickly thread the chicken on skewers, and have dinner ready in less than 30 minutes. It's one of the few times I use chicken breasts, because we want speed as much as flavor.

If the weather is lousy, a grill pan on the stove can stand in for the outside grill. Barkha often serves these with grilled cauliflower and pita. I also like them with a bitter green salad, such as Baby Escarole, Endive, Radicchio, and Blood Orange Salad (page 75). **SERVES 6**

½ cup extra-virgin olive oil

2 tablespoons minced shallots

3 garlic cloves, finely minced or pressed with a garlic press

2 tablespoons chopped fresh rosemary

Minced zest and juice of 1 lime or lemon

3 tablespoons sweet paprika

1½ teaspoons kosher salt, plus more for seasoning the chicken

1 tablespoon black peppercorns, finely ground

¼ teaspoon cayenne

2 pounds/907 grams boneless, skinless chicken breasts, each cut lengthwise into 3 equal pieces

Canola oil for the grill or grill pan

2 limes, cut into wedges, for serving

6 to 12 metal or bamboo skewers

In a ziplock bag, combine the olive oil, shallots, garlic, rosemary, lime zest and juice, paprika, 1½ teaspoons salt, black pepper, and cayenne. Seal the bag and shake until well blended. Add the chicken, seal the bag, squeezing out the air, and massage to thoroughly coat the chicken with the marinade. Marinate in the refrigerator for at least 6 but no more than 24 hours.

If using bamboo skewers, soak them in water for 40 minutes.

If grilling outside, prepare a high-heat grill.

Meanwhile, remove the chicken from the marinade. If grilling outside, reserve the marinade; if cooking inside, discard it. Thread 1 or 2 chicken strips onto each of the skewers. Season with salt and let stand at room temperature until the grill is ready.

Lightly oil the grill. Place the skewers on the grill and brush on some of the marinade; discard the remaining marinade. Grill the skewers until they release easily from the grill and are well marked, about 4 minutes. Flip them over and cook until the chicken is cooked through, about 4 minutes.

Alternatively, heat a stovetop grill pan over medium-high heat. Oil the pan. Add the skewers and cook until the chicken is well marked and cooked through, 3 to 4 minutes per side. Serve right away, with the lime wedges, if desired.

COOKING TIME: ABOUT 30 MINUTES / INACTIVE TIME: 6 TO 24 HOURS FOR MARINATING

CHAPTER TWO

Dinner for Two

MEALS TO COOK WHEN THERE'S JUST A PAIR

Cooking for many diners at once is a source of exhilaration for me, but the nights in our lives when it's just two people at home for dinner (one of whom is not always me) are where I find quiet inspiration. With dishes like a healing chicken soup, a quick salad, or a pot of steaming deliciousness in the form of mussels or coconut curry, this is the chapter that's most grounded in how my family and I eat most of the time. On the pages that follow you'll find the meals I turn to when the dinner is just for two, whether the pair is my wife, Barkha, and me, or Barkha and one of our boys, because I'm working, traveling, or cooking at a charity event. The constant is Barkha, and that is why many of these dishes in particular are designed around her preferences. (Plus, as any wise husband will tell you, if you're going to take over the kitchen, it's simply good policy to make sure that your wife likes what you're cooking.)

Although most of the recipes in this chapter are written to serve just two, every one of them is very easy to double or triple. I know this because at least once when we've made any of these recipes, one or both of the boys have peered into the pot or smelled what was cooking and asked us to "make extra" so that there will be leftovers for a late-night snack or for lunch the next day. I think this is partly because I never compromise on flavor, even when I'm preparing something simple. In a busy family like ours, when only two of us are sitting down to eat together, we want to enjoy what is most important: the person sharing the meal with us. But that shouldn't ever be at the expense of wonderful, flavorful food. I don't see simple cooking as an excuse to skimp on the use of spice and other flavor enhancers, and you don't need to either. Especially not when it's so easy to make the delicious, nourishing dishes in this chapter.

BRUSSELS SPROUTS HASH

This is a vegetarian dish I first made for the menu of the Bread Bar at Tabla. I have since included it on the menu at every one of my restaurants, although only when local sprouts are in season, no matter how many protests we get when we take it off the menu. It is among the most popular vegetarian dishes I've ever made, but please don't get the wrong idea; this is *not* a "cheffy" dish. In fact, I make it at home so often that I've come to think of it more as one of our family recipes. It makes a great side dish for Thanksgiving. It's also one of Barkha's favorites, and we often enjoy it with a piece of grilled fish. This recipe makes more than enough for the two of us, and Barkha usually takes the leftovers to work the next day. So I know that it makes great leftovers.

The trick to preparing great Brussels sprouts is to cook them *just* until they are done. Overcooked Brussels sprouts emit an awful sulfuric smell that, understandably, makes many people hesitant to cook them. To ensure that you can cook them just right, cut them to a smaller size. For this recipe, they are shaved on a mandoline, and they cook very quickly indeed. You can find the dals and fresh curry leaves at Indian and Asian grocery stores.   **SERVES 4 TO 6**

1 pound/454 grams Brussels sprouts, trimmed

3 tablespoons canola oil

1 tablespoon split black beans (*urad dal*)

1 tablespoon split yellow peas (*chana dal*)

1½ teaspoons brown mustard seeds

1 teaspoon chile flakes

1 tablespoon minced shallot

1 tablespoon minced peeled fresh ginger

1 tablespoon minced chiles, such as serrano

Leaves from 2 sprigs fresh curry leaves (optional)

Kosher salt

5 tablespoons water

Thinly slice the Brussels sprouts on a mandoline. You should have about 8 cups.

Place a large sauté pan over low heat and add the oil, black beans, and split peas. Heat until the dals just begin to color and smell toasty, 2 to 3 minutes. Add the mustard seeds, increase the heat to medium, and cook until the seeds pop, 1 to 2 minutes. Add the chile flakes and cook for 30 seconds.

Add the shallot, ginger, chiles, and curry leaves, if using. Season with salt and cook until the shallots are fragrant, 2 to 3 minutes. Add the water and simmer until the liquid is almost completely gone and the lentils soften slightly (they should still be a little crunchy but not hard), 8 to 10 minutes.

Add the Brussels sprouts to the pan, increase the heat to high, and stir-fry until the sprouts are slightly tender but with some crunch, about 2 minutes.

Season to taste with salt and serve.

COOKING TIME: 30 TO 35 MINUTES

ROASTED BEETS with ORANGE and FRESH RICOTTA

Barkha loves beets so much that I've been moved to come up with more ways to prepare them than I can count. For a long time, our favorite way to eat them was very simple: roasted and then tossed with sweet onions, olive oil, vinegar, chiles, and salt. But over the years, I've adapted that basic method in many different ways to make them a little more palatable to the boys, who don't enjoy tangy heat as much as Barkha and I do. This recipe has become one of our most frequent variations, whether I'm preparing beets for the whole family or just the two of us. Note that if you can't find baby beets, you can substitute larger ones: you'll only need one or two of each type and they'll take longer to cook (up to 3 hours if they're very large).

You'll need cheesecloth and an instant-read thermometer to make the ricotta—but please do *make* your own ricotta; flavor- and texture-wise, there's just no comparison between it and the store-bought stuff. The ricotta recipe yields a bit more than you may want on your beets, which is a good thing, because it is great on bruschetta. If you must buy it, remember to stir in the orange zest and juice and black pepper.

There's a lot of extra dressing here for a reason; I love it, especially when there's some great, crusty bread available. It drives me crazy when restaurant servers take the bread off the table too soon. That's another reason I love to cook and eat at home; no one steals my bread.   **SERVES 2**

FOR THE RICOTTA
1 quart whole milk
1 cup buttermilk
Minced zest and juice of 1 large orange
Kosher salt
Freshly ground black pepper

FOR THE BEETS
4 red baby beets, trimmed
4 golden baby beets, trimmed

1 tablespoon canola oil
Kosher salt
Freshly ground black pepper
¼ cup fresh orange juice
¼ cup extra-virgin olive oil
2 tablespoons red wine vinegar
4 drops Thai chile oil
1 tablespoon minced peeled fresh ginger
½ cup diced red onion
2 cups arugula

To make the ricotta, in a medium saucepan, heat the milk and buttermilk over very low heat, stirring occasionally so that the bottom of the pan does not scorch, until the mixture reaches 110°F on an instant-read thermometer. Turn up the heat slightly and continue to cook, stirring occasionally, until the mixture reaches 175°F. Remove the pan from the heat and set aside until curds form, about 5 minutes.

Line a colander with several layers of cheesecloth and set it over a bowl. Use a spoon to skim the curds from the whey (liquid) and place them in the colander. Let stand at room temperature until completely cooled.

Continued

Transfer the drained ricotta to another bowl (discard the whey left behind). Stir in the orange zest and juice and season to taste with salt and pepper. Set aside if serving within a few hours, or refrigerate for up to 5 days.

Meanwhile, prepare the beets: Preheat the oven to 350°F.

Place the red beets in one bowl and the golden beets in another. Drizzle with the canola oil, season with salt and pepper, and toss to coat. Wrap the beets in two separate foil packs.

Put the packs on a baking sheet and roast until the beets are tender when pierced with a paring knife, 45 minutes to 1 hour (if the beets are very fresh, check them at 30 minutes, as they may cook very quickly). Unwrap the beets and while they are still hot, rub off the skin with paper towels. Cut them into 1-inch pieces and transfer to a bowl.

Add the orange juice, olive oil, vinegar, chile oil, ginger, and salt and pepper to taste to the beets and toss to coat. Set aside to marinate at room temperature for 1 hour, or refrigerate for up to 24 hours.

Just before serving, add the onion to the beets and toss to combine. Taste for seasoning.

Place the arugula on a serving platter and spoon the beets and all the marinade over it. Place several spoonfuls of ricotta on top or place the ricotta in a bowl on the side. Serve.

COOKING TIME: 1 TO 1½ HOURS / INACTIVE TIME: 1 TO 24 HOURS FOR MARINATING

BABY ESCAROLE, ENDIVE, RADICCHIO, and BLOOD ORANGE SALAD

When I prepared this dish for the *Top Chef Masters* challenge where I cooked for Maroon 5, I got raked over the coals by the judges. They dismissed it as merely a "simple salad." This is my cookbook, however, so I get the last word. The judges were wrong; the salad may be pretty simple, but the dressing is complex and delicious. In fact, this salad is a hit pretty much everywhere I serve it. I think this is in part because it has that magical sweet-sour-spicy-bitter flavor profile.

There's really only one way that I make dressings and vinaigrettes at home: I throw everything into a Mason or jam jar and vigorously shake it until blended. I like to use a just-emptied anchovy or mustard jar so that whatever of the original contents is left in the jar gets mixed up deliciously into the dressing. This method is easy, there's no whisk or bowl to clean when I'm done, and I use the same jar to store the leftovers.

When preparing the escarole, peel off the outer leaves until you get to the tender heart, which you'll use for the salad. The outer leaves are great braised, and they can be used in place of the cabbage in the Braised Chicken Thighs with Winter Vegetables (page 170). **SERVES 2**

1 blood orange or navel orange

FOR THE VINAIGRETTE
Blood orange juice (from above)
1 tablespoon extra-virgin olive oil
1½ teaspoons red wine vinegar
1 teaspoon Dijon mustard
1 teaspoon maple syrup
Kosher salt
Freshly ground black pepper

FOR THE SALAD
1 head escarole
1 small endive
6 to 8 radicchio leaves, torn into large pieces
12 Marcona almonds, toasted (see following page) and coarsely chopped
2 teaspoons minced shallot
Coarse sea salt
Freshly ground black pepper

Use a sharp thin-bladed knife to cut off just enough of the top and bottom of the orange to expose the flesh. Set the orange cut side down on a cutting board and slice off the peel and pith, following the curve of the fruit with the knife. Holding the orange over a bowl to catch the segments and the juice, cut the segments away from the thin membranes holding them together. Then squeeze the membranes over the bowl to extract the remaining juice; discard the membranes. Pour the orange juice into a jar. Set the orange segments aside.

Add to the jar with the juice the olive oil, vinegar, mustard, maple syrup, and kosher salt and pepper to taste. Tightly close the jar and shake vigorously until well combined. Set aside.

Continued

Remove the outer leaves from the head of escarole and reserve them for another use. Tear the tender leaves from the heart into large pieces and transfer them to a large bowl.

Trim the base of the endive. Separate the leaves from the center core; discard the hard core. Stack several leaves at a time on a cutting board and cut them lengthwise into 4 or 5 thin strips each. Add the strips to the escarole.

To finish the salad, add the radicchio, the reserved orange segments, the almonds, and shallot to the bowl. Shake the vinaigrette and pour it over the salad. Toss gently until well coated. Season to taste with salt and pepper. Serve.

COOKING TIME: ABOUT 30 MINUTES

TOASTING NUTS

Toasting nuts changes their flavor and texture enormously. To toast nuts, preheat a toaster oven (I love my Breville!) or regular oven to 350°F. Place the nuts on a rimmed baking sheet and toast, shaking the pan once or twice, until they are lightly colored, 5 to 10 minutes. Immediately transfer the nuts to a plate to cool.

SPICED CHICKEN SOUP with CHICKPEA NOODLES

I believe absolutely in the healing power of many foods, and this soup is an especially good restorative. I made it for the first time one day at Tabla when Danny Meyer was feeling sick and wished aloud that he had a big bowl of chicken soup. I don't know if he meant to conjure up a soup with such a kick, but when anyone is sick, I rely on abundant spices—especially ginger, which is an anti-inflammatory warming spice (see page 27), and turmeric and black pepper, which have natural anti-inflammatory and antibiotic properties—to help cure what ails them. It must have worked for Danny. He loved the soup so much that he launched a company-wide chicken soup event for the holidays, during which time the proceeds from every bowl of chicken soup sold in the restaurant group went to Share Our Strength, an organization that fights hunger. It seems that this soup is good for body *and* soul.

You can cook the noodles one of two ways. You can drop them directly into the simmering soup or you can cook them ahead of time and then refrigerate them until you're ready to serve the soup; see the Note on the following page for instructions. **SERVES 4**

2 tablespoons canola oil

Half a 3-inch cinnamon stick

4 whole cloves

1 teaspoon cumin seeds

½ cup thinly sliced shallots (slice into half-moons)

3 small carrots, cut lengthwise in half and sliced into half-moons

2 cups sliced scallions (white and green parts)

1 tablespoon chopped peeled fresh ginger

1 to 3 teaspoons sliced fresh chiles, such as serrano

1 teaspoon turmeric

2 quarts Chicken Stock (page 337) or high-quality store-bought stock

1¼ pounds/567 grams boneless, skinless chicken thighs, excess fat removed, cut into ¼-inch dice (2½ to 3 cups)

One 6-inch rosemary sprig (optional)

Kosher salt

¼ cup thinly sliced washed and dried cilantro leaves (see page 39) with tender stems (stack the leaves a few at a time to slice)

1 tablespoon black peppercorns, finely ground

FOR THE CHICKPEA NOODLES

1 cup (4 ounces/113 grams) chickpea flour

3 tablespoons (1 ounce/28 grams) all-purpose flour

1 large egg, lightly beaten

½ cup water

Kosher salt

Freshly ground black pepper

In a stew pot, heat the oil over medium heat until it shimmers. Add the cinnamon and cloves and cook until aromatic, about 1 minute. Add the cumin seeds and cook until they sizzle, about 30 seconds. Add the shallots, reduce the heat, and cook, stirring occasionally, until translucent, about 3 minutes. Add the carrots, scallions, ginger, and chiles and cook until the scallions are softened, 3 to 4 minutes. Stir in the turmeric and cook for 1 minute.

Add the stock, chicken, and rosemary, if using. Increase the heat to medium-high and bring to a boil. Season lightly with salt, reduce the heat, and simmer until the chicken is cooked and the carrots are tender, about 10 minutes.

Meanwhile, make the noodle batter: In a large bowl, combine the chickpea flour, all-purpose flour, egg, water, and salt and pepper to taste. Whisk until the batter falls in ribbons off the whisk when you lift it. Add more water if necessary.

Remove the cinnamon stick, cloves, and rosemary sprig from the soup and discard. Hold or set a metal colander or perforated hotel pan over the pot. Pour the batter into the colander and use a plastic pastry scraper or a silicone spatula to press the batter through the holes into the soup. Then cook until the noodles rise to the top, 1 to 2 minutes.

Stir in the cilantro and season with freshly ground black pepper and salt if needed. Serve.

COOKING TIME: 35 TO 45 MINUTES

Note: If you'd like to cook the noodles ahead of time, prepare the batter as instructed. Bring a large saucepan of salted water to a boil and set a large bowl of ice water next to the stovetop. Pour the batter through a metal colander or perforated hotel pan into the boiling water as described above and cook until the noodles rise to the top. As they rise, remove the noodles with a spider or slotted spoon and immediately transfer them to the ice water to stop the cooking. When all of the noodles are cooked, drain them and lay them on a rimmed baking sheet lined with a clean kitchen towel. If keeping for longer than 1 hour or so, wrap the pan in plastic wrap and refrigerate; the noodles can be refrigerated for up to 1 day.

When the soup is ready, stir in the noodles and simmer until heated through. Stir in the cilantro, season as directed above, and serve.

SPICE-CRUSTED SWORDFISH with BRAISED ROMAINE

For years I wouldn't buy swordfish because it was so overfished that the whole population was in jeopardy. Today, however, swordfish is sustainably fished in the United States, which means that the population is monitored to prevent it from being dangerously diminished, and I am cooking with it again. When you buy it, just make sure that you're buying U.S. swordfish—and the more local, the better. For all seafood shopping, in fact, I highly recommend downloading the Seafood Watch app from the Monterey Bay Aquarium (see Sources, page 345). Whether you're at the grocery store or in a restaurant, the app will provide you with up-to-date information on the best sustainable choices for all fish and shellfish, and it'll suggest alternatives if what you're looking for or what you find isn't a good choice.

I'm very glad to be eating and serving swordfish again, because it's a wonderfully meaty fish. It lends itself to a pleasantly assertive smoky chile crust and holds up beautifully on the grill. If you can't find two smaller steaks, just cook one big piece and cut it in half before serving. **SERVES 2**

FOR THE SWORDFISH

¼ dried chipotle chile, with seeds

¼ guajillo chile, seeds removed

¼ ancho chile, seeds removed

One ½-inch piece pasilla de Oaxaca chile, with seeds

1 tablespoon coriander seeds

Two 6-ounce/170-gram swordfish steaks, about 1 inch thick

Sea salt

Canola oil

1 lime, cut into wedges

FOR THE BRAISED ROMAINE

1 tablespoon extra-virgin olive oil

1 tablespoon minced shallot

1 teaspoon minced peeled fresh ginger

1 head romaine, cut lengthwise in half and cleaned (see note)

¼ cup Chicken Stock (page 337), high-quality store-bought stock, or water

Sea salt

Freshly ground black pepper

Heat a small heavy-bottomed skillet over medium heat. Add the chipotle, guajillo, ancho, and pasilla chiles and toast, turning once, until the chipotle is colored and the other chiles are softened, about 5 minutes. Remove from the pan and let cool.

Transfer the cooled chiles to a spice/coffee grinder and finely grind, then transfer to a small bowl.

Finely grind the coriander seeds, add them to the bowl with the chiles, and stir to combine thoroughly.

Season the swordfish all over with salt and dust on both sides with the spice blend. Let stand at room temperature for 30 minutes.

If grilling the fish, prepare a medium-hot grill. Brush the steaks with canola oil. Grill the steaks for 4 to 6 minutes on each side for medium, or to the desired doneness.

If cooking the fish on the stovetop, heat a large heavy-bottomed skillet over medium heat until hot, 3 to 4 minutes. Add 2 to 3 tablespoons canola oil, then add the fish and cook for 4 to 6 minutes on each side for medium, or to the desired doneness.

Meanwhile, once you flip the swordfish over, prepare the braised romaine: Heat a skillet large enough to hold both romaine halves cut side down over medium heat. Add the olive oil, shallot, and ginger and cook until translucent, about 2 minutes. Add the romaine halves, cut side down, then add the stock, increase the heat to high, and bring to a boil. Season the romaine with salt and pepper, cover the pan, and cook until tender, 3 to 4 minutes. Remove from the heat.

Squeeze the lime juice over the steaks and serve at once, with the braised romaine halves.

COOKING TIME: ABOUT 40 MINUTES / INACTIVE TIME: 30 MINUTES FOR TEMPING THE SWORDFISH

Note: To clean the romaine, swish the halves around in a large bowl of cold water once or twice, then remove and gently shake dry.

DON'T PLAY WITH YOUR FISH!

I feel really confident advising people who are usually uncomfortable cooking fish to go ahead and cook swordfish. Its sturdiness makes it a great candidate even for novices. The only thing that I do recommend is to avoid playing hockey with the fish once it's on the grill or in the pan. In other words, don't move it around or flip it multiple times. This is the one common mistake I see many people make with fish. They mess around with it, and it breaks. If the steak you're cooking is thicker than 1 inch, you can shift it 90 degrees about three-quarters of the way through the cooking on each side to give it nice crosshatch marks. But for anything 1 inch thick or less, don't mess with it!

STEAMED COCONUT MUSSELS

Barkha and I love nothing more than sitting down to a steaming pot of these mussels and a loaf of fresh, crusty bread or a bowl of steamed rice—one or the other is definitely needed to soak up every drop of the scrumptious, aromatic coconut broth. And this dish is so easy to prepare. The most complicated part is making sure that you buy the mussels no more than 24 hours before you prepare it (or any mussel dish). Feel free to use clams if you prefer them to mussels. Whichever you use, clean them just once, right before cooking.

I sometimes add a smoky, meaty undertone to the dish by rendering a bit of diced linguiça, Portuguese chorizo, or bacon in the pan after toasting the mustard seeds.   **SERVES 2**

2 teaspoons canola oil

1 teaspoon brown mustard seeds

¼ cup quartered and thinly sliced shallots

3 garlic cloves, thinly sliced

1 teaspoon minced peeled fresh ginger

1 serrano chile, thinly sliced

1 teaspoon black peppercorns, finely ground

¼ teaspoon turmeric

1 cup Chaokoh-brand coconut milk (stir well before using)

1 teaspoon Tamarind Paste (page 340)

1½ pounds/680 grams mussels, scrubbed and debearded (see page 54)

Leaves and tender stems from 4 washed and dried cilantro sprigs (see page 39)

Leaves from 4 Thai basil sprigs, torn in half if very large

Heat a large stew pot over medium heat. Add the oil, and when it starts to shimmer, add the mustard seeds and cook until they begin to pop. Add the shallots, garlic, ginger, and chile, reduce the heat to medium-low, and cook, stirring occasionally, until the shallots are translucent, about 3 minutes. Add the pepper and turmeric and cook for 3 minutes.

Add the coconut milk, tamarind paste, and mussels, increase the heat to medium, and cover the pot. Cook until the mussels start to open, about 2 minutes. Add the cilantro and basil leaves, cover, and cook until all of the mussels have opened, 2 to 3 minutes. Discard any mussels that have not opened.

Serve immediately.

COOKING TIME: ABOUT 20 MINUTES

STEAMED RED SNAPPER with GINGER and CILANTRO

For this steamed fish dish, don't use a steamer that has a perforated or otherwise unsealed bottom. You want to preserve all the delicious liquid that the fish and vegetables give off during cooking, and steamers that are perforated or have slatted bottoms would let it all escape. (See below for how to improvise.)

I like to serve this Chinese-style with the fish, vegetables, and liquid in one bowl and the steamed rice in another bowl, so you can use chopsticks to add as much rice to each bite as you like. Jasmine rice, sticky rice, and basmati rice are all very nice with this. I use a bottle of Sriracha sauce too, for anyone who wants to add a little kick. If you can't find good fresh red snapper, use sea bass, sole, fluke, or flounder in its place.   **SERVES 2**

Two 6-ounce/170-gram thin skin-on
   red snapper fillets
Sea salt
Freshly ground black pepper
1 tablespoon salted butter, softened
½ small carrot, sliced into matchsticks
   (about 2 tablespoons)
1½ teaspoons fresh ginger matchsticks
   (peel before slicing)

½ serrano chile, cut into thin slices
Leaves and tender stems from 4 washed
   and dried cilantro sprigs (see page 39),
   leaves left whole and stems sliced on
   the bias
1 scallion (white and green parts), thinly
   sliced on the bias
½ cup mung bean sprouts
Steamed rice for serving

Prepare your steamer: Have ready a deep wok or pot with a tight-fitting lid and a glass pie plate or shallow baking dish that fits inside the wok. Place a few upside-down ramekins, an inverted bamboo steamer, or the perforated insert of a pressure cooker in the wok to hold the pie plate above the bottom of the pot and allow the steam to circulate.

Season the fish with salt and pepper. Brush the fillets on both sides with the butter. Lay the fish skin side up in the baking dish and sprinkle the carrots, ginger, chile, cilantro, and scallions on top.

Bring 2 inches of water to a simmer in the wok. Place the baking dish on top of the ramekins, cover the pan, and steam until there is no resistance when the fish is pierced with a very thin roasting fork, about 8 minutes. Remove the steamer from the heat.

Alternatively, you can steam the fish in the oven: Place each fillet on a large sheet of aluminum foil or parchment and top it with its share of aromatics. Seal each package tightly and bake in a 350°F oven for about 12 minutes.

Divide the mung bean sprouts between two warmed bowls. Place a fillet on top of each and spoon the vegetables and juices on top. Divide the steamed rice between two warmed bowls. Serve.

COOKING TIME: ABOUT 20 MINUTES

EGGS POACHED in TOMATO CURRY

One of my pet peeves about Indian restaurants is that you don't see enough eggs on the menu. This is true even in India, which is why we made sure to have a couple of egg dishes on the menu at the Bombay Canteen, my restaurant in Mumbai. Eggs are actually extremely popular in India, probably in large part because they are just an amazing source of protein. This particular dish was inspired by Parsi cuisine, which is not well represented in most Indian restaurants but in which eggs play a very big role.

If you want to increase the heartiness of the dish, stir some vegetables into the tomato base: spinach or kale during colder months or in-season peas or zucchini during the spring and summer. It's also good served over pasta. And note that this is a great make-ahead dish, since you can prepare the tomato base up to 3 days in advance.   **SERVES 2**

2 tablespoons canola oil or Ghee (page 342)

1 cup thinly sliced onion

¼ serrano chile, thinly sliced

2 garlic cloves, minced

One ½-inch piece fresh ginger, peeled and minced

¼ teaspoon turmeric

¼ teaspoon cumin seeds, finely ground

A pinch of cayenne

1½ large beefsteak tomatoes, cored and diced (about 2½ cups)

½ cup water, or as needed

Leaves and tender stems from 4 washed and dried cilantro sprigs (see page 39), sliced

Kosher salt

4 extra-large eggs

2 tablespoons sliced mint leaves

Freshly ground black pepper

Heat a medium rondeau or stew pot over medium heat. Add the oil and heat until it shimmers. Add the onion and cook, stirring frequently, until almost caramelized, about 10 minutes.

Stir in the chile, garlic, ginger, turmeric, cumin, and cayenne and cook until fragrant and the garlic is beginning to color lightly, about 1 minute. Stir in the tomatoes and water, increase the heat to medium-high, and cook for 1 minute. Reduce the heat to medium and simmer, stirring occasionally, until the tomatoes begin to break down, about 20 minutes. Add more water if necessary to help the tomatoes break down. You don't want to let the sauce get too thick, or it will be difficult to cook the eggs. (The dish can be made up to this point, cooled, and stored in the refrigerator for up to 3 days. Reheat the tomato base in the stew pot until simmering before continuing.)

Fold in the cilantro. Taste and season with salt. Reduce the heat to a gentle simmer. Working quickly, crack each of the eggs into a cup and then drop them one by one into the sauce; do not stir. Make sure that the tomato sauce does not come to a boil. Cover and cook gently for 8 to 12 minutes.

Continued

Sprinkle the mint over the eggs, season with black pepper, and serve immediately.

COOKING TIME: 30 TO 40 MINUTES

POACHING EGGS

The fastest, neatest way to add eggs to a pan of simmering liquid is to crack each one into a cup—a teacup with a handle works best, but a ramekin is a fine substitute. If you have the counter space, crack all the eggs into their own cups while the liquid simmers so that you can very quickly slip them into the pan one at a time.

I always give a wide range of cooking time for poaching eggs to accommodate different preferences. If you like your poached eggs with the whites just barely set and the yolks very runny, cook the eggs for the shorter time listed, on average 2 minutes in water and up to 8 in thick sauces. For firm whites and yolks that are more set, cook for the longer time, usually about 4 minutes in water and about 12 minutes in thick sauces.

PETER'S ORANGE-and-MUSTARD GRILLED CHICKEN with CHICKPEAS

My son Peter lived in Cleveland for an internship a few years ago, and one night he called to get advice on what to make for dinner. He wanted it to be a one-pot meal, and he wanted to use what was already in his kitchen. He told me which ingredients "we" had to work with, and by the time I hung up, I was nursing a pretty strong hankering for the oranges, mustard, and chicken I'd just virtually concocted into a stew. Not being in the mood for stew myself, though, I conjured up instead an orange-and-mustard marinade for the chicken. The chickpea side dish came to pass because we had many beet greens in the garden. Knowing that oranges are delicious with beets—check out the Roasted Beets with Orange and Fresh Ricotta (page 71) in case you need proof of this glorious pairing—it occurred to me that beet greens might be pretty tasty with oranges too. And so it was proven true; the beet greens marry beautifully with the sweet orange.

The great thing about this dish, besides its fabulous flavors, is that you can make it all in advance; it's very nice served at room temperature. You can use red Swiss chard leaves in place of the beet greens; the effect is just as good. Whichever you use, if the stems are very thick and fat, cook them a bit before adding the leaves so that they become properly softened. And feel free to use boneless, skinless chicken breasts in place of the thighs.

Incidentally, I heard from Pete the day after his call that the stew was delicious. The marinade is pretty great too.   **SERVES 2**

FOR THE CHICKEN

Minced zest and juice of 1 orange
1½ tablespoons canola oil
1½ teaspoons minced peeled fresh ginger
2 garlic cloves, finely minced
1½ teaspoons Colman's mustard powder
    or ground yellow mustard seeds
1½ teaspoons coriander seeds, pounded
    in a mortar with a pestle
¾ teaspoon black peppercorns, coarsely
    ground
Leaves from one 6-inch rosemary sprig,
    coarsely chopped
Kosher salt
4 boneless, skinless chicken thighs
    (about 1 pound/454 grams), excess fat
    removed

FOR THE CHICKPEAS AND BEET GREENS

12 beet leaves or 6 Swiss chard leaves
    and stems, washed
2 tablespoons extra-virgin olive oil
3 tablespoons thinly sliced shallots
2 garlic cloves, crushed
1 teaspoon minced peeled fresh ginger
One 3-inch rosemary sprig
1 cup cooked chickpeas (see page 341) or
    canned chickpeas, rinsed and drained
¼ cup fresh orange juice
1½ teaspoons fresh lemon juice
1 tablespoon minced orange zest
1 tablespoon minced lemon zest
Kosher salt
Freshly ground black pepper

Canola oil for the grill
1 lemon, halved

Continued

To marinate the chicken, in a large ziplock bag, combine the orange zest and juice, canola oil, ginger, garlic, mustard powder, coriander, pepper, rosemary, and salt to taste. Seal the bag and shake until the marinade is well blended. Add the chicken to the bag, seal it, and massage the bag to thoroughly coat the chicken with the marinade.

Marinate the chicken in the refrigerator for at least 4 hours, and up to 12 hours.

Prepare a medium-hot grill. Remove the chicken from the refrigerator and let stand at room temperature while the grill is heating.

Meanwhile, prepare the chickpeas and beet greens: Separate the beet leaves from the stems. Cut both into ½-inch pieces. Set aside, keeping the stems separate from the leaves.

In a large sauté pan, heat the olive oil over medium heat. Add the shallots, garlic, ginger, and rosemary and cook, stirring occasionally, until the shallots are translucent, about 3 minutes. Add the chickpeas, orange juice, lemon juice, and the reserved beet stems. Cover and cook gently until the stems are slightly softened, 2 to 4 minutes. Add the reserved beet leaves, the orange and lemon zest, and salt and pepper to taste, cover, and cook until the stems are tender and the leaves wilted, about 4 minutes. Set aside, covered, to keep warm.

Oil the grill grate. Remove the chicken from the bag and place it on the grill (discard the marinade). Grill until the chicken is cooked through but still juicy, 6 to 8 minutes on each side.

Transfer the chicken to a platter and sprinkle with the juice of the lemon. Add the chickpeas and greens to the platter and serve.

COOKING TIME: 40 TO 45 MINUTES / INACTIVE TIME: 4 TO 12 HOURS FOR MARINATING

OSSO BUCO BRAISED with WARMING SPICES

Often the same people who think nothing of buying and preparing short ribs or oxtail will hesitate when faced with veal shanks, also sold under the name osso buco. There's a sort of aura of exclusiveness around osso buco that leads some to be a little intimidated by it. But I think any recipe for short ribs or oxtail can also be done with osso buco. These are very similar cuts and are pretty interchangeable, so no one should shy away from osso buco and miss out on experiencing its divine flavor at home, and the fun of braising this tough cut until it becomes melt-in-your-mouth tender. I like to make this dish during the winter, when we can especially appreciate the effects of cinnamon and cloves, richly warming spices that help build heat in the body.

Although you could eat this right after preparing it, it will taste so much better if you refrigerate it for a day or so before serving. Serve the osso buco with hearty, crusty bread or noodles, risotto, or steamed rice, any of which will work to absorb the flavorful sauce. **SERVES 2**

2 large (1½-pound/680-gram) osso buco (veal shanks)

Kosher salt

Freshly ground black pepper

10 dried shiitake mushrooms

1½ cups boiling water

2¼ teaspoons black peppercorns

2¼ teaspoons cumin seeds

2¼ teaspoons coriander seeds

2¼ teaspoons brown mustard seeds

Half a 3-inch cinnamon stick

4 whole cloves

1 tablespoon sweet paprika

½ teaspoon turmeric

¼ cup canola oil

2 cups diced onions

1 cup diced carrots

1 cup diced celery

⅓ cup thinly sliced peeled fresh ginger (sliced crosswise)

4 garlic cloves, smashed

1 serrano chile, sliced lengthwise in half

2 small bay leaves

4 cups canned diced fire-roasted tomatoes, preferably Muir Glen brand, with their juice (from three 14.5-ounce/411-gram cans)

½ cup red wine, such as pinot noir or cabernet

2 cups Chicken Stock (page 337), high-quality store-bought stock, or water

Tie each osso buco around the center with kitchen string, as if you're tying a belt around it. Generously season with salt and pepper and set aside at room temperature for 20 to 30 minutes.

Meanwhile, place the shiitakes in a medium bowl and cover with the boiling water. Set aside to soak until softened, about 20 minutes.

Lift the mushrooms out of the soaking liquid and drain them in a strainer; reserve the soaking liquid. Remove and discard the mushroom stems and cut the caps into quarters. Set aside. Strain the soaking liquid through a mesh strainer lined with a coffee filter or several layers of cheesecloth. Set the liquid aside.

Place the peppercorns, cumin seeds, coriander seeds, mustard seeds, cinnamon stick, and cloves in a spice/coffee grinder and finely grind them. Transfer the ground spices to a small bowl. Add the paprika and turmeric and mix until well combined. Set aside.

Place an oven rack in the center of the oven and preheat the oven to 325°F.

Heat the oil in a 7- to 8-quart heavy-bottomed ovenproof pot over medium-high heat until shimmering. Add the osso buco and sear until nicely browned on both sides, about 4 minutes on each side. Remove and set aside.

Add the onions, carrots, celery, ginger, garlic, chile, and bay leaves to the pot and cook until the vegetables are softened and beginning to brown, about 10 minutes. Stir in the tomatoes, wine, and reserved spice blend and cook for 5 minutes.

Stir in the reserved mushrooms and then return the osso buco to the pot, nestling them between and under the vegetables. Add the stock and the reserved mushroom soaking water. Season with salt. Bring the braise to a boil and simmer for 10 minutes.

Tightly cover the pot with a lid or foil, transfer to the oven, and cook until the meat is fork-tender, about 2 hours. Remove the pot from the oven, uncover, and let cool to room temperature.

Transfer the meat, vegetables, and sauce to a container and seal. Refrigerate the osso buco for at least 1 day, and up to 3 days.

When ready to serve the osso buco, remove and discard the solidified fat from the surface. Transfer the vegetables and sauce to a pot and bring the liquid to a boil over medium heat. Skim any remaining fat from the surface with a ladle.

Add the meat to the sauce to reheat. Serve hot.

COOKING TIME: ABOUT 3 HOURS, OR 1¼ HOURS IN THE PRESSURE COOKER / INACTIVE TIME: 20 TO 30 MINUTES FOR TEMPING AND FOR SOFTENING THE MUSHROOMS, PLUS AT LEAST OVERNIGHT IF MAKING AHEAD (RECOMMENDED)

PRESSURE-COOKER FRIENDLY

To prepare the osso buco in a pressure cooker, follow the recipe as written, searing the osso buco in the pressure cooker, softening the vegetables, and returning the osso buco to the pot. Continue as directed, adding only as much chicken stock as needed to reach the pressure cooker's "fill to" line. Bring to a simmer. Seal the pressure cooker. Follow the manufacturer's instructions to bring it up to pressure (it will begin to steam) and cook for 20 minutes, adjusting the heat as necessary to keep steady pressure. Remove the pressure cooker from the heat and let stand, covered, until the pressure releases, then open the cooker and continue as directed.

BARKHA'S MANGO-POMEGRANATE COCKTAIL

Barkha could eat mangoes or drink mango juice pretty much all day and all night and never grow tired of them. I feel the same way about pomegranates. A blend of the two was no doubt destined to be a Cardoz house specialty, but it was the addition of the dark rum that really guaranteed its status. The aroma and flavor of any decent dark rum instantly transports us both back to India, and it reminds me of my younger days, when my school buddies and I often enjoyed a healthy amount of Old Monk rum, the rum most likely to be imbibed by everyone in India. So great is its iconic stature that on the cocktail menu for the Bombay Canteen, my restaurant in Mumbai, we list only one liquor by brand name: Old Monk. It is the defining ingredient in the delicious Dark Monsoon, which I highly recommend you try the next time you're in Mumbai. In the meantime, break out your favorite rum and enjoy a sip of this, Barkha's favorite cocktail.   **SERVES 2**

Crushed ice
4 fluid ounces dark rum
6 fluid ounces pomegranate juice
6 fluid ounces mango juice
Juice of 1 lime

Club soda
2 lime slices for garnish
2 large slices candied ginger, threaded
    on cocktail picks, for garnish

Half-fill two tall highball glasses with crushed ice. Divide the rum between the glasses. Pour over the pomegranate juice. Then pour over the mango juice and then the lime juice. Top off each glass with club soda.

Garnish each drink with a slice of lime and candied ginger and serve.

COOKING TIME: 5 TO 10 MINUTES

CHAPTER THREE

Essentially Vegetables

SALADS, SOUPS, MAINS, AND SIDES THAT BRING
OUT THE WONDERS OF VEGGIES

My childhood relationship with vegetables was one that applies to many kids: I hated them. Unfortunately for me, my family was very traditional. Not only were the kids not consulted about what was served for dinner every—or any—night, we had to eat everything on our plates. Even worse, my family's cook was not great when it came to preparing vegetables. Our go-to vegetable dish was an ordinary salad. If the cook got really creative, we'd have boiled carrots, cauliflower, or cabbage, or the occasional Goa-style vegetable (which is to say, a very simple and unadorned preparation). Not the stuff childhood memories are made of.

When I married Barkha, she opened up a whole world of vegetables that I didn't know existed. I was exposed to a way of treating vegetables that I had never seen before. Every night our table was graced with a different kind of vegetable prepared with love and care. To me it was a revelation, and it turned out to be the launch of my education. Many years later, I began my next level of vegetable studies when I joined chef Gray Kunz's kitchen at Lespinasse. Gray had an unusual gift for preparing and presenting vegetables in a way that was both elegant and respectful of the raw materials. He was one of the first chefs I know who started a seasonal vegetarian tasting menu; he did it long before it was trendy to do so.

My love for seasonality grew exponentially when I was introduced to the Union Square Greenmarket, the local farmers' market in New York City. I had never seen so many different kinds of potatoes, beans, and greens! By the time I opened Tabla, just a few blocks north of the Greenmarket, playing around with vegetables had become second nature to me. I was very excited and inspired by what I could do—the possibilities seemed endless.

On the home front, my evolution overlapped with the growth of my kids, who began to enjoy the vegetables I made for the family. I used different techniques and seasonings with them and tried to vary the ingredients I cooked with, often employing my tried-and-true method of introducing new vegetables and methods by combining them with ingredients they already knew and loved. At first I'd accommodate their meat-loving tendencies by adding bacon, shrimp, anchovies, chicken stock, or meaty leftovers to the vegetables. I'm happy to say that these days I don't need to add meat "compromises" very often. Our boys are nothing like the picky, choosy vegetable hater I once was. They are both true vegetable lovers now.

Along the way, we began gardening at home, thanks in large part to my former chef de cuisine, Ben Pollinger, who has a real passion for what he calls home farming. I discovered what every home gardener knows: The produce I pull out of my garden bursts with flavor, has amazing texture and color, and cooks more quickly than any vegetables one can buy, since it is as fresh as it can be. The possibilities really are endless.

These days we normally have at least one thoughtfully prepared vegetable at every meal, by which I don't mean an extravagant or it-took-hours-to-make vegetable, as you'll see from many of the selections in this chapter. It's just that we always want the vegetable dish to be just as tasty as everything else we're serving. Vegetables are some of the best ways to introduce texture and color to a meal, and the more texture a meal has, the better it tastes.

Finally, a word about the most important thing to remember when you're cooking vegetables: Don't overcook them! When vegetables are cooked too long, they lose all their charm and are rendered just as boring as that dreary boiled cauliflower I grew up (not) eating. In general, the trick for cooking veggies just right is to cook them over high heat and keep the cooking time relatively brief. And now to the vegetable patch!

"UPMA" POLENTA with WILD MUSHROOMS

Upma is an unassuming breakfast dish that is hugely popular in India. My version became a bit of a phenomenon when I prepared it for the last *Top Chef Masters* challenge and won the season. After the finale aired worldwide, "#upma" became the top-trending hashtag on Twitter in India, where it was dubbed the "Hundred-Thousand-Dollar Upma," a tongue-in-cheek reference to the *Top Chef* prize money I won for the Young Scientist Foundation.

The funny thing about this recipe is that at first blush (and bite), it might not seem like a "wow" dish you'd prepare to blow people away. It's unpretentious and even a little homely. But take another bite, and then another, and with each taste, you're very likely to love it more. This upma dish has been on my restaurant menus for years, first at Tabla, then at North End Grill, and now at Paowalla. It is so popular that people often request it even when it isn't on the menu.

In India, upma is usually made simply, from semolina and water with some mustard seeds, chiles, and sometimes a bit of vegetable; it's typically very stiff and dry. It's served for breakfast or maybe at teatime with no more fanfare than Americans might give toast. My preparation of upma, on the other hand, is creamy and lush and has many layers of flavors, not only from mustard seeds and chile, but also from earthy cumin, aromatic ginger and shallots, tangy kokum, grassy cilantro, and rich coconut milk. Plus, I always serve it with a topping inspired by the season. Here I share two of my favorite toppings, the wild mushroom fricassee—perfect in the fall—that I made on the show, and a bright green springtime variation made with asparagus, spring onions, and sugar snap peas (see page 103).

Indian semolina is a lot softer than American semolina, so if you use the latter, you'll need to use more liquid. However, if you use instant semolina, keep the proportions given here. Indian semolina can be found at Indian and often Asian groceries or online, as can black cumin seeds, fresh curry leaves, and wet kokum. **SERVES 6**

FOR THE WILD MUSHROOMS
¼ cup canola oil

1½ pounds/680 grams wild mushrooms, brushed clean and cut into bite-sized pieces

Kosher salt

4 tablespoons salted butter

¼ cup minced shallots

¼ cup minced peeled fresh ginger

2 tablespoons sliced fresh chiles, such as serrano or cayenne

½ cup white port

2 teaspoons black cumin seeds (*shahi jeera*)

Freshly ground black pepper

1 cup washed and dried cilantro leaves (see page 39), stacked a few at a time and thinly sliced

FOR THE UPMA
4 cups Vegetable Stock (page 339), Chicken Stock (page 337), or high-quality store-bought stock, or as needed

4 cups Chaokoh-brand coconut milk, or as needed (stir well before using)

2 tablespoons canola oil

1 teaspoon mustard seeds

½ teaspoon cumin seeds

Leaves from 2 sprigs fresh curry leaves (optional)

2 tablespoons salted butter

2 tablespoons minced shallots

2 tablespoons minced peeled fresh ginger

1 tablespoon sliced fresh chiles, such as serrano or cayenne

1½ cups Indian semolina (*suji* or *sooji*)

4 quarter-sized pieces wet kokum, seeded and thinly sliced

¼ cup washed and dried cilantro leaves (see page 39), stacked a few at a time and thinly sliced

Kosher salt

Freshly ground black pepper

To make the wild mushroom fricassee, heat a large heavy-bottomed stew pot or Dutch oven over medium-high heat for 2 minutes. Add the oil. When the oil starts to shimmer, add the mushrooms and reduce the heat to medium. Season the mushrooms with salt and cook, stirring constantly, until lightly colored and softened, 3 to 5 minutes.

Add the butter, shallots, ginger, and chiles and cook until very fragrant and the shallots are softened, 2 to 3 minutes. Add the port and deglaze the pot, using a wooden or metal spatula to scrape up the browned bits on the bottom. Add the black cumin seeds and simmer for 2 minutes more. Taste and add salt and black pepper if needed. Set aside, covered to keep warm, while you make the upma.

In a medium saucepan, heat the stock and coconut milk over medium-low heat until hot. Keep warm.

Meanwhile, heat a heavy-bottomed 3-quart stew pot over medium heat. Add the oil and heat until it shimmers, about 2 minutes. Add the mustard and cumin seeds and cook until the mustard seeds pop, 1 to 2 minutes. Add the curry leaves, if using, and cook for 30 seconds. Add the butter, shallots, ginger, and chiles and cook until the shallots are translucent, about 2 minutes.

Add the semolina and cook, stirring constantly, until it is lightly colored and smells toasty, 8 to 10 minutes.

Whisking constantly, add the hot stock and coconut milk to the semolina, then bring to a boil over medium heat; this will happen almost immediately. Add the kokum, cilantro, and salt and pepper to taste. Cook, stirring constantly, until all the liquid is absorbed and the mixture has a creamy texture, 3 to 4 minutes. (If you are using a different kind of semolina, you may need to add more liquid to achieve the proper texture.)

If necessary, rewarm the wild mushroom fricassee over low heat. Stir in the cilantro.

For each serving, place a generous spoonful of upma in the center of a shallow bowl. Spoon the wild mushrooms around the upma. Serve.

COOKING TIME: 40 TO 50 MINUTES

Continued

Note: The recipe can be prepared through the toasting of the semolina with the spices up to 1 week in advance. Store in the refrigerator. Reheat the semolina in the stew pot and heat the stock and coconut milk before continuing with the recipe.

FRICASSEE OF ASPARAGUS AND SPRING ONIONS

Serve this topping, with its abundant spring onions, asparagus, and sugar snap peas, to usher in spring. Then, a month or so later, swap in summer squash and fresh tomatoes. As you can see, upma can be served year-round.

2 tablespoons extra-virgin olive oil

2 cups thinly sliced spring onions (white and green parts, sliced on the diagonal)

1 spring garlic (white and green parts), sliced

1 bunch pencil asparagus (about 1 pound/454 grams), washed (see below) and cut into 1½-inch pieces

8 ounces/227 grams sugar snap peas, cut diagonally in half (about 2 cups), strings removed

2 tablespoons minced shallots

2 tablespoons minced peeled fresh ginger

1 teaspoon sliced fresh chile, such as serrano or cayenne

4 quarter-sized pieces wet kokum, seeded and thinly sliced

Kosher salt

Freshly ground black pepper

2 tablespoons finely chopped washed and dried cilantro (see page 39)

2 tablespoons chopped chives

Unless you have a 14-inch skillet, use a large roasting pan. Place it over two burners set to medium heat. Add the olive oil, then add the spring onions, spring garlic, and asparagus and sauté, stirring constantly, until the asparagus is bright green and the spring onions are very soft, about 4 minutes.

Add the sugar snap peas, shallots, ginger, chile, and kokum and cook, stirring constantly, until the asparagus is crisp-tender, 3 to 4 minutes. Season to taste with salt and pepper. Keep warm while you make the upma, then add the cilantro and chives and stir to mix.

For each serving, place a generous spoonful of upma in the center of a shallow bowl. Spoon the asparagus around the upma. Serve.

COOKING TIME: ABOUT 10 MINUTES

WASHING ASPARAGUS

Asparagus needs thorough rinsing to get rid of all the sand that can hide in its tight leaves and tips. To wash it well, place the asparagus tips down in a cylindrical container, such as a wine bucket or a thermos. Fill the container with cold water and let stand for 20 minutes, periodically shaking the asparagus to get the dirt out. Remove the asparagus from the water and shake dry.

DAD'S PEA SOUP

Like every man of his age I knew when I was growing up, my father rarely set foot in the kitchen and he certainly *never* cooked. But he loved to shell peas. He would set up at the table on Saturday afternoon with a beer and a bushel of peas and get to work. This shelling was the only "cooking" he ever did, which I guess explains why none of us listened to him when week after week he repeated his counsel to my mother that she should get the cook to make a stock out of the shells. Anyone within earshot would roll their eyes and go back to what they were doing, pretty certain that he had no idea what he was talking about. At some point, though, I finally heeded my father's suggestion and discovered that if the peas are really fresh, the shells do indeed add wonderful flavor to stocks. And now I put them to good use both at home and in the restaurant, where we simmer them along with the other ingredients to make our daily vegetable stock.

In this recipe, I prepare a pea puree separately from the rest of the soup and stir it in only at the end in order to keep its beautiful bright green color. To further ensure that the soup has that vivid color, use only white, not dark, liquor. If you don't have white port, use sweet white sherry instead. Don't use regular port, because the color will make the soup look muddy.

Depending on what I have on hand or am in the mood for, I usually stir in a bit of crabmeat or chicken at the end—although you can certainly prepare the soup without either. Use fish stock if adding crabmeat or chicken stock if adding chicken. Stirring the coriander in right at the end preserves its toasted, citrusy flavor. **SERVES 4**

Kosher salt

3 cups shelled fresh peas plus ½ cup for finishing (about 3½ pounds/ 1.59 kilograms in the shell)

3 cups sugar snap peas (about 10 ounces/ 283 grams), strings removed

3 tablespoons canola oil

2 green cardamom pods, cracked with the side of a large knife

1 teaspoon brown mustard seeds

1 cup sliced onion

¾ cup sliced shallots

3 garlic cloves, sliced

One ½-inch piece ginger, peeled and sliced into coins

¼ cup white port or sweet white sherry

4 cups White Fish Stock (page 338), Chicken Stock (page 337), Vegetable Stock (page 339), or high-quality store-bought stock

1½ teaspoons coriander seeds, toasted (see page 20) and finely ground

1½ teaspoons black peppercorns, toasted (see page 20) and finely ground

½ cup fresh or high-quality canned crabmeat, picked over to remove shells, or ½ cup diced cooked chicken (optional)

2 tablespoons sliced mint leaves (stack a few leaves at a time to slice)

Blanch, shock, and drain the peas and snap peas separately (see page 33).

When the peas and snap peas are completely cool, drain them well (keep them separate). Set aside ½ cup of the peas for finishing the soup. Puree the remaining peas in a blender, adding just enough water to make a smooth but

thick puree. Transfer to a bowl and puree the snap peas in the same way. Combine with the pea puree and set aside.

Heat a large stew pot or Dutch oven over medium heat. Add the oil, and when it starts to shimmer, add the cardamom and mustard seeds and cook until the mustard seeds begin to pop, 1 to 2 minutes. Add the onion, shallots, garlic, and ginger and cook until translucent, 4 to 6 minutes.

Add the port and cook for 3 minutes. Add the stock and bring to a boil, then reduce the heat and simmer for 15 minutes. Remove from the heat.

Let the soup cool slightly, then puree it until smooth in a blender, in batches if necessary. Strain the pureed soup through a chinois or medium-mesh strainer, using a wooden spoon if necessary to push it through.

Return the strained soup to the pot and bring to a boil over medium heat. Stir in the pea and snap pea puree, coriander, and pepper. Season with salt to taste.

Stir in the reserved peas, the crab or chicken if using, and the mint. Divide the soup among four warmed bowls and serve.

COOKING TIME: ABOUT 1¼ HOURS

MUNG BEANS with POBLANO and TOMATILLOS

There was a point in my life when I absolutely despised mung beans. It took some time, but I eventually realized that this was not really the beans' fault. Rather, it was because during a culinary school internship, I ate most of my meals in a dining hall where mung beans were cooked one way, and one way only, every single day of the week.

Since those monotonous days, I've come around, and now I consider mung beans one of the staples of my home pantry for several reasons. First, and this is important from the home-cooking perspective, they are a good, inexpensive source of protein and other nutrients. Second, and this is essential from a culinary perspective, they are a fabulous blank slate. You can do anything at all with them (except cook them the same way every day), and they'll always please. I had never seen them with tomatillos, for instance, so I tried it one day, and the recipe you see here has become a regular in our home dinner rotation. Add mung beans to your pantry, and look at them as an easy starting point if you want to try something a little different. (See page 109 for more on how to cook them.) This comes together really quickly in a pressure cooker, but you can also make it using a regular pot (see page 109). I sometimes serve this stew with steamed whole buckwheat groats, whose nutty flavor and chewy texture go really nicely with the toothsome beans.

When I cook this dish, I like to use cilantro and tomatillos from my garden. I never actually intended to grow tomatillos, but one spring, some tomatillo plants just popped out of my compost, the happy consequence of my composting some grocery store tomatillos the year before. When volunteers (the term for these sorts of plants that pop up unexpectedly in gardens or compost) come up in my garden, I always do my best to nurture them. A wholly planned garden, like a wholly planned meal, isn't half as much fun as a spontaneous one. **SERVES 4**

1 pound/454 grams whole mung (moong) beans, picked over and rinsed well

3 tablespoons canola oil

1 teaspoon cumin seeds

½ cup sliced shallots

1 tablespoon minced peeled fresh ginger

2 garlic cloves, minced

1 large poblano pepper, roasted (see page 202), peeled, seeded, and minced

1 cup minced husked and rinsed tomatillos (about 8 ounces/227 grams)

1 teaspoon turmeric

1 teaspoon black peppercorns, coarsely ground

5 cups water

¼ cup washed and dried cilantro leaves (see page 39)

Kosher salt

Place the beans in a large bowl and cover by 2 inches with cold water. Set aside to soak overnight, then drain, rinse well, and drain again. Set aside.

Continued

In a pressure cooker, heat the oil over medium heat until it shimmers. Add the cumin seeds and cook until the oil bubbles around them and they are fragrant, about 2 minutes. Add the shallots, ginger, and garlic and cook until translucent, about 4 minutes. Stir in the poblano pepper, drained beans, tomatillos, turmeric, pepper, and water and bring to a boil. Seal the pressure cooker. Follow the manufacturer's instructions to bring it up to pressure (it will begin to steam), then cook for 8 minutes, adjusting the heat as necessary to keep steady pressure. Remove the pressure cooker from the heat and let stand, covered, until the pressure releases.

Open the pressure cooker and stir in the cilantro and salt to taste. If the mixture is too thick, stir in water and return to a boil. Serve hot.

COOKING TIME: ABOUT 30 MINUTES / INACTIVE TIME: OVERNIGHT SOAKING

Note: If you don't have a pressure cooker, you can use a large stew pot instead. Proceed as directed above, and once the mixture comes to a boil, reduce the heat and simmer, uncovered, until the beans are tender, about 45 minutes; add more water as necessary to keep the beans just covered. Add the cilantro and salt and serve.

MUNG (MOONG) BEANS

Americans in general are more familiar with mung bean sprouts—the thick, crunchy, roughly 2-inch-long whitish sprouts with a wisp of yellow germ at one end that are common in Chinese and Thai stir-fries—than they are with mung beans. Well, those sprouts have to begin somewhere, and it's with beans, which are germinated to make those sprouts. The bean is ubiquitous in India. Mung beans come three different ways: whole beans, which are green; with skin and split, which are also green; and without skin and split, which are yellow. Split mung beans are often referred to as green or yellow mung dal. Cooking times vary widely. When cooked on the stovetop, yellow mung dal take only about 15 minutes; green mung dal (with skin) take about 30 minutes; and the whole beans take around an hour. And no matter what I just said, beans that have been stored for a long time will take longer to cook. As in this recipe, the pressure cooker shaves off a lot of time, but I use it only for whole beans, never split. I choose which form of mung bean to cook according to the texture I'm looking for and how much time I have to cook them. Whole beans keep their distinct form and have a nice bite. Split mung dal are softer.

GRILLED EGGPLANT and NECTARINE SALAD with TOMATO VINAIGRETTE

One summer day at North End Grill, we'd just seeded and juiced a huge quantity of tomatoes to use in a dish, and we had a great vat of seeds and juice left over. Often I use these leftovers in stock, but on that day, I looked around for what else was in my kitchen. Strangely, until then, I'd never used eggplant, nectarines, and tomatoes together in the same dish, even though they are all in season together every summer. As it turns out, they are quite excellent companions in this dish, where their unique sweet, acid, and earthy qualities meld beautifully.

Now I don't wait to have leftover tomato juice to make this vinaigrette and instead use whole fresh tomatoes, which are even more flavorful. This is a vegetarian dish that can be served with lots of crusty bread for soaking up all of the vinaigrette (there's a lot of it intentionally—once you taste it, you'll know why!). Or serve it on top of grilled or toasted country bread for bruschetta. **SERVES 6**

FOR THE VINAIGRETTE
3 medium-large beefsteak tomatoes, cored and cut into chunks (about 6 cups)
½ cup extra-virgin olive oil
2 tablespoons sherry vinegar
¼ teaspoon Thai chile oil

FOR THE SALAD
1 large eggplant (about 1¼ pounds/ 567 grams)
Kosher salt

Extra-virgin olive oil
2 small red onions, quartered, leaving the root ends intact (about 1½ cups)
Freshly ground black pepper
6 nectarines, halved, pitted, and sliced
2 cups fresh basil leaves, stacked a few at a time and thinly sliced
Fresh lemon juice
2 cups thinly sliced arugula
⅓ cup walnut halves, toasted (see page 76) and roughly chopped

To make the vinaigrette, puree the tomatoes in a food processor or blender. Transfer the puree to a medium saucepan and bring to a simmer over medium heat. Meanwhile, fill a large bowl with ice and water.

Strain the tomato juice through a fine-mesh sieve into a medium bowl, using a spoon to push it through. Place the bowl of tomato juice in the bowl of ice water to cool it quickly; stir occasionally to speed the process along. You should have 3 cups tomato juice.

Transfer the tomato juice to a large jar with a lid, add the olive oil, vinegar, and chile oil, cover, and shake vigorously until well combined. Set aside. (The vinaigrette can be made ahead and stored in the refrigerator for 1 day.)

Cut the eggplant lengthwise into slices no thicker than ¼ inch. Place the slices in a large bowl and add cold water to cover. Add salt until the water tastes like the ocean. Place a plate on top of the eggplant to keep it submerged if necessary and set aside to soak for at least 15 minutes, and up to 30 minutes.

While the eggplant is soaking, prepare a medium-high-heat grill.

Remove the eggplant from the saltwater and pat it dry. Brush on both sides with olive oil and grill until softened and well marked, 5 to 7 minutes per side. Remove from the grill and set aside while you grill the onions.

Season the onions with salt and pepper. Brush all over with olive oil. Grill on all sides directly on the grill, or use a grill basket and toss the onions occasionally, until well marked and softened, about 10 minutes. Remove the onions from the grill.

Cut each eggplant slice lengthwise in half and then cut each half crosswise into 1-inch-wide pieces. Transfer to a bowl.

Cut off the root end from each onion wedge and discard. Separate the onion layers and add them to the bowl with the eggplant.

Add the nectarines and half of the vinaigrette to the eggplant and onions and gently mix with your hands or a spatula. Add the basil and salt and pepper to taste and gently mix. Add lemon juice to taste.

Just before serving, add the arugula and mix gently. Arrange the salad on six salad plates. Spoon or pour the remaining vinaigrette around the salads; there will be a generous amount of vinaigrette. Sprinkle the walnuts over each salad and serve immediately.

COOKING TIME: ABOUT 1½ HOURS

PAN-ROASTED BROCCOLI with LIME, HONEY, and CHILE FLAKES

I think the reason Americans don't generally like broccoli is because it is easy to overcook it. Not only does overcooked broccoli smell horrible, it tastes that way too—if it tastes like anything at all. One excellent way to avoid the overcooking scourge is *never* to cook broccoli in water. Instead, grill, panfry, or roast it to bring out the vegetable's natural sweetness while retaining its pleasing, crunchy texture. Adding some sweet-and-spicy notes, as I do in this dish, makes it even more interesting. This method is simple enough to do on a weeknight, and it elevates this underappreciated vegetable far beyond "just broccoli." It works great with cauliflower too. **SERVES 6**

2 large or 4 small heads broccoli
   (2 pounds/907 grams), ends trimmed
3 to 4 tablespoons extra-virgin olive oil,
   or as needed
Kosher salt

Freshly ground black pepper
1 teaspoon chile flakes
2 tablespoons honey
2 tablespoons fresh lime juice

Cut the stems off the broccoli just below the florets. Use a paring knife to remove the stems' tough skin. Cut the peeled stems into ¼-inch-thick coins. Separate the broccoli heads into spears; try to cut them so that each one has at least one long flat side that will lie flat on the pan bottom.

Heat a large sauté pan over medium heat. Add 3 tablespoons olive oil and the broccoli, increase the heat to high, and cook, stirring, until the broccoli is bright green and slightly tender, 2 to 3 minutes. (It is important not to crowd the pan, or the broccoli will steam rather than brown. It's fine to do this in two batches or to use two pans if necessary; use 2 tablespoons oil per batch.) Season the broccoli with salt and pepper. Reduce the heat to medium. Cover the pan and cook, stirring occasionally, until the broccoli is crisp-tender, 3 to 4 minutes. Stir in the chile flakes. (If cooking in two batches, keep the first batch warm in a very low oven while you cook the remaining broccoli.)

Meanwhile, in a small bowl, combine the honey and lime juice.

When the broccoli is cooked, pour the honey mixture over it and toss to coat. Serve hot.

COOKING TIME: 15 TO 20 MINUTES

Note: You can also roast the broccoli in the oven. Preheat the oven to 450°F. Toss the broccoli with the olive oil, chile flakes, and salt and pepper to taste. Spread it in a single layer on one or two rimmed baking sheets. Roast until crisp-tender and lightly browned in spots, 10 to 15 minutes. Remove from the oven, toss with the honey and lime juice, and serve.

YELLOW LENTIL "DAL"

Yellow lentils are actually pink when dried (which is how you buy them). They turn a lovely shade of yellow during cooking. This dish, known in India as *masoor dal,* is one of the simplest I make, and it's a great introduction to cooking with spices and with lentils. It's also a really flexible recipe. You can add greens when you have them for a bit of extra bulk. Using the eggs will help thicken the dal and contribute a lovely, smooth richness.

You can serve this two different ways: as soup or as bruschetta. For soup, simply serve it in warmed bowls. For bruschetta, cut the water by half and spoon the stew on top of grilled bread to eat out of hand. Garnish the bruschetta with small sprigs of cilantro if you want to dress it up. **SERVES 4**

3 tablespoons salted butter

3 garlic cloves, smashed

1½ cups pink lentils, picked over and rinsed well

1 medium onion, sliced

½ cup diced tomatoes

½ serrano chile, sliced into thin rings

½ teaspoon turmeric

4 cups water

Kosher salt

2 cups kale or baby spinach, sliced into thin strips (optional)

2 large eggs (optional)

¼ cup washed and dried cilantro leaves (see page 39), coarsely chopped

Melt the butter in a small stew pot over medium-low heat. When the bubbles begin to disappear, add the garlic and cook, shaking the pan occasionally, until the butter and garlic are light brown and the butter has a nutty smell. Keep a close eye on it once the butter begins to brown, as it can burn quickly.

Add the lentils, onion, tomatoes, chile, turmeric, and water, increase the heat to high, and bring to a boil. Reduce the heat and simmer until the lentils are tender, 8 to 12 minutes. Season to taste with salt.

If you are adding greens, add the kale about 6 minutes before the lentils are cooked or the spinach about 4 minutes before the end of cooking.

If you are adding eggs, whisk them in a glass measuring cup. After the lentils are cooked, slowly pour the eggs into the simmering lentils while slowly stirring with a wooden spoon.

Add the cilantro and cook for another minute. Serve hot.

COOKING TIME: 30 TO 35 MINUTES

TANTO'S TOMATO-POTATO CURRY

Tanto was the nickname we gave one of my close childhood friends. He is a priest today, and I sometimes wonder if anyone who knows him as Father Francis realizes that once upon a time, his irreverent friends affectionately renamed him after the elephants (*tantors*) in the land of Tarzan, whose comic books we consumed voraciously.

When we were young, a bunch of us went camping together a lot. Each of us was responsible for a meal, and for whatever reason, Tanto always made a tomato-potato curry. Truth be told, this is nothing at all like his original dish, but I still think of him every time I make it. Some memories are funny that way. This curry is hearty and delicious; it's not very saucy, so don't be surprised by that (for more on what a curry is and is not, see page 19). **SERVES 4 TO 6**

1½ pounds/680 grams fingerling
    potatoes
Kosher salt
2 tablespoons canola oil
1 tablespoon coriander seeds,
    coarsely ground
1 tablespoon fennel seeds, coarsely
    ground
1 teaspoon black peppercorns,
    coarsely ground

3 whole cloves
4 garlic cloves, thinly sliced
1 dried chipotle chile
1 cup minced onion
One 2-inch piece fresh ginger, peeled
    and sliced into thin coins
4 cups diced ripe red tomatoes with
    juice (about 3 large tomatoes)
1 cup mint leaves

Place the potatoes in a large pot. Add cold water to cover by at least 1 inch and several generous pinches of salt and bring to a boil over medium-high heat. Reduce the heat and simmer the potatoes until they are tender when pierced with the tip of a sharp knife, 10 to 15 minutes. Drain thoroughly and set aside.

Heat the oil in a large stew pot over medium heat until it shimmers. Add the coriander, fennel, pepper, and cloves and cook until aromatic, about 1 minute. Add the garlic and chipotle and cook until fragrant, about 2 minutes. Add the onion and ginger and sauté until translucent, about 3 minutes.

Add the tomatoes and salt to taste. Cover the pan, reduce the heat, and cook until the tomatoes start to break down, about 10 minutes.

Meanwhile, cut the drained potatoes in half—or into quarters, if they are very large. Add the potatoes to the pot, along with salt to taste. Cook, uncovered, to blend the flavors and heat the potatoes through, about 4 minutes.

Remove and discard the cloves. Remove the chipotle (you can chop it up and return it to the curry if you want a little more heat). Stir in the mint and serve.

COOKING TIME: 45 TO 50 MINUTES

CRACKED-WHEAT PILAF with SPRING PEAS

I came up with this dish one spring when I wanted to create a showcase for a *lot* of peas: a pressing issue, since they were pouring out of my garden faster than I could cook them. I also wanted to make sure that the sugar snaps were prepared in such a way that there was minimal risk of overcooking them, which I think is too often their unhappy fate. Peas are very nice paired with cracked wheat, an ingredient that I once thought of only in the context of breakfast. The nutty flavor and chewiness of the cracked wheat complements the sweet sugar snaps and English peas. Pureeing some of the peas and stirring the puree into the wheat underscores that fresh, green flavor that tells us spring is here.

This is substantial enough to be a main course for four people. Or serve it as a side with just about any lamb dish, such as Grilled Lamb Shanks with Salsa Verde (page 248).

SERVES 4 TO 6

2 cups Chicken Stock (page 337) or high-quality store-bought stock

2 teaspoons canola oil

½ teaspoon cumin seeds

2 whole cloves

One ¼-inch piece cinnamon stick

1 bay leaf

½ small onion, finely chopped

1 tablespoon minced peeled fresh ginger

1 tablespoon minced serrano chiles

2 cups medium-fine cracked wheat

Kosher salt

4½ cups shelled fresh peas (about 4½ pounds/2 kilograms in the shell)

1 tablespoon salted butter

2 cups sugar snap peas (about 6 ounces/170 grams), cut into 1-inch pieces, strings removed

1 cup loosely packed mint leaves

Freshly ground black pepper

Gently heat the stock in a small saucepan. Keep warm.

Meanwhile, in a 4-quart saucepan, heat the oil over medium heat until shimmering. Add the cumin, cloves, cinnamon, and bay leaf and cook, stirring and shaking the pan, until fragrant, 2 to 3 minutes. Add the onion, ginger, and chiles and cook, stirring occasionally, until the onion is translucent, 2 to 3 minutes.

Stir in the cracked wheat and cook, stirring occasionally, until it is lightly colored and smells toasted, 5 to 6 minutes. Stir in the warm chicken stock and salt to taste and bring to a boil over high heat. Remove the pan from the heat, cover, and let the pilaf stand until all the liquid is absorbed, about 30 minutes.

Blanch, shock, and drain 2 cups of the peas (see page 33); reserve. Set aside to cool completely.

Return the pan of water to a boil. Add the remaining peas and boil until they are very soft, 3 to 4 minutes. Drain thoroughly, transfer to a food processor, and process until pureed. Set aside.

Continued

When the pilaf is ready, remove and discard the cloves, cinnamon stick, and bay leaf. Stir in the reserved pea puree and gently warm over low heat.

Meanwhile, in a large sauté pan, combine the butter and sugar snap peas and sauté over medium-high heat, stirring often, until the snap peas are crisp-tender, about 5 minutes. Drain the blanched peas and add them to the pan, along with the mint and salt and pepper to taste. Cook until heated through.

To serve, spoon the pilaf into shallow bowls and spoon the peas and mint over the top. Serve hot.

COOKING TIME: ABOUT 1 HOUR

GINGERED SPINACH

I'm not opposed to using frozen spinach for a puree, but for this side dish, I always use fresh (or even the prewashed spinach in those gloriously large bags that Barkha or I buy every time we're at Costco). The dish needs big spinach flavor, and frozen contains too much water to allow that to come through. If the fresh spinach available to you looks disappointing, use other fresh greens such as collards, kale, Swiss chard, or escarole instead. The cooking time will be longer than for spinach.   **SERVES 4**

3 tablespoons extra-virgin olive oil
1 teaspoon minced peeled fresh ginger
1 pound/454 grams trimmed spinach,
    washed and drained

Kosher salt
Freshly ground black pepper

Place a large sauté pan over high heat. Add the olive oil and minced ginger and cook for 15 seconds. Add the spinach and cook until wilted, using tongs to move the wilted leaves out of the way to make room on the bottom of the pan for the uncooked leaves.

Season to taste with salt and pepper. Serve.

COOKING TIME: ABOUT 5 MINUTES

STEEL-CUT-OAT RISOTTO with KALE PUREE

Steel-cut oats lend themselves to being slowly cooked the way rice is for risotto, and you can add just about anything to enhance the flavor or increase the healthful quotient along the way. After making this with kale, I realized that pretty much any vegetable would work beautifully here. Since then, I've made oat risotto with garden greens such as spinach and mustard as well as carrots, tomatoes, peas, and just about anything else that can be pureed. Go ahead and stretch the limits of your own imagination and pantry with this great "playing around" dish. **SERVES 6**

12 ounces/340 grams Tuscan kale or baby kale

Kosher salt

¼ cup canola oil

One 3-inch cinnamon stick

4 whole cloves

6 tablespoons salted butter

1 cup thinly sliced shallots

2 tablespoons minced peeled fresh ginger

4 garlic cloves

1 cup Irish steel-cut oats

2 quarts Chicken Stock (page 337), Vegetable Stock (page 339), or high-quality store-bought stock

¼ cup freshly grated peeled fresh horseradish

If using Tuscan kale, cut the stems from the leaves. Chop the leaves and set aside. Chop any stems that are no thicker than a pencil (discard thicker stems). If using baby kale, just coarsely chop the leaves and tender stems. (You should have about 10 cups chopped kale.)

Blanch, shock, and drain the kale leaves and stems (see page 33).

Transfer the drained kale to a blender and puree, adding a bit of water if necessary to keep the greens moving. You should have 2 cups. Set aside.

In a large stew pot, heat the oil over medium heat until it shimmers. Add the cinnamon and cloves and cook until aromatic, about 1 minute. Add the butter, shallots, ginger, and garlic and cook until the shallots are translucent, about 3 minutes.

Add the oats and reduce the heat. Cook, stirring occasionally, until the oats have a rich, nutty aroma, 10 to 15 minutes.

Meanwhile, in a small saucepan, bring the stock to a simmer. Stirring constantly, add the warm stock to the oats 2 cups at a time, waiting until the oats have completely absorbed the stock after each addition before adding more. Then continue cooking and stirring until the oats are creamy and tender. The whole process will take 30 to 35 minutes.

Remove and discard the cinnamon stick, cloves, and garlic cloves.

Stir in the reserved kale puree and the horseradish and gently heat through. Taste and adjust the seasoning and serve.

COOKING TIME: ABOUT 1¼ HOURS

CHAPTER FOUR

Family Style

THE CARDOZ SUNDAY-NIGHT FAVORITES

I come from a family of food lovers. All of us—from my kids and my wife to my brothers and sisters and their families—can happily discuss our next meal while enjoying the present one. My wife, Barkha, and I have been blessed with two boys who love food as much as we do, so cooking for them is always a pleasure—although sometimes that gift can have unintended consequences. Once when my son Peter was just six years old, I made pasta with truffle butter and wild mushrooms for a Sunday dinner. At around 3:30 on Monday afternoon, the head reservationist at Tabla interrupted me during a meeting to inform me that my son was on the phone—for the fourth time that day! I rushed to the phone, bracing myself for a terrible emergency. I immediately asked Pete if he was okay. He replied that no, he was certainly *not* okay. He could not find the leftover wild mushroom pasta with truffle butter!

Cooking for my family is very important to me—and not only because it can provide valuable teachable moments about the definition of a true emergency and when it is and is not appropriate to bother Dad at work. (In fairness to Pete, though, this was actually a pretty good example of the type of "emergencies" we tend to have at home: food-related ones.) I believe food is a vital component of culture and, further, that our children form many of their identity-defining memories around what we eat when we are together. When the kids were young, Barkha and I began a tradition of having family dinner on Sunday nights, since running a restaurant meant that I couldn't be with them on weekday nights. We often served dishes that Barkha or I had grown up eating, and we'd share with the boys whatever family stories the food brought to mind. I like to think that the boys will do the same thing with their own children someday, passing on our stories just as we have passed on our parents' and grandparents' stories.

We sometimes played a game to see who could identify the different ingredients and flavors in whatever dish we were eating. Our son Justin usually won; he has the most discerning palate. Of course, this was not only a fun dinnertime diversion; it was also a nice bit of highly effective parental trickery. The best way to win was to eat everything on their plates, since they needed to take more and more bites to identify all the ingredients and flavors.

You don't have to be a chef to instill the same love of flavor, food, and culture in your own family. All you need is to feel a love for cooking and eating and sharing, and the rest will follow. There are days when I prepare a meal with many courses and there are days when we enjoy much simpler fare. No matter what I cook, when I'm doing it for the family, it gives me great pleasure. The love and comfort that flow from and to me when I'm cooking for my family help me produce some of my very best, most flavorful dishes.

CORN ON THE COB "ELOTE" with COTIJA CHEESE

When doing research for El Verano Taqueria, the taco stands in the baseball stadiums of the New York Mets and the Washington Nationals for which I created the food and menu, I traveled to taco joints all over the country. Outside of what seemed like every single taqueria I visited, there would be a lady selling *elote,* steamed corn on the cob slathered in mayonnaise and generously coated with cheese. When I describe this to most Americans, I see a reflection of *my* initial reaction when I first encountered it. People often assume a vaguely horrified look that can be summed up as, "Why, *why* would you smear mayonnaise all over perfectly fabulous corn on the cob?"

That's probably why it wasn't until my very last taqueria visit, to the one that was practically in my backyard—on 116th Street in Manhattan—that I finally tasted a sample, and at last I understood. This corn is amazing. It may sound like an odd combination, but it absolutely works: sweet, spicy, salty, and creamy. Trust me: You've just got to taste it to appreciate how very good it is.

You'll find cotija cheese—often grated, in sealed bags or plastic tubs—in Hispanic supermarkets or at other grocery stores with a good selection of Hispanic foods. If you can't find it, Pecorino Romano and Parmigiano-Reggiano are good substitutes.

Use very fresh corn. This is a summer thing. Just like baseball. **SERVES 6**

Kosher salt
6 ears corn, husked
2 cups grated cotija cheese
(8 ounces/227 grams)

½ cup mayonnaise, preferably Hellmann's
Cayenne
1 lime, cut into 6 wedges (optional)

Fill a large pot with water, add sufficient salt to make it taste like seawater, and bring to a boil over high heat. Add the corn, cover, and simmer for 5 minutes.

While the corn is cooking, place the cheese on a rimmed baking sheet.

Drain the corn. While it is still hot, brush each ear with mayonnaise and roll it in the cheese so that it is completely covered with cheese. Dust the corn with cayenne and serve with the lime wedges, if desired.

COOKING TIME: 20 TO 25 MINUTES (INCLUDING 10 TO 15 MINUTES TO BRING THE WATER TO A BOIL)

STEAMED BOK CHOY with GINGER and SHALLOTS

This recipe was inspired by a main-course meat-based stir-fry I made one night, which included everything here, all playing a supporting role to the meat. Along the way it occurred to me that the seasonings would work well with bok choy all on its own. You can find toasted peanut oil at well-stocked grocery stores and Asian markets. **SERVES 6**

3 tablespoons toasted peanut oil

¼ cup minced shallots

One 2-inch piece fresh ginger, peeled and sliced into thin strips (see page 32)

Kosher salt

Freshly ground black pepper

Six 4- to 5-inch-long bok choy, split lengthwise in half, washed, and dried (see below)

Place a large stew pot over medium heat. Add the oil and shallots and cook until the shallots are translucent, 3 to 4 minutes. Reduce the heat, stir in the ginger, and cook until fragrant, about 1 minute. Season with salt and pepper.

Arrange the bok choy cut side down in the pot; it's best if they are in a single layer, but it's okay if you have to place a few on top of the first layer. Season with salt and pepper. Sprinkle 3 tablespoons water over the bok choy, increase the heat to high, cover, and steam until it is tender, about 4 minutes.

Transfer the bok choy to a platter and spoon the ginger and shallot mixture over it. Serve immediately.

COOKING TIME: ABOUT 15 MINUTES

CHANGING IT UP

Adjust the flavor profile of the bok choy depending on what else you're serving. With an Asian-inspired main dish, add a couple of tablespoons of oyster sauce along with the water and finish with a couple of tablespoons of very thinly sliced kimchi. Or, if you're serving it with something like Tabasco Chipotle–Marinated Pork Chops (page 286), substitute extra-virgin olive oil and use garlic in place of the shallots and ginger. Or, to up the umami factor, use olive oil, omit the ginger, and add a few finely chopped anchovies along with the water.

CLEANING BOK CHOY

Bok choy can be very sandy, so it needs a good cleaning before cooking. Soak the halved bok choy in cold water for 20 minutes. Drain, place the halves in a salad spinner with the cut sides facing out, and spin until well dried.

BRAISED ESCAROLE with MUSTARD

This is a great method for preparing bitter or hearty greens, which take well to spicy heat and saltiness. The grated potato helps to thicken and bring it all together. I typically use escarole because in my experience it's more acceptable to kids than other greens, but this method works equally well with kale, Swiss chard, collards, and even broccoli rabe. If you use greens such as kale, Swiss chard, or collards, pull the thick stems off the leaves before cleaning and chopping them. Or, for superconvenient prep, pick up one of those handy bags of braising greens available at many supermarkets and farmers' markets these days.

Serve the greens as a side with steak or grilled chicken. **SERVES 4**

1 head escarole, leaves separated

3 tablespoons extra-virgin olive oil or bacon fat

3 garlic cloves, smashed

1 small onion, finely minced (about ¾ cup)

1 teaspoon chile flakes

1 cup Chicken Stock (page 337), high-quality store-bought stock, or water

1 russet (baking) potato, peeled

Kosher salt

Freshly ground black pepper

2 tablespoons freshly grated peeled horseradish

1 tablespoon whole-grain mustard

Wash the escarole and spin dry in a salad spinner. Cut into 2-inch pieces. Set aside.

Place the olive oil and garlic in a large wide pot and heat over medium-low heat. When the garlic begins to lightly color, add the onion and chile flakes and cook, stirring occasionally, until the onion is translucent, 7 to 9 minutes.

Add the escarole, then add the stock and bring to a boil over medium heat.

Meanwhile, grate the potato on the large holes of a box grater.

Add the potato and salt and pepper to taste to the pot and stir until well combined. Cover, reduce the heat, and cook until the greens are tender and the potato is cooked, 10 to 12 minutes.

Stir in the horseradish and mustard. Taste and adjust the seasoning. Serve.

COOKING TIME: ABOUT 30 MINUTES

CHANGING IT UP

To add some extra interest and funk (see page 25) to the flavor profile, add 4 chopped anchovy fillets right before you take the greens off the stove.

"BERYL'S SUNDAY LUNCH" BASMATI RICE

My mom, Beryl, made this dish so often for Sunday lunch when I was young that my memories of those afternoons are inextricably linked with rice. It was her Sunday standby, because it can be served with so many different main courses. It works really well as an accompaniment to roasted chicken or pork, pretty much anything that is grilled or panfried, or stew. I've also seen people pile their plates high with *just* the rice and nothing more, or the rice with a simple salad of cucumbers and tomatoes. Serve with the Romaine-Cucumber Salad with Lime and Thai Chile (page 39) for an easy and satisfying lunch—perfect for Sundays.

There is one ingredient in this recipe sure to cause a few raised eyebrows: bouillon cubes. I know, a chef who recommends store-bought bouillon instead of a homemade stock in even *one* of his recipes? But bouillon cubes are very common in most Asian countries and the Caribbean. For this reason, you're sure to see them prominently displayed in any Asian or Hispanic grocery store you enter. I honestly have no idea how they came to be so popular in India, but I grew up with them, and there's always a jar in my pantry today. This is one of the places where all my rules about making things from scratch go right out the window, because I love them, especially the brand my mother used when I was growing up: Maggi. Bouillon cubes add that salty-savory umami flavor that chicken stock alone can't provide. True, sometimes this is helped by the addition of MSG, but you can find plenty of brands that don't include it.

One thing to note is that in spite of a wide perception that bouillon cubes are extremely salty, they really do vary quite a bit from brand to brand, and once they've mingled with the rice, water, and other ingredients below, you'd be surprised at how little overall saltiness there is. So be sure to taste and add salt if needed. Also note that bouillon cubes come in different sizes: Use two small squares or one of the large rectangular cubes in this dish. **SERVES 6**

3 tablespoons canola oil

One 1-inch piece cinnamon stick

3 whole cloves

1 cup finely chopped white onion

4 scallions (white and green parts), thinly sliced

2 bay leaves

2 cups white basmati rice, rinsed, soaked, and drained (see following page)

1½ cups diced tomatoes

2 small or 1 large chicken bouillon cube, preferably Maggi brand

3 cups boiling water

Kosher salt

Heat the oil in a 4-quart stew pot over medium heat until shimmering. Add the cinnamon stick and cloves and cook until fragrant, about 1 minute. Add the onion and scallions and cook, stirring, until softened (don't let them color), about 3 minutes.

Continued

Add the bay leaves and drained rice, stirring to coat the rice with the oil. Cook, stirring frequently, until the rice starts to stick to the bottom of the pot, 4 to 6 minutes.

Add the tomatoes, bouillon cube, and water, taste, and add salt as necessary. Increase the heat and bring the mixture to a boil. Gently stir the rice with a silicone spatula a couple of times and cover the pot. Reduce the heat to medium and cook, stirring occasionally, until most of the liquid has evaporated, about 15 minutes. Turn off the heat and let the pilaf stand, covered, for 15 minutes.

Fluff the pilaf with a fork. Remove and discard the cinnamon stick, cloves, and bay leaves and serve.

COOKING TIME: ABOUT 45 MINUTES / INACTIVE TIME: ABOUT 35 MINUTES FOR SOAKING AND RESTING THE RICE

RINSING AND SOAKING BASMATI RICE

It is very important to clean the starch and grit from basmati rice before cooking it. And after a thorough rinsing, soaking the rice for several minutes helps it cook a little faster and more evenly and results in cooked rice with longer grains.

To rinse and soak basmati rice, put the rice in a large bowl and fill the bowl with cold water. Swish the grains around gently with your hand, then pour off the water. Repeat at least 10 times, or until the washing water remains clear.

Cover the rice with lukewarm water and soak for 20 minutes. Drain the rice in a sieve.

QUICK MASHED POTATOES

I have to tip my hat to one of my *Top Chef Masters* teammates, Alessandro Stratta, for this recipe. We were doing the RV challenge, where we had to cook a full family-style meal for the band Maroon 5 in a ridiculously small space. Alex asked if I'd ever made mashed potatoes this way—cooking the potatoes directly in the milk and butter that you usually use to mash them, rather than boiling the potatoes separately in water. It was the very first time I'd done it this way, but I'll never go back to the other way—it's so very easy and nothing goes to waste. In fact, I love this streamlined method so much that I adopted it for the mashed potatoes at my restaurants.

As for the milk, there's no great mystery behind why I use fat-free; it's simply because that's what's in our fridge at home. Convenience aside, though, I do actually prefer it. The fact is that I rarely use cream in my cooking, and I'll go so far as to avoid it when I eat out as well. There's already enough butter here to give the potatoes good body and a nice creaminess; any more fat would be unpleasant.

And, yes, you're reading the nutmeg right. Add a full half nutmeg; it's what puts these potatoes over the top. Serve them with roast chicken, grilled steak, or the Osso Buco Braised with Warming Spices (page 92). **SERVES 6**

4 large russet (baking) potatoes (about 1½ pounds/680 grams), peeled and cut into roughly 2-inch pieces

3 cups fat-free milk, plus more if needed

8 tablespoons (1 stick) salted butter

Kosher salt

Freshly ground black pepper

½ nutmeg

In a large pot, combine the potatoes, milk, and butter and bring to a boil over medium heat. Reduce the heat and simmer until the potatoes are tender, about 25 minutes.

Drain the potatoes in a colander set over a bowl, reserving the milk and butter mixture.

Rice the potatoes back into the hot pot or return them to the pot and use a masher to mash them by hand. Place the pot over medium-low heat and season the potatoes with salt and pepper. Slowly pour in the milk-butter mixture, stirring until the potatoes have reached the desired consistency. Add more milk, if desired, for a looser consistency. Grate the nutmeg into the mashed potatoes and stir to blend. Serve hot.

COOKING TIME: ABOUT 45 MINUTES

EGGS in PEANUT-COCONUT CURRY

This is the kind of curry that we ate often at home in Bombay when I was growing up—especially during Lent, when we abstained from meat on Fridays. Our family wasn't unusual; egg curries are very common in India, and it's easy to see why. Poaching eggs in gently simmering, spiced liquid results in a slightly loose, brothy curry made even more delicious by the rich egg yolks, which are incorporated into the mix only when broken by the diners' forks. If you prefer not to cook the eggs directly in the sauce, you can cut warm hard-cooked eggs in half and serve them with the curry. **SERVES 4**

1 teaspoon cumin seeds

½ teaspoon black peppercorns

¾ cup grated unsweetened coconut

¼ cup unsalted roasted peanuts

4 garlic cloves

3 cups Chicken Stock (page 337), high-quality store-bought stock, or water

1 tablespoon sweet paprika

1 teaspoon turmeric

2 tablespoons canola oil

¾ cup sliced onion

One 13.5-fluid-ounce can Chaokoh-brand coconut milk (stir well before using)

1 fresh chile, preferably Anaheim, halved lengthwise

1 tablespoon Tamarind Paste (page 340)

Kosher salt

8 extra-large eggs

Crusty bread or steamed rice for serving (optional)

Finely grind the cumin seeds and peppercorns in a spice/coffee grinder. Set aside.

In a blender, combine the coconut, peanuts, garlic, and 1 cup of the stock and puree until smooth. Transfer the coconut paste to a bowl and add the pepper and cumin mixture, the paprika, and turmeric. Whisk to blend. Set aside.

In a large wide stew pot, heat the oil over medium heat until it shimmers. Add the onion and cook, stirring often, until translucent, 6 to 8 minutes.

Add the coconut-spice paste and cook, stirring, for 2 to 3 minutes. Add the remaining 2 cups stock, the coconut milk, chile, tamarind paste, and salt to taste. Simmer for 10 to 15 minutes to allow the flavors to blend.

Reduce the heat. Working quickly, crack each of the eggs into a cup and drop them one by one into the sauce; do not stir. Cook for 4 to 8 minutes, depending on how you like your eggs cooked.

Serve in warmed shallow bowls with bread or rice, if desired.

COOKING TIME: 30 TO 45 MINUTES

CHANGING IT UP

To make a filling for the best egg sandwiches you'll ever have, don't add the eggs to the sauce, or use leftover sauce. Simmer the sauce until very reduced and add chopped hard-cooked eggs to the warm (or room-temperature) sauce.

BRAISED STRIPED BASS with BABY ROOT VEGETABLES

Once a year, my boys and I love to take a fishing trip for striped bass. Striped bass is my favorite northeastern fish. It is meaty yet delicate and easy to cook. I think the fact that the bass eats so many mollusks and small fish makes it especially tasty. This dish came about after a particularly good catch one year. I like this method of cooking fish—slipping it into a simmering broth and cooking it, covered, over a very low flame—because it keeps the fish very silky. Be sure to use fish with the skin still on; the gelatin in the skin gives the stock a lot of body. When preparing the vegetables, cut them all into roughly the same size (even if they aren't quite the same shape) to ensure that they cook evenly.

The spices and orange juice also work very well with grouper and red snapper, so feel free to use either in place of the striped bass. If possible, use fresh clam juice (I buy it frozen at Whole Foods). Shelf-stable bottled clam juice can be salty, so adjust the salt in the dish as necessary if you use it.   SERVES 4

1 cup golden raisins

½ to ⅔ cup white wine

8 garlic cloves, very thinly sliced

2 tablespoons extra-virgin olive oil

½ cup very thinly sliced shallots

One 2-inch piece fresh ginger, peeled and sliced into thin strips

3 tablespoons anise seeds, finely ground

3 tablespoons coriander seeds, finely ground

2 dried chipotle chiles, seeded and finely sliced

6 cups Chicken Stock (page 337), Vegetable Stock (page 339), or high quality, store-bought stock

4 cups fresh or bottled clam juice or water

4 cups fresh orange juice (from 8 to 12 oranges)

Four 5-ounce/142-gram skin-on striped bass fillets

Sea salt

Freshly ground black pepper

1 cup sliced (quarter-sized slices) fingerling potatoes

1 cup halved or quartered baby carrots

1 cup halved or quartered baby turnips

Place the raisins in a small saucepan and pour over enough wine just to cover. Bring to a boil, then reduce the heat, cover the pan, and simmer until the wine is absorbed and the raisins are soft, about 10 minutes. Set aside.

In a large stew pot, combine the garlic and olive oil and heat over medium-low heat until the oil begins to gently bubble around the garlic and it begins to soften, about 5 minutes. Add the shallots and ginger and cook until translucent, about 3 minutes. Add the anise, coriander, and chipotle and cook until fragrant, about 1 minute.

Continued

Add the stock, clam juice, and orange juice. Increase the heat to medium, bring to a simmer, and simmer for 10 minutes.

Meanwhile, lightly season the fish on both sides with salt and pepper. Let stand at room temperature until needed.

Add the potatoes to the pot and cook until almost tender, about 7 minutes. Add the carrots and turnips and cook until beginning to soften, 4 to 5 minutes. Add the reserved raisins and adjust the seasoning with salt and pepper.

Add the fish to the pot, reduce the heat to a very low simmer, cover, and cook until just opaque throughout, about 8 minutes.

Spoon the broth and vegetables into four shallow bowls. Place a piece of fish in each bowl and serve.

COOKING TIME: ABOUT 1 HOUR

SHRIMP CURRY with CAULIFLOWER

When I was growing up in Bombay, this was a very common lunch dish at our house. Once Barkha and I had kids and I began to serve it in our own home, I quickly realized why it's such a great family meal. Adults appreciate the excellent taste of the mild, tender cauliflower and sweet, toothsome shrimp simmered in coconut milk with lots of aromatic flavors. Kids just really enjoy it because it's yummy and different without being particularly spicy. And everyone agrees that it makes the kitchen smell delectable while it's cooking. My mom taught me the trick of simmering the throwaway parts of the shrimp—the heads and shells—to quickly make a really flavorful stock. (If you're pressed for time, though, you can use peeled shrimp in place of the head-on shrimp called for here, and use 3 cups of fish stock instead of making stock from the shrimp heads and tails.)

We always eat this with steamed white rice or "Beryl's Sunday Lunch" Basmati Rice (page 135) to soak up all the delicious coconut curry broth.

If you have leftovers, use them for breakfast the next morning. Place the curry in a wide pot and simmer over medium-low heat until thick. Serve with fried eggs and crusty bread. **SERVES 6**

1½ pounds/680 grams (21–25 count)
   head-on shrimp
Sea salt
1 tablespoon canola oil
1½ cups thinly sliced onions
5 garlic cloves, finely minced
1 tablespoon turmeric
1½ teaspoons cumin seeds, ground
1 teaspoon black peppercorns, finely
   ground

1 serrano chile, sliced lengthwise in half
1 tablespoon Tamarind Paste (page 340)
1 tablespoon cider vinegar
3 cups cauliflower florets
One and a half 13.5-fluid-ounce cans
   Chaokoh-brand coconut milk (stir well
   before measuring)

Remove the heads and shells from the shrimp, reserving both. Devein the shrimp and rinse them well. Season the shrimp with salt and refrigerate.

Place the shrimp heads and shells in a medium saucepan, add cold water to cover, and bring to a boil over medium heat. Reduce the heat and simmer until the liquid is reduced to 3 cups, 25 to 30 minutes. Strain the stock and set aside.

Heat the oil in a 4- to 6-quart pot over medium-high heat until shimmering. Add the sliced onions and cook, stirring occasionally, until translucent, 3 to 4 minutes. Add the garlic, turmeric, cumin, and pepper and cook until the garlic is lightly colored and the spices are fragrant, 2 to 3 minutes.

Add the reserved stock, the chile, tamarind paste, and vinegar and bring to a boil. Reduce the heat and simmer for 5 minutes.

Add the cauliflower and coconut milk and bring to a boil over medium-high heat. Season with salt. Reduce the heat and simmer gently until the cauliflower is just beginning to soften, 3 to 4 minutes.

Stir in the shrimp and cook until the shrimp are firm, 5 to 7 minutes. Remove and discard the serrano, if desired. Taste and adjust the seasoning. Serve hot.

COOKING TIME: ABOUT 1 HOUR

CHANGING IT UP

Sometimes I make this with fish instead of shrimp, using one 4- to 5-ounce (113- to 142-gram) halibut or fluke steak per person. (The steaks come from cutting a whole fish crosswise into ½- to 1-inch-thick slices. It's a very pretty cut, resulting in a nice oblong shape with a bone in the middle and the skin ringing the steak.) Use fish stock or plain water in place of the shrimp stock; the fish's bones and skin add depth and richness to the curry, just as the shrimp shells do. Add the fish steaks where the recipe instructs you to add the shrimp and cook until the fish is opaque and flakes easily.

ROASTED CITRUS-BRINED CHICKEN with PAN-TOASTED CROUTONS

I've roasted more chickens than I can count in my life, professionally and at home, but this particular version, which came about one day when Barkha and I were preparing dinner together, has become the Cardoz family gold standard. We had already brined the chicken, which I do whenever I have the time, even though it runs contrary to my more spontaneous style of cooking at home, because brining seasons the chicken all the way through and helps keep it moist.

Our dinner plan was chicken and a salad—simple enough that when the chicken went into the oven, we began thinking about the salad. The boys love croutons, and I thought about using the pan juices from the chicken to make some extra-savory ones. When the chicken had come out of the oven and was resting, I reduced the pan juices, dropped in several handfuls of cubed cheese bread, and popped the pan back in the oven. After just ten minutes, we had the most delectable croutons the boys had ever tasted (we tossed them with lightly dressed arugula) and a savory accompaniment that seems to just underline everything that is good about the chicken.

There are specifics below, but the truth is that this delicious accompaniment to roasted chicken will be a little different every time you make it, depending on what kind of bread you use. At our house, that depends on what is in the freezer. We often serve bread with dinner. Sometimes it might be a plain white rustic loaf, but usually it's olive or cheese bread. And since I am genetically programmed to be incapable of throwing away bread, when dinner is over, we cut any leftovers into cubes and pop them into a ziplock bag in the freezer. So I'm always prepared to create this quick and delicious flourish right before we eat. Incidentally, this method—the brining and croutons alike—also works for turkey. **SERVES 4 TO 6**

FOR THE BRINE

2 lemons, thinly sliced

1 orange, thinly sliced

2 cups white wine

1 large head garlic, halved horizontally

1¼ cups kosher salt

2 tablespoons black peppercorns, coarsely ground

Three 6-inch rosemary sprigs

4 quarts water

One 2½-pound/1.13-kilogram chicken

FOR ROASTING THE CHICKEN

Kosher salt

Freshly ground black pepper

2 teaspoons chopped rosemary

FOR THE CROUTONS

1½ cups Chicken Stock (page 337), high-quality store-bought stock, or water

4 loosely packed cups cubed (1-inch) bread

Thyme or rosemary sprig (optional)

Continued

Squeeze the juice from the lemon and orange slices into a large bowl or pot and then add the slices. Add the wine, garlic, salt, pepper, rosemary sprigs, and water and stir until well combined. Add the chicken. Place in the refrigerator for at least 12 hours, and up to 24 hours.

Remove the chicken from the brine and pat it dry with a paper towel. Remove the garlic, lemon and orange slices, and rosemary sprigs from the brine and set aside. Discard the brine.

Put the chicken breast side up in a large heavy-bottomed flameproof baking pan, preferably enameled cast iron. Stuff the cavity with some of the reserved brine ingredients (discard the remainder). Tie the legs together using kitchen string. Season the chicken lightly with salt and pepper and sprinkle with the chopped rosemary. Let stand at room temperature for 30 to 45 minutes.

Preheat the oven to 425°F.

Roast the chicken, basting it occasionally with the pan juices, for about 1 hour, or until the juices run clear when the thickest part of the thigh is pierced with a sharp knife. Remove the pan from the oven (leave the oven on). Lift up the chicken and tilt it to let the cavity juices run into the pan. Transfer the chicken to a cooling rack to rest while you prepare the croutons.

Skim off and discard most of the fat from the cooking liquid. Add the stock to the pan and place the pan over medium heat. Bring to a boil, using a metal spatula to scrape up all of the stuck bits from the bottom of the pan. Reduce the heat and simmer until the liquid is reduced by one-half. Add the bread cubes and press them down so that they soak up all of the liquid. Add the thyme sprig, if desired.

Place in the oven and bake until the bread is lightly toasted on top, 12 to 16 minutes.

Cut up the chicken and serve with the toasted croutons.

COOKING TIME: 1 HOUR AND 15 MINUTES / INACTIVE TIME: 12 TO 24 HOURS FOR BRINING THE CHICKEN AND 30 TO 45 MINUTES FOR TEMPING

Note: You can reuse the brine once more the following day if you keep it refrigerated. Use it for another whole chicken or bone-in chicken thighs.

STEWED CHICKEN with FRESH TOMATOES

There comes a time every summer—right around when the garden kicks into high gear and there is a plethora of tomatoes—when my kids invariably declare that they have developed an acute allergy to raw tomatoes and could not possibly consider eating another one. Ever. A few summers back, I responded to their "allergy" with this stew, which was deemed delicious by all and certain to aggravate allergies in no one.

The number of tomatoes you need will naturally depend on their size and how many seeds they have, but I suggest a ballpark weight that should yield right around the amount that works best.

For the chiles, I usually use smoky dried chipotles, but sometimes I switch it up and use fresh serranos, especially when they're in season during the summer. Use whichever you prefer or have on hand. If you want a spicier dish, cut the chile you use crosswise into slices. If you want less spice, slice the chile lengthwise in half and remove it at the end of cooking.   **SERVES 6**

---

2 pounds/907 grams boneless, skinless chicken thighs, excess fat removed, cut in half

Kosher salt

3 tablespoons canola oil

1 tablespoon brown mustard seeds

3 whole cloves

1 teaspoon cumin seeds

1 dried chipotle or 1 fresh serrano chile, sliced crosswise or cut lengthwise in half (see headnote)

5 garlic cloves, minced

One 1-inch piece fresh ginger, peeled and minced

1 tablespoon turmeric

1 bay leaf

4 large ripe tomatoes (about 3 pounds/1.36 kilograms), peeled and seeded (see opposite), if desired, and diced (about 6 cups)

1 tablespoon Tamarind Paste (page 340)

1 tablespoon honey

Freshly ground black pepper

Leaves from 1 generous bunch Thai basil

1 cup washed and dried cilantro leaves (see page 39) with tender stems

---

Season the chicken with salt. Set aside at room temperature.

Heat a large stew pot over medium heat. Add the oil, and when it starts to shimmer, add the mustard seeds and cloves. Cook until the mustard seeds begin to pop, 1 to 2 minutes, then add the cumin seeds, chipotle, and garlic and cook until very fragrant, 2 to 3 minutes.

Add the ginger, turmeric, and bay leaf and cook for 1 minute. Add the tomatoes (and the strained tomato juice if you seeded them) and bring to a boil. Reduce the heat and simmer for 5 minutes.

Add the chicken, tamarind paste, honey, and salt and pepper to taste and bring to a boil over medium heat. Reduce the heat and simmer until the chicken is tender when pierced with a knife, 12 to 15 minutes.

Remove the bay leaf and cloves, and the halved chile, if desired. Season the stew to taste with salt and pepper. Fold in the basil and cilantro leaves and serve.

COOKING TIME: ABOUT 40 MINUTES

CHANGING IT UP

This wonderful stew has lots of rich sauce, and although we often manage to eat it all, occasionally we have some left over. In those cases, I like to replace 1 cup of the water or stock in a pilaf (such as "Beryl's Sunday Lunch" Basmati Rice, page 135) with 1 cup of this sauce. If you have some stewed chicken left over too, tuck it into the rice during the last 10 minutes of cooking to warm it through. If there is no meat left over, or if you just want to make it a heartier dish, add 1 pound ground turkey or chicken to the pilaf when you add the liquid.

PEELING AND SEEDING TOMATOES

I don't often peel and seed tomatoes for family dishes because the skin and seeds are a great source of fiber. That said, when a recipe needs something more refined, this is how I do it.

To peel tomatoes, bring a large pot of water to a boil. Have ready a bowl of ice water. Cut a shallow X through the skin on the bottom of each tomato. Blanch the tomatoes in the boiling water for about 20 seconds, then immediately plunge them into the ice water until cold. Use a paring knife to pull the skin off the tomatoes and discard it. (If the skin does not peel easily from the flesh, repeat the blanching process.)

To seed the tomatoes, cut each tomato crosswise in half. If using the juice in the recipe, set a medium-mesh strainer over a bowl and squeeze the seeds and juice from the tomatoes into the strainer. When all of the tomatoes have been seeded, discard the seeds in the strainer and set the strained juice aside. If you are not using the juice, simply squeeze the seeds and juice into a container and store in the refrigerator or freezer; use in stock.

CHICKEN TAGINE with OLIVES, CHICKPEAS, and PINE NUTS

Whenever I use butcher's twine in cooking, I remember this dish. There is no exotic connection between these two events other than the fact that we store both the spools of twine and our tagine in the laundry room, where—I admit—I only ever go if I'm looking for twine. Invariably while searching for the twine, I see the tagine and begin craving this meal. But there's far more to this dish than happenstance. It's a hearty and nourishing one-pot dinner that comes together quickly once the ingredients are chopped. And while the ingredients list might look long at first glance, it's made up entirely of pantry and freezer staples. Which is a good thing, because I go on the hunt for twine pretty often!

Traditional tagines are made of clay, but the one I use has a heavy stainless steel base and a terra-cotta lid. It's durable and easy to clean, and it can be placed directly on a burner, unlike the traditional versions. You can also use a Dutch oven or stew pot.

Throw in the whole chipotle for milder flavor or cut it in half if you want bolder flavor. **SERVES 6**

1½ pounds/680 grams boneless, skinless chicken thighs, excess fat removed, cut in half

Kosher salt

Freshly ground black pepper

2 lemons

¼ cup extra-virgin olive oil

One 1-inch piece cinnamon stick

2 whole cloves

1 teaspoon cumin seeds

2 cups minced onions

4 garlic cloves, smashed

1 tablespoon minced peeled fresh ginger

2 tablespoons sweet paprika

1 teaspoon turmeric

2 red or green bell peppers, cored, seeds and ribs removed, and diced

2 cups cooked chickpeas (see page 341) or canned chickpeas, rinsed and drained

One 14.5-ounce/411-gram can diced fire-roasted tomatoes, preferably Muir Glen brand, with their juice

¼ cup raisins

¼ cup pine nuts

¼ cup pitted drained kalamata or Niçoise olives packed in oil

1 dried chipotle chile, halved if desired (see headnote)

3 thyme sprigs

2 bay leaves

1 cup water, or as needed

Steamed couscous for serving (optional)

Season the chicken with salt and pepper. Set aside at room temperature.

Remove the zest from the lemons using a vegetable peeler and juice them. Set the zest and juice aside.

Continued

In a flameproof tagine, a large stew pot, or a Dutch oven, heat the olive oil over medium heat until it shimmers. Add the cinnamon stick and cloves and cook, stirring, until they are fragrant and little bubbles form around the spices, about 1 minute. Add the cumin seeds and cook for 30 seconds. Add the onions, garlic, and ginger and cook, stirring occasionally, until translucent, 3 to 4 minutes. Add the paprika and turmeric and cook for 2 minutes.

Add the chicken, peppers, chickpeas, tomatoes, raisins, pine nuts, olives, the reserved lemon zest and juice, the chipotle, thyme, and bay leaves, stir, and cook for 5 minutes. Add the water, cover, and cook until the chicken is cooked through, about 10 minutes. Uncover the pot. The consistency should be between that of a pot roast and a stew; add up to another 1 cup water if the mixture is very dry. Taste and adjust the seasoning. Remove the cinnamon stick, cloves, chipotle, thyme sprigs, and bay leaves.

Serve, with couscous, if desired.

COOKING TIME: ABOUT 40 MINUTES

GRILLED HANGER STEAK with RED WINE SAUCE

I much prefer hanger steak, with its strong, beefy flavor and pleasing chewiness, to more popular cuts such as tenderloin, which I find bland and even kind of mushy. But unlike with more mild and tender cuts, you can't just throw a little seasoning on hanger steak and slap it on the grill. This recipe requires some advance planning, since hanger steak is best when it is marinated before cooking. A bold marinade complements the assertively flavored meat and tenderizes it a bit as well. Here I use a red wine with big flavor both to marinate the meat and in a reduced sauce—which incorporates the marinade after the meat is grilled. This way nothing—including all that great flavor—goes to waste. Demiglace is a highly reduced, flavorful sauce based on dark veal stock. It is a time-consuming process to do at home, so I recommend buying good-quality demi-glace (see Sources, page 345).

Use the widest saucepan you have to make the sauce. The wider it is, the more quickly the sauce will reduce to the proper consistency. **SERVES 6**

FOR THE MARINADE

2 cups red wine, preferably cabernet or pinot noir

⅓ cup sliced shallots

4 garlic cloves, sliced

One 1-inch piece fresh ginger, peeled and sliced into coins

Leaves from two 4-inch rosemary sprigs, lightly chopped

1 tablespoon black peppercorns, coarsely ground

2 pounds/907 grams hanger steak, trimmed into evenly sized steaks

Kosher salt

FOR THE SAUCE

2 cups red wine, preferably cabernet or pinot noir

6 allspice berries, coarsely pounded in a mortar with a pestle

One 2-inch rosemary sprig

2 tablespoons red wine vinegar

½ to 1 tablespoon black peppercorns, ground medium fine

1½ teaspoons brown sugar, plus more if necessary

Kosher salt

½ cup demi-glace

Reserved marinade

To prepare the marinade, in a large ziplock bag, combine the wine, shallots, garlic, ginger, rosemary, and pepper. Seal the bag and shake it to blend the marinade. Place the steaks in the bag, seal it tightly, and massage the bag to thoroughly coat the meat with the marinade. Refrigerate for at least 4 hours, and up to 24 hours.

Meanwhile, to prepare the sauce, in a medium saucepan, combine the wine, allspice, rosemary, vinegar, pepper, brown sugar, and salt to taste and bring to a boil over medium heat. Reduce the heat to medium-low and simmer until the

sauce is reduced to one-quarter of its original volume (roughly ⅔ cup), about 30 minutes. Stir in the demi-glace. (The sauce can be prepared to this point up to 1 day in advance and stored in the refrigerator.)

When ready to grill the steaks, prepare a high-heat grill.

While the grill heats, remove the steaks from the bag; reserve the marinade. Pat the steaks thoroughly dry with paper towels. Season with salt. Set aside.

If necessary, bring the sauce back to a simmer over medium heat. Add the reserved marinade and bring to a boil. Reduce the heat and simmer until reduced to a sauce consistency (the sauce should coat the back of a spoon), about 20 minutes. Taste and season with salt and/or brown sugar if necessary.

While the sauce simmers, grill the steaks for 4 to 5 minutes per side for medium-rare, or the desired doneness. Remove the steaks from the grill, transfer to a cooling rack, and let rest for about 6 minutes.

Meanwhile, strain the sauce and discard the solids.

Thinly slice the steaks against the grain. Serve with the sauce.

COOKING TIME: ABOUT 1 HOUR / INACTIVE TIME: 4 TO 24 HOURS FOR MARINATING

VANILLA-BEAN KULFI with CITRUS FRUIT in ROSE WATER SYRUP

Kulfi is a creamy frozen treat popular in India. Served with fruit and sweet syrup, as in this recipe, it was one of the most requested desserts at Tabla. It remains a fixture at my home—so much so that I've had to find ways to serve it all year long. It's not hard to adapt the fruit to match the season. During the summer, I use peaches or cherries, and in the fall I change to diced apples, replacing the rose water with a cinnamon stick and warming the apples for a few minutes in the hot syrup before letting the whole thing steep and cool together.

Although it's sometimes referred to as Indian ice cream, kulfi has enough heavy cream that the mixture would turn to butter if it were actually churned in an ice cream maker. Instead, the cream and milk are simmered until the liquid has reduced almost to the consistency of a fluid custard. Then it's divided into small portions and frozen. This is not at all a difficult dessert to make. I especially like it because both the kulfi and the fruit are prepared in advance and simply put together at the last minute. But it does need a bit of loving attention. When simmering the cream and milk, you want two things most of all: for the mixture to reduce quickly and for it to reduce sufficiently. If it takes too long to reduce, the kulfi will discolor and become sticky, and if it doesn't reduce enough, sugar crystals will form, so make sure to use a saucepan that is wide rather than high and just keep an eye on it and follow the indications given in the recipe.   **SERVES 6**

FOR THE KULFI

2¾ cups heavy cream

1 cup milk

1 vanilla bean, preferably Tahitian, split lengthwise in half

3 ounces/85 grams (⅓ cup plus 1½ tablespoons) sugar

A pinch of fine sea salt

FOR THE CITRUS FRUIT

⅓ cup water

2⅜ ounces/67 grams (⅓ cup) sugar

1 vanilla bean, preferably Tahitian, split lengthwise in half

One 1-inch piece fresh ginger, peeled and sliced

2 to 4 citrus fruits, such as oranges, grapefruit, clementines, tangerines, and blood oranges, or as needed

½ teaspoon rose water

To make the kulfi, pour the cream and milk into a wide heavy-bottomed saucepan. Scrape the seeds from the vanilla bean and add them to the milk, along with the pod. Bring to a simmer over medium heat and cook, stirring often, until the liquid has reduced to one-third of its original volume and coats the back of the spoon—when you run your finger through the mixture, the trail of your finger should remain; this will take about 50 minutes.

Continued

Add the sugar and cook, stirring, until dissolved. Stir in the salt. Remove and discard the vanilla bean. Transfer the mixture to a bowl set in a larger bowl of ice water and let cool to room temperature, stirring occasionally.

Pour the kulfi into six 4½-ounce molds (I use Dixie cups) and freeze until solid, at least 24 hours. (The kulfi can be frozen for up to 2 weeks.)

To prepare the citrus fruit, combine the water and sugar in a small saucepan, place over medium heat, and cook, stirring occasionally, until the sugar has dissolved. Remove the pan from the heat, add the split vanilla bean and sliced ginger, cover, and let stand for 30 minutes.

Remove the lid and cool the syrup to room temperature. Strain and set aside.

Meanwhile, use a sharp thin-bladed knife to cut off just enough of the top and bottom of one of the citrus fruits to expose the flesh. Set the citrus cut side down on a cutting board and slice off the peel and pith, following the curve of the fruit with the knife. Holding the peeled fruit over a bowl to catch the segments and the juice, cut the segments away from the thin membranes holding them together. Then squeeze the membranes over the bowl to extract the remaining juice; discard the membranes. Repeat with the remaining citrus until you have 3 cups segments. Set aside.

Stir the rose water into the reserved syrup. Pour the syrup over the fruit and stir gently to combine. Let steep for at least 1 hour at room temperature, and up to 4 hours in the refrigerator.

When ready to serve, divide the fruit among six shallow bowls. Spoon over some of the syrup and unmold one kulfi into each bowl (I just tear the paper cups off). Serve.

COOKING TIME: ABOUT 45 MINUTES / INACTIVE TIME: 24 HOURS FOR FREEZING AND 1 TO 4 HOURS FOR STEEPING

CHANGING IT UP

The flavor of the kulfi can be varied by adding a puree such as mango, strawberry, or pistachio. Add about ¼ cup puree to the chilled mixture before dividing it among the cups.

TAHITIAN VANILLA BEANS

I prefer Tahitian vanilla beans because they have very nice flavor and are easy to find in good markets. Store vanilla beans in a ziplock bag in the refrigerator for 6 to 8 months.

MY DOG SHADOW'S FAVORITE DINNER

A dog bit me when I was a kid, and it instilled in me a fear of dogs so strong that I wouldn't even touch, let alone feed, a dog for most of my life. Then came my sons, Peter and Justin, seemingly born with a deep longing for a dog of their own. Few forces in the world are as persuasive as the yearning of little boys to have a puppy. And so we became the human family to Shadow, a Labrador–pit bull mix that soon grew to seventy pounds.

It took me years to be fully comfortable with Shadow, and although I eventually learned to embrace him both literally and figuratively, I'm not sure I'll ever be keen on letting him take food directly from my hands. I'll happily put food in his dish, however, which I did for a few years before it dawned on me that I give so much time and attention to cooking for everyone else in the house, it was about time I gave Shadow's dinner a little of both. I did some online research about what dogs can—and, more important, cannot—eat. The first time I prepared food for him, I concocted it using what I had in the pantry. He loved it, and before long it became more or less the formula I make all the time. I've shared the recipe with a few friends who report that their dogs love it too, so although I can't personally vouch for the good flavor here, I feel confident that it's been thoroughly dog tested and approved. We give Shadow ½ cup of this every other night along with his dry kibble. Check with your vet to see what would be best for your dog. Woof! **MAKES ABOUT 6 CUPS**

½ cup steel-cut oats

½ cup medium-grind bulgur wheat

½ cup diced carrots

½ cup diced peeled potatoes

½ cup peas

½ cup ½-inch pieces green beans

½ cup (3 ounces/85 grams) ground beef

½ cup (4 ounces/113 grams) chicken livers

3 cups Chicken Stock (page 337) or high-quality store-bought stock

1¼ cups water

In a pressure cooker, combine the oats, wheat, carrots, potatoes, peas, and green beans. Add the ground beef and chicken livers, breaking them up with your fingers as you add them. Add the stock and water and use your hands to mix it all together. Bring to a boil over high heat, stirring constantly. Seal the pressure cooker. Follow the manufacturer's instructions to bring it up to pressure (it will begin to steam), then cook for 10 minutes, adjusting the heat as necessary to keep steady pressure. Remove the pressure cooker from the heat and let stand, covered, until the pressure releases.

Open the pressure cooker and stir to combine the ingredients well. Transfer to a bowl to cool completely.

Divide the mixture into individual servings and place each in a small ziplock bag. Freeze for up to 1 month.

To serve, thaw a bag of the dinner overnight in the refrigerator. Add to the dog's dish with his or her regular dry kibble dinner.

COOKING TIME: ABOUT 30 MINUTES

CHAPTER FIVE

Cooking for Tomorrow

BRAISES, STEWS, AND MEALS THAT
YOU CAN PLAN AHEAD

As much as I love cooking spontaneously, in a busy household it's not a practical approach to getting dinner on the table every night. That's where braises and stews come in. These slow-cooked dishes, based on forgiving ingredients like short ribs, chicken thighs, oxtail, or salt cod, benefit from sitting in the fridge for a day or so. While some of them can certainly be eaten right away (the recipes indicate when this is the case), the flavors of braises and stews deepen and develop beautifully over time; they actually taste even better a day or more after they are prepared.

Braises and stews aren't the only method I use to "cook for tomorrow" and help get ahead for the week. Since Sunday is the day I'm most often able to cook at home, it's the day I usually prepare both that night's dinner and whatever else I can to make the rest of the week easier on everyone. When I'm grilling, I'll throw some extra vegetables or chicken thighs on the grill for the next day's meal. If the oven is on for roast chicken, I might roast two so that my wife, Barkha, can turn the second one into sandwiches in a day or two. Perhaps I'll roast a bunch of vegetables in addition to whatever I'm making for dinner. Roasted and grilled veggies are delicious the day after they are prepared, whether served at room temperature with a sauce or vinaigrette, stirred into a risotto, or tossed with pasta.

Braises and stews may take a little extra deliberation, but they allow you to pull together a meal with complex flavors much more quickly than usual a day or two later. The flexibility of stews and braises also allows you to easily multiply the recipes to serve more (or to serve them for more days) if your week or family demands it—with absolutely no loss in flavor or quality. Sometimes I'll kill two birds with one stone, putting a braise in the center of the oven and roasting vegetables or a couple of chickens on the bottom rack, or making two different braises at the same time. If you can't afford to give over several hours to making these, invest in an inexpensive (and now very safe) pressure cooker (see page 29), which will significantly cut down on the cooking time. The recipes in this chapter that are well suited to the pressure cooker include a "Pressure-Cooker Friendly" variation.

So go ahead and pull out those pots to cook dinner . . . for tomorrow. Your taste buds and your future self will thank you for it!

GREAT NORTHERN BEAN and GREEN MUSTARD STEW

I like mustard greens here, but you can also use kale, spinach, or any leafy green that happens to be in abundance either in your garden or at the market.

If you've ever followed a recipe for a roux-thickened sauce, you might have noticed that often after the butter and flour are cooked, warm stock or cream is added. Conventional wisdom is that doing this prevents lumps, but in my experience, a far better way to avoid lumps is to add an unheated liquid to the roux and whisk well, as in this recipe. **SERVES 4 TO 6**

3 tablespoons chickpea flour

Kosher salt

1 pound/454 grams mustard greens, stems removed

2 tablespoons canola oil

1 tablespoon brown mustard seeds

3 tablespoons salted butter

1 tablespoon minced shallot

1 tablespoon minced peeled fresh ginger

1 teaspoon Aleppo pepper

1 tablespoon minced rosemary

1 to 2 cups Chicken Stock (page 337) or high-quality store-bought stock

4 cups cooked Great Northern beans (see page 341) or canned beans, rinsed and drained

2 tablespoons whole-grain mustard

Freshly ground black pepper

In a small skillet, toast the chickpea flour over medium heat, stirring, until lightly browned, 4 to 6 minutes. Immediately transfer it to a bowl; set aside.

Blanch, shock, and drain the mustard greens (see page 33). Puree the greens in a blender, adding just enough water to keep the greens moving and to make a smooth, thick puree. Set aside. (The puree can be made ahead and stored in a covered container in the refrigerator for up to 24 hours.)

Heat a small stew pot or Dutch oven over medium heat. Add the oil, and when it starts to shimmer, add the mustard seeds. Cook until they begin to pop, 1 to 2 minutes. Add the butter. When it starts to melt, add the shallot and ginger and cook until softened, 1 to 2 minutes. Add the toasted chickpea flour, Aleppo pepper, and rosemary and cook until the mixture is fragrant and beginning to color slightly, 2 to 3 minutes.

Slowly pour in 1 cup of the stock, whisking constantly, and continue to whisk until the mixture starts to thicken, about 3 minutes. Stir in the beans. (The beans can be made ahead. Let cool and store in a covered container in the refrigerator for up to 3 days. Reheat over medium heat, stirring, before proceeding.)

Reduce the heat to medium-low. If the mixture is very thick, add a little stock to loosen it. Stir in the reserved mustard green puree and cook, stirring, until the mixture is well blended and heated through. It should be slightly loose; add more stock if it becomes very thick upon heating.

Stir in the mustard and season with salt and black pepper. Serve hot.

COOKING TIME: ABOUT 35 MINUTES

SALT COD STEW with FINGERLING POTATOES and FENNEL

My grandmother Esme was a huge fan of *bacalao* (salt cod). She made all sorts of dishes, especially stews, with it. The funny thing is, though, that I had never actually tasted authentic Portuguese *bacalao* stew until I had it in a restaurant in New York City! I loved it so much that I came up with this version, which is best eaten with bread. **SERVES 4**

Four 3-ounce/85-gram pieces *bacalao* (salt cod)
2 tablespoons extra-virgin olive oil
3 garlic cloves, thinly sliced
1 tablespoon coriander seeds
1 teaspoon fennel seeds
½ teaspoon black peppercorns
1 dried peri peri chile or ¼ teaspoon chile flakes
2 whole cloves

½ teaspoon turmeric
2 cups ¼-inch-thick half-moons fingerling potatoes (10 ounces/283 grams)
1 cup ¼-inch-diced onion
½ cup ¼-inch-diced carrot
½ cup ¼-inch-diced fennel, plus fennel fronds for garnish
1½ cups Chicken Stock (page 337) or high-quality store-bought stock
Sea salt if needed

Place the salt cod in a large bowl and cover generously with cold water. Cover and refrigerate for 2 days, changing the water twice (usually the first night and then again the next morning). Drain and discard the soaking water.

Preheat the oven to 375°F.

Meanwhile, in a large ovenproof stew pot or Dutch oven, combine the olive oil and sliced garlic. Place the pot over low heat and cook until the garlic starts to brown, about 5 minutes.

While the garlic cooks, combine the coriander seeds, fennel seeds, peppercorns, peri peri chile, if using, and cloves in a spice/coffee grinder and finely grind.

Add the ground spices, chile flakes, if using, turmeric, potatoes, onion, carrot, and diced fennel to the pot. Stir until all the ingredients are evenly coated with spices. Increase the heat to medium and cook, stirring occasionally, for 5 minutes.

Add the stock and bring to a simmer. (The stew base can be made ahead to this point. Remove from the heat and cool. Store in a covered container in the refrigerator for up to 2 days. When ready to finish, preheat the oven. Return the stew base to the pot and bring to a simmer over medium heat.)

Add the soaked salt cod, cover the pot, place in the oven, and cook until the potatoes are tender and the flavors well blended, about 30 minutes. Taste and add salt if necessary. Garnish the stew with the reserved fennel fronds and serve hot.

COOKING TIME: ABOUT 1 HOUR / INACTIVE TIME: 2 DAYS FOR SOAKING THE SALT COD

BRAISED CHICKEN THIGHS with WINTER VEGETABLES

This great one-pot dinner came about when I was asked by the Partnership for a Healthier America to come up with a healthy meal that cost less than $5 per person. It is now a dish I often prepare when I have the oven on for cooking other things. Then we refrigerate it and reheat it later in the week. Marinating the chicken in a fragrant but simple mixture adds an extra layer of flavor to this dish. Longer marinating is better, but if you're pressed for time, you can just marinate for 1 hour. Serve it with couscous or your favorite grain or pilaf to soak up all the delicious juices. We especially like it with a cracked-wheat pilaf like the one on page 119, simply made without the peas.

This is really nice with the Baby Escarole, Endive, Radicchio, and Blood Orange Salad (page 75)—and you can use the leftover outer leaves from the escarole in place of the cabbage here if you'd like.   **SERVES 4**

¼ cup extra-virgin olive oil

1 tablespoon minced peeled fresh ginger

1 tablespoon coriander seeds, finely ground

Leaves from two 6-inch rosemary sprigs

4 bone-in chicken thighs (about 1 pound/454 grams), skin removed

Kosher salt

Freshly ground black pepper

½ cup (2 ounces/57 grams) medium-diced bacon

4 garlic cloves, smashed

1 sweet onion, such as Vidalia, cut into ¾-inch wedges

1 large russet (baking) potato, peeled and cut into 1-inch pieces

4 medium carrots, cut into ½-inch pieces

2 cups Chicken Stock (page 337) or high-quality store-bought stock

¼ small Savoy cabbage, cored, thick ribs removed, and cut into ½-by-2-inch strips

1 tart apple, such as Mutsu or Granny Smith, peeled, cored, and cut into ½-inch pieces

¼ teaspoon chile flakes

2 tablespoons Dijon mustard

In a large bowl, combine 3 tablespoons of the olive oil, the ginger, coriander, and rosemary. Add the chicken thighs and turn once or twice to coat them. Cover the bowl with plastic wrap and refrigerate for at least 1 hour, and up to 24 hours.

When ready to cook the chicken, preheat the oven to 375°F. Remove the chicken from the refrigerator and let stand at room temperature while the oven heats.

Remove the chicken from the marinade and pat dry; discard the marinade. Season the chicken with salt and pepper.

In a Dutch oven or other large ovenproof pot with a tight-fitting lid, heat the remaining 1 tablespoon olive oil over medium-high heat until it shimmers. Add the chicken and cook until browned on both sides, about 6 minutes per side. Transfer the chicken to a plate.

Reduce the heat to medium, add the bacon and garlic to the pot, and cook until the bacon fat is rendered, about 5 minutes. Add the onion, potato, and carrots and season with salt and pepper.

Cover the pot, transfer to the oven, and cook for 20 minutes.

Meanwhile, bring the stock to a simmer.

Remove the pot from the oven and stir in the chicken and hot stock. Return the uncovered pot to the oven and cook until the chicken is almost cooked through, about 20 minutes, stirring halfway through. (The chicken can be made in advance. Let cool thoroughly and transfer to a tightly sealed container. Store in the refrigerator for up to 4 days. When ready to serve, return the braised chicken to the pot and bring to a boil over medium heat.)

Add the cabbage, apple, chile flakes, and mustard, cover, reduce the heat, and simmer until the cabbage is tender, 7 to 10 minutes.

To serve, place the pot on the table and spoon the braise into shallow bowls, making sure to include lots of vegetables and flavorful broth in each serving.

COOKING TIME: ABOUT 1 HOUR AND 10 MINUTES / INACTIVE TIME: 1 TO 24 HOURS FOR MARINATING

PORK BUTT with TOMATOES, OLIVES, and FENNEL

You can serve this delicious stew on its own or as a ragù on top of spaghetti, elbow macaroni, or ziti. Like many stews, it gets even better when it sits for a day or so; but hold off on adding the mint until just before serving.

Another nice thing about this recipe is that it often leads to one of my favorite lunches the next day. Chop up some of the leftover meat, heat it, and put it in a bulky roll with a little of the warmed sauce—a truly great hero sandwich.

To me, this stew is at its absolute best when a few anchovies and a bit of the oil they come in are stirred in at the last minute. It makes the dish a little more complex. **SERVES 4**

1 pound/454 grams boneless pork butt, cut into 1½-inch cubes

Kosher salt

Freshly ground black pepper

5 tablespoons extra-virgin olive oil, or as needed

6 garlic cloves, smashed

One 1-inch piece fresh ginger, peeled and sliced into thin coins

3 whole cloves

1 tablespoon fennel seeds

One 1-inch piece pasilla de Oaxaca chile or 1½ teaspoons chile flakes

2 bay leaves

One 28-ounce/794-gram can crushed fire-roasted tomatoes, preferably Muir Glen brand, with their juice

2 cups Chicken Stock (page 337), high-quality store-bought stock, or water

2 tablespoons honey

One 6-inch rosemary sprig

⅓ cup Niçoise, kalamata, or gaeta olives, pitted

3 to 5 anchovy fillets, chopped, with some of their oil (optional but strongly recommended)

¼ cup mint leaves

Cooked spaghetti, elbow macaroni, or ziti for serving (optional)

Season the pork with salt and pepper and let stand at room temperature for 20 to 30 minutes.

In a large heavy-bottomed stew pot or Dutch oven, heat 2 tablespoons of the olive oil over medium heat until it shimmers. Add the pork (do not crowd the pot—cook in batches if necessary, adding a little more oil as needed) and brown on all sides. Transfer the pork to a bowl and set aside.

Reduce the heat to medium-low and add the remaining 3 tablespoons olive oil to the pot. Add the garlic and cook until lightly golden, 1 to 2 minutes. Add the ginger, cloves, fennel seeds, chile, and bay leaves and cook until you can really smell the spices, 3 to 5 minutes.

Continued

Add the reserved pork and any juices, along with the crushed tomatoes, stock, honey, and rosemary, to the pot. Increase the heat to medium and bring to a simmer, then reduce the heat to medium-low, cover, and simmer, stirring occasionally, until the meat is tender when pierced with a fork, about 1 hour and 15 minutes.

Stir in the olives, adjust the seasoning, and cook for 5 minutes.

Remove the cloves, bay leaves, chile, if using, and rosemary sprig. Stir in the anchovies, if using, and mint and serve, with pasta if desired.

COOKING TIME: ABOUT 1 HOUR AND 45 MINUTES, OR 45 MINUTES IN THE PRESSURE COOKER / INACTIVE TIME: 20 TO 30 MINUTES FOR TEMPING

PRESSURE-COOKER FRIENDLY

To prepare the stew in a pressure cooker, follow the recipe as written, browning the pork and blooming the spices in the uncovered pressure cooker. Then, once everything is in the cooker and brought to a simmer as instructed above, seal the pressure cooker. Follow the manufacturer's instructions to bring it up to pressure (it will begin to steam) and cook for 15 minutes, adjusting the heat as necessary to keep steady pressure. Remove the pressure cooker from the heat and let stand, covered, until the pressure releases.

Open the cooker, stir in the olives, and cook for 5 minutes. Continue as directed above, adding the mint and anchovies just before serving.

PORK CARNITAS with ORANGE and CHIPOTLE

There are strong correlations between the cooking of Mexico and that of India. Sauce, heat, and spice all play integral roles in so many dishes in both cuisines, as they do in this dish. When I was developing it, we immediately knew it was a winner; everybody who ate it absolutely loved it. It quickly became not only the centerpiece of the menu at El Verano Taqueria but also a favorite at home.

You can store the carnitas in the refrigerator for up to 2 weeks, but make sure that the meat is submerged in fat and that there is at least ½ inch of fat above it. As for that fat, you can get great free-range, no-hormone lard online (see Sources, page 345). And try to get a piece of pork butt that still has a good amount of fat on it. In addition to the accompaniments listed here, you may like to serve this with your favorite salsa or pico de gallo. **SERVES 4**

2 pounds/907 grams boneless pork butt with some fat, cut into 1-by-3-inch chunks

Kosher salt

Freshly ground black pepper

1 pound/454 grams good-quality lard

½ cup sliced onion

3 garlic cloves

One 1-inch piece cinnamon stick

5 allspice berries

1 dried chipotle chile, broken into pieces

Zest of 1 orange—removed with a vegetable peeler

½ cup fresh orange juice (from 1 to 2 oranges)

2 tablespoons fresh lemon juice

2 tablespoons fresh lime juice

FOR SERVING

8 to 12 tortillas, warmed

2 cups finely shredded cabbage

1 avocado, halved, pitted, peeled, and diced

Leaves from 1 small bunch cilantro, washed and dried (see page 39)

1 to 2 serrano chiles, chopped

1 to 2 limes, cut into wedges

Season the pork with salt and pepper. Let stand at room temperature for 20 minutes.

In a large stew pot, heat the lard over medium-low heat until shimmering; it should register about 250°F on an instant-read thermometer. Turn off the heat to prevent an overflow and add the seasoned pork, along with the onion, garlic, cinnamon, allspice berries, chipotle, and orange zest.

Turn the heat to medium and cook, stirring occasionally, until the pork is tender, 1½ to 2 hours. (Alternatively, cover the pot and cook in a preheated 350°F oven for the same amount of time.)

Add the orange, lemon, and lime juices (return the pot to the stovetop if you cooked the pork in the oven), increase the heat to high, and cook for 5 minutes.

Continued

Turn off the heat and let stand for at least 1 hour. The carnitas taste even better the next day; let cool completely, transfer to a storage container, and refrigerate. For longer storage, make sure that the meat is completely submerged in fat (use a narrow, tall container to ensure this) and refrigerate for up to 2 weeks.

When ready to serve, use a spoon to scoop off as much fat as possible (discard or strain and save it in the refrigerator for another use). Try not to remove any of the delicious dark *fond* at the bottom of the container, though; there's a lot of heavenly flavor in there.

Transfer all of the remaining contents of the storage container to a large saucepan and heat the carnitas slowly over low heat. Once the remaining fat has melted, move the mixture to a smaller pan. Use a spoon to skim off any fat that floats to the top, then stir to gently shred the meat. It does not need to be perfectly shredded, just small enough that it can be spooned into tacos. Remove and discard the cinnamon stick and allspice. Season the carnitas to taste with salt.

Transfer to a bowl and serve with the tortillas, cabbage, avocado, cilantro, chiles, and limes. Let your guests form their own tacos.

COOKING TIME: 2¼ TO 2¾ HOURS / INACTIVE TIME: 20 MINUTES FOR TEMPING AND 1 HOUR FOR COOLING

LAMB STEW with YOGURT and COCONUT

Years ago, when I was sous-chef at the Oberoi Hotel in Bombay, I worked with one of the most incredible young cooks I've ever known, Syed Nasir. He couldn't have been more than about sixteen then but I learned so much from this insanely talented kid. Syed of course cooked whatever he needed to for work, but his real passion was Hyderabadi cuisine, which is a very specific kind of cooking. It involves an intricate balance of spices and layers of flavor, and there's a great amount of ritual surrounding the food. This dish, with a thick sauce that is reminiscent of a korma, is among my favorites that he made, although I've tweaked it over the years to accommodate both the preferences of the people I make it for and the ingredients available to me. He always made it with goat, not lamb, and I usually prefer baby goat to lamb; it's an extremely healthy meat and is great in simmered stews like this one. As goat becomes more common in the United States, I hope that more people will discover all that it has to offer. When choosing a chile for this dish, keep in mind that you don't want to make the stew too spicy; use a moderately hot dried chile, such as the ones listed below. **SERVES 6**

2½ pounds/1.13 kilograms boneless lamb shoulder, cut into 1-inch cubes

Kosher salt

2½ tablespoons coriander seeds

1½ teaspoons cumin seeds

1 teaspoon black peppercorns

One 3-inch cinnamon stick

6 whole cloves

3 moderately spicy dried chiles, such as Kashmiri or chipotle

12 garlic cloves

One 1½-inch piece fresh ginger, peeled and sliced into thin coins

1 cup unsweetened shredded dried coconut

2 cups sliced onions

1 cup plain yogurt

1½ cups (6 ounces/170 grams) cashews

About 3½ cups water

3 tablespoons canola oil

4 black cardamom pods

Steamed rice for serving

Season the lamb with salt. Let it stand at room temperature for about 30 minutes.

Meanwhile, in a large heavy-bottomed skillet toast the coriander seeds over medium-low heat, shaking the pan frequently, until fragrant and several shades darker, about 3 minutes. Transfer to a large bowl to cool. Repeat, one spice at a time, with the cumin seeds, peppercorns, cinnamon stick, and cloves, adding them to the bowl with the coriander seeds. Set aside.

Add the chiles to the pan and toast, turning once, until slightly colored on both sides, about 5 minutes. Transfer to a bowl to cool.

Add the garlic and ginger to the pan and toast until lightly browned, 3 to 5 minutes. Remove from the pan and set aside.

Add the coconut to the pan and toast until lightly browned, about 1 minute.

Remove from the pan and set aside.

Add the onions to the pan and toast, stirring occasionally, until lightly browned, 5 to 7 minutes. Remove from the pan and set aside.

Finely grind all the toasted spices and the chiles in a spice/coffee grinder. Set aside.

Place the yogurt in a blender. Add the toasted garlic, ginger, coconut, and onions, then add the cashews and puree until smooth, adding about ½ cup of the water to keep the mixture moving. Transfer to a medium bowl. Stir in the ground spice mix. Set aside.

In a large stew pot, heat the oil over medium heat until it shimmers. Add the black cardamom pods and cook for 2 minutes. Increase the heat to medium-high and add the seasoned lamb (avoid crowding the pot; do this in batches if necessary). Sear until the lamb is nicely browned on all sides, 10 to 12 minutes.

Reduce the heat and stir in the yogurt puree and 3 cups water, then increase the heat and bring to a boil. Reduce the heat and simmer until the lamb is fork-tender, 45 to 60 minutes.

Remove and discard the cardamom pods. Cool the stew, then transfer to a covered container and refrigerate for at least 1 day, and up to 4 days.

When ready to serve, reheat the stew over medium-low heat, adding water as necessary so that the consistency is like heavy cream. Serve over rice.

COOKING TIME: 1¾ TO 2 HOURS, OR ABOUT 1¼ HOURS IN THE PRESSURE COOKER

PRESSURE-COOKER FRIENDLY

To prepare the stew in a pressure cooker, follow the recipe as written, toasting and browning all the ingredients and searing the lamb in the uncovered pressure cooker. Then, once everything is in the cooker and brought to a simmer as instructed above, seal the pressure cooker. Follow the manufacturer's instructions to bring it up to pressure (it will begin to steam) and cook for 15 minutes, adjusting the heat as necessary to keep steady pressure. Remove the pressure cooker from the heat and let stand, covered, until the pressure releases.

Open the cooker and continue as directed above.

BRAISED SHORT RIBS with PEANUTS and ANCHOVIES

At Tabla, we had a staff Thanksgiving celebration every year for which I asked each employee to cook a dish from his or her own culture. One year a Filipino cook, Anton, made a traditional dish called *kare kare,* an unbelievably good oxtail and peanut stew. This is my take on it, adjusted here and there to accommodate my pantry and preferences. Sometimes I use long beans or bok choy in place of the cabbage in this dish, and it works beautifully.

The original recipe used dried shrimp paste. The first time I made it myself I didn't have the paste on hand, so I tried it without, but the dish was definitely lacking. It really needs the deep flavor added by the paste, which is made from fermented shrimp. However, shrimp paste is not so easy to find. Anchovies, on the other hand, are very easily found and are always in my pantry because they are, in fact, my go-to ingredient for the type of funk this and certain other dishes need.

The first time I ate this dish, it was with rice, its traditional accompaniment.   **SERVES 4**

1½ pounds/680 grams boneless beef
    short ribs, cut into 2-inch cubes, or
    2½ to 3 pounds/1.13 to 1.36 kilograms
    bone-in ribs
Kosher salt
3 tablespoons canola oil
1½ teaspoons black peppercorns
1 dried chipotle chile, broken in half
2 bay leaves

1½ cups sliced onions
4 garlic cloves, smashed
One 1-inch piece fresh ginger, peeled
    and sliced into thin coins
7½ cups water
1 small head Savoy cabbage
1 cup unsalted roasted peanuts
4 anchovy fillets, minced
Steamed rice for serving (optional)

Season the ribs with salt. Set aside at room temperature for at least 20 minutes.

In a large stew pot, heat the oil over medium heat until it shimmers. Add the peppercorns, chipotle, and bay leaves and cook, stirring, until they are fragrant and little bubbles form around the spices, about 1 minute. Add the onions, garlic, and ginger and cook until translucent, 3 to 4 minutes.

Add the seasoned ribs, 6 cups of the water, and a pinch of salt (don't add too much here). Bring to a boil, then reduce the heat, cover, and simmer until the meat is tender when pierced with a fork, 2½ to 3 hours.

Meanwhile, separate the cabbage leaves and cut the ribs out of each one. Stack the leaves a few at a time and cut into 2-inch pieces. Set aside 4 cups for this dish and reserve the remainder for another use.

Place the peanuts in a blender with the remaining 1½ cups water and puree until smooth.

Continued

Add the anchovies to the stew pot, along with the reserved cabbage and the peanut puree. Bring to a simmer, stirring to prevent sticking, and simmer, uncovered, stirring occasionally, until the cabbage is tender, about 10 minutes. Taste for seasoning.

Remove the pot from the heat and remove and discard the bay leaves. Serve in shallow bowls, with rice if desired.

COOKING TIME: 3 TO 3½ HOURS, OR ABOUT 1 HOUR IN THE PRESSURE COOKER / INACTIVE TIME: ABOUT 20 MINUTES FOR TEMPING

PRESSURE-COOKER FRIENDLY

To prepare the braise in a pressure cooker, follow the recipe as written, blooming the spices and cooking the aromatics in the uncovered pressure cooker. Use only 5 cups water (or less—do not go above the "fill to" line inside the pressure cooker), and bring the water to a boil. Seal the pressure cooker. Follow the manufacturer's instructions to bring it up to pressure (it will begin to steam) and cook for 25 minutes, adjusting the heat as necessary to keep steady pressure. Remove the pressure cooker from the heat and let stand, covered, until the pressure releases.

Open the cooker and stir in the anchovies, cabbage, and peanut puree. Continue as directed above.

ANCHOVY OIL

I always save the oil that anchovies are packed in. It's not good to cook with because the bits of fish left behind will burn too easily, but it's an extremely flavorful finishing oil for fish or pasta dishes. Prepare a vinaigrette with it or drizzle a little over grilled fish, or toss some pasta with a little anchovy oil and some freshly shaved Parmigiano-Reggiano, and you'll see what I mean.

SLOW-COOKED OXTAILS with WINTER VEGETABLES

This recipe makes great use of the few vegetables that are truly seasonal in the cold winter months, and preparing (and then eating) it is an extremely satisfying way to spend a little time on the first cold day of the year. The warm spices—cloves, allspice, and star anise—and the chipotle accentuate the warming effect of the oxtails (see page 290). If you prefer, though, you can use short ribs in place of the oxtails. You can use any extra winter vegetables in the Braised Chicken Thighs with Winter Vegetables (page 170). I also like to slice the leftover daikon and eat it raw, sprinkled with salt, for a crunchy snack. **SERVES 6**

3 pounds/1.36 kilograms oxtails, trimmed
    of most fat
Kosher salt
Freshly ground black pepper
6 cups cold water
3 whole cloves
6 allspice berries
2 star anise
1 dried chipotle chile
2 medium onions, diced
4 garlic cloves, smashed

One 3-inch piece fresh ginger, peeled and
    sliced into thin coins
2 large carrots, cut into 1-inch pieces
1½ cups 1-inch pieces turnips or trimmed
    whole baby turnips
1½ cups 1-inch pieces daikon radish
1 cup 1-inch pieces peeled rutabaga
1 leek, split, washed, and cut into 1-inch
    pieces
2 tablespoons dark soy sauce
1-inch pieces chives for garnish

Season the oxtails generously with salt and pepper and let stand at room temperature for 20 to 30 minutes.

Place the cold water and oxtails in a large, wide stew pot, season the water generously with salt, and slowly bring up to a boil over medium heat, skimming off the foam as necessary.

Meanwhile, tie the cloves, allspice berries, star anise, and chipotle in a sachet or wrap them in a 6-inch square of cheesecloth and tie with kitchen string.

Add the onions, garlic, ginger, and spice sachet to the pot. Make sure that the oxtails are covered with water by at least ½ inch, and return to a boil. Reduce the heat, cover, and simmer until the oxtails are tender when pierced with a roasting fork, about 2 hours. (The dish can be prepared to this point up to a day in advance and refrigerated. Remove and discard the solidified fat on top of the broth and reheat the oxtails and liquid in the same pot before continuing with the recipe.)

Add the carrots, turnips, daikon, rutabaga, leek, and soy sauce to the pot and bring to a simmer. Cook until all the vegetables are fork-tender, about 30 minutes.

Continued

Remove and discard the spice sachet. Taste for seasoning. Serve, sprinkled with chives. Or, if serving later, cool, transfer to a covered container, and store in the refrigerator for up to 4 days.

COOKING TIME: ABOUT 3¼ HOURS, OR ABOUT 1¾ HOURS IN THE PRESSURE COOKER / INACTIVE TIME: 20 TO 30 MINUTES FOR TEMPING

PRESSURE-COOKER FRIENDLY

To prepare the oxtails in a pressure cooker, follow the recipe as written in the uncovered pressure cooker (use less water if necessary; do not go above the "fill to" line inside the pressure cooker). Then, once everything is in the cooker and brought to a simmer as instructed on page 183, seal the pressure cooker. Follow the manufacturer's instructions to bring it up to pressure (it will begin to steam) and cook for 25 to 30 minutes, adjusting the heat as necessary to keep steady pressure. Remove the pressure cooker from the heat and let stand, covered, until the pressure releases.

Open the cooker. Continue as directed above, adding the carrots, turnips, daikon, rutabaga, leeks, and soy sauce and continue cooking, uncovered, until fork-tender. Serve as above.

RENDANG SHORT RIBS

A traditional Indonesian *rendang* is a braise that requires long and very slow cooking on the stovetop until the meat is tender. My version is less labor-intensive, but the result is still meltingly tender. Former *Saveur* magazine editor in chief James Oseland loves it so much that the first time he tasted the dish, it brought actual tears to his eyes—something I wouldn't believe if I hadn't seen it myself. James calls it a "reverse braise" because instead of being caramelized and then simmered in liquid, the meat is first cooked in lots of liquid and then the lid is removed so that the liquid reduces and the meat is glazed with the resulting succulent sauce. We serve a version of this made with goat at the Bombay Canteen in Mumbai, where we call it My Uncle's Mutton Curry in a nod to James.

The ingredients list may look daunting, but it's mainly just a matter of throwing it all into the pot. And the ingredients can be found in any well-stocked Asian grocery store. That's where you'll find fried shallots and fresh, frozen, or dried galangal (all are fine here—if using dried, toss in 3 or 4 coins). Frozen pandan leaves, or screwpine leaves, are widely used in Asian cooking to impart a lovely fragrance. **SERVES 4**

8 whole bone-in beef short ribs
   (about 3 pounds/1.36 kilograms)
Kosher salt
½ cup chopped shallots, plus 1 cup
   sliced shallots
¼ cup sliced lemongrass, plus
   2 lemongrass stalks, trimmed
   and lightly crushed
One 2-inch piece fresh ginger, peeled
   and minced
1 serrano chile, halved
1 tablespoon cumin seeds
1 tablespoon coriander seeds
One 2-inch piece pasilla de Oaxaca
   or dried chipotle chile
½ teaspoon turmeric
⅛ teaspoon cayenne
2 tablespoons canola oil
One 3-inch cinnamon stick
5 whole cloves

½ cup store-bought fried shallots
6 garlic cloves, smashed
One 1-inch piece galangal, peeled and
   sliced into coins (see headnote)
2 pandan leaves
4 Kaffir lime leaves
Four 6-inch rosemary sprigs
4 cups Chaokoh-brand coconut milk
   (stir well before using)
4 cups Chicken Stock (page 337) or
   high-quality store-bought stock
1 teaspoon Tamarind Paste (page 340)
½ teaspoon brown sugar
1 fresh Thai chile
4 cups water
½ cup ground cashews
1 cup washed and dried cilantro leaves
   (see page 39) for garnish
Steamed jasmine rice for serving

Season the short ribs lightly with salt and let stand at room temperature for at least 20 minutes.

Continued

Meanwhile, in the work bowl of a food processor, combine the chopped shallots, sliced lemongrass, ginger, and serrano chile and process until finely chopped. Set aside.

In a spice/coffee grinder, combine the cumin seeds, coriander seeds, and pasilla de Oaxaca and finely grind. Combine with the turmeric and cayenne and set aside.

In a large ovenproof stew pot or Dutch oven, combine the oil and the reserved shallot and lemongrass mixture and cook over medium heat, stirring, until the mixture is slightly colored and releases some oil, about 15 minutes.

Add the cinnamon stick, cloves, and the reserved ground spice mixture and cook until fragrant, 2 to 4 minutes.

Add the seasoned short ribs, sliced shallots, fried shallots, garlic, galangal, crushed lemongrass stalks, pandan leaves, lime leaves, rosemary sprigs, coconut milk, stock, tamarind paste, brown sugar, Thai chile, water, and a pinch of salt, increase the heat to high, and bring to a boil. Cover the pot, reduce the heat, and simmer slowly, stirring occasionally, until the meat is tender when pierced with a fork, 4 to 5 hours.

Toward the end of cooking, preheat the oven to 325°F.

Add the cashews to the pot and transfer, uncovered, to the oven. Cook, basting the short ribs every 5 minutes, until the liquid has reduced enough to form a glaze on the meat and the fat has begun to separate out, 20 to 30 minutes.

Remove and discard the lemongrass stalks, cinnamon, cloves, galangal, lime leaves, pandan leaves, rosemary sprigs, and Thai chile. Taste for seasoning. Sprinkle with the cilantro and serve.

COOKING TIME: 5 TO 6 HOURS, OR ABOUT 2 HOURS IN THE PRESSURE COOKER

PRESSURE-COOKER FRIENDLY

Cooked in the pressure cooker, rendang is soupier than when braised in a regular pot. To achieve the same consistency as the original, reduce the sauce on the stovetop after cooking.

Follow the recipe as written, browning all the ingredients in the uncovered pressure cooker. Then, once everything is in the cooker and brought to a simmer as instructed above, seal the pressure cooker. Follow the manufacturer's instructions to bring it up to pressure (it will begin to steam) and cook for 30 minutes, adjusting the heat as necessary to keep steady pressure. Remove the pressure cooker from the heat and let stand, covered, until the pressure releases.

Open the cooker. To reduce the sauce further, set the pot over medium heat, bring to a simmer, and simmer until the liquid has reduced enough to form a glaze on the meat and the fat has begun to separate out, 20 to 30 minutes. Remove and discard the aromatics as described above before serving.

CHAPTER SIX

Rise and Shine

BREAKFAST AND BRUNCH DISHES TO FLAVOR YOUR DAY

It may be a cliché to say that breakfast is the most important meal of the day, but it is true. It's a shame that so many people just skip it, either because of the misguided notion that they're doing themselves a favor by freeing up more calories to use later in the day—on "real" meals—or because they're so rushed that they don't have time to think about it. On busy mornings, it can seem easier to just grab a bowl of cereal before dashing out the door, or eat a granola bar on the run, or have nothing at all.

I know this only too well, for when our boys were younger, my wife, Barkha, and I were under so much pressure to get everyone out the door to school and work on time that we relied heavily on quick fixes in lieu of real food in the morning. As the boys got older, though, we realized that for much of the day, they were presented with a distressing number of opportunities to make bad food choices. It became clear that our best option was to exercise control over the very first thing they ate each day. So we made a concerted effort to refocus on the one meal in our house that had become almost an afterthought. We got away from sugary cereals and other store-bought breakfast foods that tend to be way too sweet, lack flavor, and don't really satisfy anyone. Instead, we began playing around during the very first meal of the day with the same interesting tastes and spices we use later in the day in order to pique the kids' interest—and appetites.

Thankfully, my family loves eggs as much as I do, and they quickly became my morning staple. As you'll see in this chapter, eggs are often my first choice for easy, and usually very quick, meals. And I say "meals" intentionally, as these egg dishes are also good for lunch or dinner, and even as an appetizer. Spoon scrambled eggs onto small pieces of toasted or grilled bread or into mini tart shells, garnish with a fresh herb, and you've got yourself an elegant and delicious hors d'oeuvre with minimal fuss. And eggs are a great forum for incorporating interesting flavors like cumin, chiles, and turmeric, which all marry beautifully with eggs.

Naturally, eggs aren't the *only* dish for breakfast around here (although spend a week with my family, and you might think otherwise!). In this chapter there are also a few of our other favorites, such as grilled fresh peaches folded into steel-cut oatmeal and a parfait of dried figs and lime. And for those days when there's no reason to rush, you can turn a regular breakfast into a festive brunch when you mix up a batch of Masala Marys, a welcome reminder that lazy mornings are the best ones of all.

SCRAMBLED EGGS with WILD MUSHROOMS

I first tasted eggs cooked this way on a trip to Spain, where the dish was made with porcini (also known as cèpes). I was just blown away by how earthy and delicious those eggs with wild mushrooms were. Since then, I've made the dish dozens of times using one or more types of whatever wild mushrooms are in season. Whether it's morels in spring, chanterelles in summer, or hen-of-the-woods in fall, this dish is always a sure way to enjoy whatever mushrooms are having their seasonal moment. And even mushrooms that are available year-round—such as hon shimeji (also called brown beech) and shiitakes—are delicious this way.

It's easiest to sauté the mushrooms in one large pan—they'll shrink a bit—and then divide them between two large sauté pans to cook the eggs. It's difficult to give precise timing for the mushrooms, since it depends on what type you're using: Just cook over high heat until they are nicely browned. Once the eggs go into the pan, the mushrooms won't cook much more, because you'll be using high heat and cooking the eggs fast, a method that produces scrambled eggs that lie like folded sheets of silk and are neither hard nor creamy. It's a texture that holds up well against the roasted mushrooms. **SERVES 6**

12 extra-large eggs

Kosher salt

Freshly cracked black pepper

2 tablespoons canola oil

3 cups sliced fresh wild mushrooms,
    such as hen-of-the-woods, morels,
    or hon shimeji

3 tablespoons minced shallots

4 tablespoons salted butter or bacon fat

2 tablespoons chopped chives

Toasted or grilled bread for serving

In a large bowl, beat the eggs with salt and cracked pepper to taste.

Heat a large sauté pan over high heat. When the pan is hot, add the oil and mushrooms and cook, stirring occasionally, until the mushrooms are softened and lightly browned if they are pale colored. Add the shallots and cook for 1 minute. Season to taste with salt.

Transfer half of the mushrooms and shallot mixture to a second large sauté pan and place it over high heat as well. Divide the butter between the pans, then add half the eggs and chives to each pan and cook, folding once or twice with a silicone spatula, until the eggs start to set, about 3 minutes. Take care not to let the eggs get too firm.

Serve immediately, over toast or grilled bread.

COOKING TIME: 10 TO 15 MINUTES

JUSTIN'S SLOW-COOKED EGGS

One morning when my son Justin was six years old, I could not get him to eat any of his usual favorites. I came up with this dish for him and turned the whole process into an interactive cooking class. I opened the fridge and asked Justin to help decide what we would put in scrambled eggs. I chose tomatoes for their sweetness (and in a sly effort to ensure that he got some fiber in him that day) and he chose all the bits of leftover cheeses we had (we called these "Justin's five-cheese eggs" for years because it seemed like there was always that amount in the cheese drawer). I've streamlined the recipe since those early days (I guess we eat less cheese now), but you can certainly use whatever cheese or cheeses you have in your refrigerator instead—especially if you're looking for a way to use them up. Soft cheeses such as fresh goat's-milk or blue cheese can be crumbled instead of grated.

My "reward" for coming up with this trick to get Justin to eat was that from then on whenever his friends came over, I *had* to make these eggs for them—while he helped, of course. Once the eggs went into the pan, Justin was my "stirrer in chef," which is a nice help, since the eggs are ideally stirred constantly. In fact, it was by making these eggs over and over again that Justin became a master of the "8" stirring technique. It's true that this technique takes a little time, but if you love soft, creamy scrambled eggs and want to achieve them without any cream, this is the way to go. **SERVES 6**

4 tablespoons salted butter
2 cups diced tomatoes
A pinch of chile flakes
Kosher salt
Freshly ground black pepper

12 extra-large eggs
½ cup low-fat or whole milk
1 cup grated Parmigiano-Reggiano, cheddar, or other cheese (or a combination of cheeses)

In a large sauté pan, melt the butter over medium heat. Add the tomatoes, chile flakes, and salt to taste, reduce the heat to medium-low, cover, and cook, stirring occasionally to make sure that the tomatoes do not stick, until they have broken down, about 20 minutes. Add pepper to taste.

Meanwhile, in a large bowl, whisk the eggs just enough to break up the whites and yolks. (You want them fairly well blended but not overbeaten.) Add the milk and grated cheese and whisk gently just to combine.

Reduce the heat to low and add the eggs to the tomatoes. Cook gently, stirring constantly with a silicone spatula in a figure-8 motion, until the eggs begin to thicken and are soft and silky, 20 to 30 minutes. Serve immediately.

COOKING TIME: ABOUT 50 MINUTES

BOMBAY SCRAMBLED EGGS

We eat this dish for breakfast at least one weekend a month and sometimes for dinner too, spooned onto grilled bread as it is here. I love it because it's quick to prepare and very adaptable. If it's tomato season and you have a lot of tomatoes to eat up, double the amount called for below. Or, if you have a bit of spinach, toss that in right at the end of cooking. But even when I change up the other ingredients, I almost always keep the flavorings and spices as they are. The layers of flavor that come from the turmeric, ginger, chiles, and black pepper make the dish really complex.

Like Justin's Slow-Cooked Eggs (page 196), these scrambled eggs are creamy, not lumpy. I like them this way because they taste better and never have that sulfuric smell that eggs sometimes do when they're cooked longer. The trick to getting your eggs creamy—and keeping them that way—is to stir them constantly while they cook over low heat, moving the spatula in the form of a figure 8, and to remove the pan from the heat a few seconds *before* you think they're done.   **SERVES 4**

8 extra-large eggs

¼ cup thinly sliced washed and dried cilantro leaves (see page 39; stack the leaves a few at a time to slice)

Kosher salt

3 tablespoons canola oil

1 cup diced onion

1 teaspoon turmeric

One 1-inch piece fresh ginger, peeled and minced

1 serrano chile, minced

1 cup diced tomatoes

Freshly ground black pepper

Toasted or grilled bread for serving

Place the eggs in a large bowl with the cilantro and a pinch of salt. Whisk just enough to break up the whites and yolks. (You want them fairly well blended but not overbeaten.) Set aside.

Place a large sauté pan over medium heat and add the oil. When the oil is shimmering, add the onion and cook, stirring often, until golden brown, 5 to 8 minutes. Add the turmeric, ginger, chile, and tomatoes and cook, stirring occasionally, until the tomatoes have broken down, 3 to 4 minutes. Season with salt and pepper to taste.

Reduce the heat to low, add the eggs, and cook, stirring constantly with a silicone spatula in a figure-8 motion, until the eggs begin to thicken and are soft and silky, 20 to 30 minutes.

Divide the grilled bread among four warmed plates. Spoon the eggs over and serve.

COOKING TIME: ABOUT 40 MINUTES

OVEN-BAKED EGGS with POBLANOS and FINGERLING POTATOES

Here eggs are nestled in a flavorful bed of fingerling potatoes, tomatoes, and roasted poblanos and gently baked so that their yolks remain soft. I think that most people don't really know what to do with poblanos, beyond stuffing and baking them. I love their earthy, grassy flavor, and this is a really nice way to marry that flavor with sweet fingerlings and onions and rich egg yolks. Just make sure that the poblanos you use are not too spicy; poblanos tend to be spiciest during the hottest months. And if you prefer sweet bell peppers, feel free to substitute. Whichever pepper you use, if you have a gas stove, you can roast them on one burner while the potatoes cook on another.

I give a range for the amount of serrano chile because this is one dish in particular where you don't want chile heat to overwhelm the eggs. **SERVES 4**

10 ounces/283 grams fingerling potatoes

Kosher salt

3 tablespoons canola oil

1 tablespoon cumin seeds

½ cup diced onion

1½ tablespoons minced peeled fresh ginger

½ to 1 serrano chile

1 teaspoon turmeric

1½ cups diced ripe tomatoes or one 14.5-ounce/411-gram can diced fire-roasted tomatoes, preferably Muir Glen brand, with their juice

2 poblano peppers or 1 red and 1 green bell pepper, roasted (see page 202), peeled, seeded, and diced

Freshly ground black pepper

8 extra-large eggs

Preheat the oven to 350°F.

Place the potatoes in a medium saucepan and add cold water to cover by 2 inches. Add a few generous pinches of salt and bring to a boil over high heat. Reduce the heat to medium and boil gently until the potatoes are just tender when pierced with a sharp knife, about 10 minutes. Drain and set aside until cool enough to handle.

Slice the potatoes into ½-inch-thick coins.

Heat a large sauté pan over medium heat. Add the oil and heat until it shimmers, 2 to 3 minutes. Add the cumin seeds and cook until they start to sizzle, about 1 minute. Add the onion, ginger, serrano, and turmeric and cook until the onion is translucent, about 5 minutes.

Add the tomatoes, roasted peppers, and the reserved potatoes and season with salt and pepper. Transfer the potato and pepper mixture to a large baking dish and spread evenly. (The dish can be prepared up to this point up to a day in advance. When ready to proceed, reheat the mixture in the oven until very warm.)

Continued

Make 8 indentations in the pepper and potato mixture. One at a time, crack each egg into a glass measuring cup or small bowl and pour it into one of the indentations.

Bake until the egg whites are set, 20 to 25 minutes. Sprinkle with salt and pepper and serve hot.

COOKING TIME: ABOUT 1 HOUR

ROASTING PEPPERS

Roasting peppers is so straightforward—and, frankly, satisfying—that I don't think you should ever buy jarred roasted peppers. It is easiest to do on a gas stove, although the grill and broiler are equally effective. You just want to make sure that you char the skin all over, then put the peppers in a bowl and cover with a towel until cool. Don't use plastic wrap, because a tightly enclosed environment will steam the peppers and drain away a lot of the smoky flavor. Once the peppers are cooled, the blackened skin will slip easily away, leaving only the smoky-sweet flesh behind. You can certainly roast a pepper or two for a single recipe when called for, but I usually roast a few extras while I'm at it. They store well in a tightly sealed container in the refrigerator for several days and once they're in there, you can reach for them whenever you want to add a little of that flavor to a sauce, a stew, or scrambled eggs.

To roast peppers on a gas stovetop, lay each pepper on a grate and turn the flame to high. Turn the peppers occasionally until the skin is charred all over. Transfer the peppers to a bowl, cover the bowl with a dry kitchen towel, and set aside until cool. Then use a paper towel to rub the skin off the peppers, and remove and discard the core and seeds.

Alternatively, prepare a hot grill or heat an oven broiler to high, with the oven rack about 4 inches from the heat source. Grill or broil the peppers, turning them occasionally, until blackened all over. Remove from the heat and proceed as above.

SUNDAY MORNING MASALA OMELET

This dish always reminds me of my days as a young college student when I often traveled overnight on Indian Railways to visit far-off cities. When the trains pulled into stations at dawn, vendors ran up and down the tracks shouting out the names of the foods they were hawking: *"Vada pao!" "Garam chai!"* and *"Masala amlate!"* Those masala omelets were almost white, with just a trace of turmeric, and bits of onion, green chile, and cilantro lightly sprinkled in. After a night of sipping Indian rum, this basic meal was a welcome remedy at 5:00 a.m.

After I came to the United States, that omelet became a favorite breakfast for me, and it remains so on Sunday mornings or on any day when I know I will not be eating lunch until late. I have adapted the recipe to make it more nutritious and wholesome by adding about five times more vegetables (although it's still a pretty good morning-after cure). When my son Peter makes it for a post-workout meal, he takes it even further in that direction by adding spinach, thinly sliced zucchini, or chopped asparagus to the tomatoes and onions.

Now this longtime favorite of both my family and me has a little extra glamour attached to it, compliments of Hollywood. When the director of the film *The Hundred-Foot Journey,* on which I was a consulting chef, asked me for an omelet for one of the pivotal scenes in the film, I gave him an only slightly altered version of this one. **SERVES 6**

2 cups diced tomatoes

2 cups minced onions

½ cup roughly chopped washed and
   dried cilantro (see page 39)

1 serrano chile, minced

1 tablespoon turmeric

¼ teaspoon cayenne

Kosher salt

Freshly ground black pepper

12 extra-large eggs

3 tablespoons canola oil

In a large bowl, combine the tomatoes, onions, cilantro, chile, turmeric, cayenne, and salt and black pepper to taste and mix well. Divide into 6 equal portions.

In a small bowl, combine 2 eggs and one portion of the vegetable mixture and mix well with a fork. Heat 1½ teaspoons of the oil in a medium nonstick pan over medium heat. Add the egg and vegetable mixture and spread evenly. Reduce the heat and let the eggs cook until set, about 15 minutes.

Increase the heat and flip the omelet in the pan. (Or, if it's easier, just fold it in half.) Cook until firm, 2 to 3 minutes. Transfer to a plate and serve.

Repeat with the remaining eggs, vegetables, and oil, serving each omelet as soon as it comes out of the pan.

COOKING TIME: 15 TO 20 MINUTES FOR THE FIRST OMELET AND ABOUT 10 MINUTES FOR EACH SUBSEQUENT ONE

CODDLED EGGS with CRAB, GRITS, and LEEKS

One of the contradictions of having a job that entails preparing meals for other people is that, like most chefs I know, I typically miss a regularly scheduled lunch and dinner when I'm working. This makes me especially resolved to eat properly when I'm not at the restaurant. This recipe is the happy result of that determination to never miss one of those meals. One Thanksgiving a few years ago, I realized around midmorning that we had no plans for food all day until we headed out for dinner later in the evening. I knew that we—okay, I—needed some sort of lunch, but as all the nearby grocery stores were closed, I had only what was in the fridge to work with. It must have been holiday good luck, because the result was so tasty that it ended up on the opening menu at North End Grill.

There is always smoked cured sausage in my freezer, because I love to add a bit of it to just about anything I cook. Basically any time I want to "kick it up a notch," as Emeril would say, and increase the complexity and interest in a dish, I reach for Portuguese chorizo, linguiça, andouille, or even smoked Chinese sausage. Each of these will add something slightly different, but all will add an extra layer of flavor that often pushes a dish you make from good to great. **SERVES 4**

2 cups water

Sea salt

½ cup coarse-ground grits, preferably Anson Mills

1 ounce/28 grams thick-cut smoky bacon, sliced crosswise into ½-inch pieces (¼ cup)

Bacon fat (see following page) or canola oil as needed

3 garlic cloves, thinly sliced

1 tablespoon minced peeled fresh ginger

½ cup small-dice peeled celery root

4 ounces/113 grams linguiça or Portuguese chorizo, casing removed, quartered lengthwise, and sliced (1 cup)

One 4-inch piece pasilla de Oaxaca or dried chipotle chile, broken in two

½ cup sliced leeks (white and light green parts only)

Two 4-inch thyme sprigs

Two 4-inch rosemary sprigs

1 cup canned diced fire-roasted tomatoes, preferably Muir Glen brand, with their juice

½ cup fresh or high-quality canned lump or jumbo lump crabmeat, picked over to remove shells

1 teaspoon chopped tarragon

Freshly ground black pepper

4 extra-large eggs

In a small saucepan, bring the water to a boil over medium-high heat. Add a pinch of salt and slowly stir in the grits. Reduce the heat and simmer gently, stirring occasionally, until the water is absorbed and the grits are creamy, about 40 minutes. Remove the pan from the heat, cover, and set aside.

Preheat the oven to 400°F.

Continued

Place a medium sauté pan over low heat, add the bacon, and cook until the fat is rendered. With a slotted spoon, transfer the bacon to a small dish; set aside.

Add enough additional bacon fat (or canola oil) to the fat in the pan to make a total of 3 tablespoons. Add the garlic and cook slowly until very lightly colored, 1 to 2 minutes. Add the ginger, celery root, linguiça, and pasilla and cook until they soften slightly, 2 to 3 minutes. Add the leeks and a pinch of salt (be careful not to overseason, as the bacon and sausage are salty) and cook until the leeks are softened, about 5 minutes.

Add the reserved bacon, the thyme, rosemary, and tomatoes and cook, stirring occasionally, until everything blends together, about 5 minutes.

Stir in the reserved grits. The mixture will be slightly thick, not runny. Remove and discard the pasilla and thyme and rosemary sprigs. Gently fold in the crab-meat, making sure not to break up the meat. Add the tarragon and season to taste with salt and pepper (again, be careful not to overseason). Take the pan off the heat.

Meanwhile, bring a kettle of water to a boil. Place a folded kitchen towel in the bottom of a baking pan large enough to hold four 10-ounce ramekins.

Fill the ramekins with the crabmeat mixture. Crack an egg on top of each one. Place the ramekins in the baking pan. Pour enough boiling water into the baking pan to come halfway up the sides of the ramekins. Bake until the egg whites are set, 15 to 20 minutes. Remove from the oven. Sprinkle each serving with salt and pepper. Serve.

COOKING TIME: ABOUT 1½ HOURS

BACON DRIPPINGS

Bacon drippings are delicious used in place of or along with whatever oil you usually use to sauté vegetables or meat; they add really nice flavor to all sorts of dishes. To save bacon drippings, I let them cool slightly in the pan and pour them into a take-out soup container (you can use an empty mustard jar or whatever is handy; just make sure that the drippings are cool enough that they won't break or melt the container). Store in the refrigerator for up to several months and just scoop out what you want when you need it. You can pour new drippings on top of what's already in the container. Even if you only prepare bacon for a special meal every once in a while, save the drippings. They will accumulate quickly, and a little goes a long way.

STEEL-CUT OATS with GRILLED PEACH COMPOTE

I hated oatmeal when I was growing up. At some point along the way, though, I decided that I had to learn to love—or at least tolerate—oatmeal, so I added peaches, which I've always loved, and finally figured out how good oats can be. This works very well as an approach to cooking and eating (especially for kids!): Always pair something you love with something you are not so fond of. It'll give you a whole new appreciation of whatever you're resisting. Nowadays I have oats at home all the time, and my sons even ask me to make my variations, like this one—nutty steel-cut oatmeal paired with grilled peaches flavored with maple syrup and fresh ginger and topped with pumpkin seeds. It's an enormously satisfying way to start the day. **SERVES 4**

FOR THE PEACHES

3 ripe peaches
Canola oil or softened salted butter
¼ cup maple syrup
1 teaspoon minced peeled fresh ginger

FOR THE OATS

2 cups steel-cut oatmeal, preferably
  McCann's brand
4 cups water
Half a 3-inch cinnamon stick
¼ cup raw pumpkin seeds for serving
Maple syrup for serving

Prepare a high-heat grill. (Alternatively, heat an oven broiler to high, with the oven rack about 6 inches from the heat source. Or use a toaster oven.)

Split the peaches in half and remove and discard the pits. Rub the peach halves all over with oil. Grill or broil the peaches for 3 minutes on each side. Remove from the heat and set aside until cool enough to handle.

When the peaches are cool, remove and discard the skin. Dice the peaches and transfer to a medium bowl. Stir in the maple syrup and ginger. Cover and place in the refrigerator for at least 2 hours, and up to overnight.

Place the oats in a medium saucepan, add the water, and soak the oats for 20 minutes.

Add the cinnamon to the oats and bring to a boil over medium-high heat. Reduce the heat and simmer until the water is absorbed and the oats are tender but still have some bite, about 20 minutes. Stir in the peaches and their syrup and cook for 2 minutes longer.

Remove and discard the cinnamon stick. Transfer the oatmeal to bowls, spoon 1 tablespoon pumpkin seeds on top of each serving, and serve hot, with maple syrup.

COOKING TIME: ABOUT 45 MINUTES / INACTIVE TIME: 2 HOURS TO OVERNIGHT FOR MARINATING THE PEACHES AND 20 MINUTES SOAKING FOR THE OATS

ORANGE RICOTTA PANCAKES with SUMMER STRAWBERRIES

My mom loves strawberries and whipped cream, and fresh strawberry compote is all the excuse we need in my house to heap giant clouds of whipped cream onto our plates in her name. The compote is easy to prepare and makes a perfect topping for pancakes, as here, and also waffles, ice cream, and, my personal favorite, oatmeal. So use whichever one of those you want to serve as a base for the compote, and then pass the whipped cream, please. **SERVES 4; MAKES 12 TO 14 PANCAKES**

FOR THE SUMMER STRAWBERRIES

1 quart strawberries, hulled, cored, and quartered

¼ cup maple syrup

¼ cup slivered almonds, toasted (see page 76)

2 tablespoons diced candied ginger

1 teaspoon grated peeled fresh ginger

Half a 3-inch cinnamon stick

FOR THE PANCAKES

1½ cups (7½ ounces/213 grams) all-purpose flour

1 tablespoon baking powder

⅛ teaspoon ground cinnamon

¼ teaspoon fine sea salt

1 cup ricotta cheese

¾ cup milk

3 large eggs, separated

3 tablespoons sugar

Minced zest of 1 orange

½ cup fresh orange juice (from 1 to 2 oranges)

Canola oil for cooking the pancakes

Whipped Cream (see page 329) for serving

To make the strawberries, in a medium saucepan, combine the berries, syrup, almonds, candied ginger, fresh ginger, and cinnamon stick. Place the pan over medium heat and bring the mixture to a boil. Reduce the heat and simmer for 5 minutes. Remove from the heat and remove and discard the cinnamon stick. Set aside.

To make the pancakes, in a medium bowl, whisk together the flour, baking powder, cinnamon, and a pinch of the salt.

In a large bowl, combine the ricotta, milk, egg yolks, sugar, and orange zest and juice and whisk together until smooth. Add the flour mixture to the bowl and stir with a wooden spoon until just combined.

In a large bowl, using a whisk or an electric mixer, beat the egg whites until frothy. Add the remaining salt and continue beating until soft peaks form. Using a silicone spatula, fold one-third of the egg whites into the ricotta mixture, then gently fold in the remaining whites.

Preheat a lightly oiled cast-iron griddle over medium heat until hot. Ladle ⅓ cup batter onto the griddle for each pancake. Cook until bubbles form on top and the pancakes are golden on the bottom, 1 to 2 minutes. Flip the pancakes and cook for 1 minute more. Serve on a warmed plate with some of the strawberries and whipped cream. Repeat with the remaining batter to make more pancakes, serving them with the toppings.

COOKING TIME: ABOUT 30 MINUTES

CHANGING IT UP

For a slightly different flavor profile in the Summer Strawberries, prepare the recipe as written, but add the zest and juice of 1 lemon or orange to the saucepan with all the other ingredients.

DRIED FIG PARFAIT

For years, I made this parfait only with dried Indian white apricots, but it can be so challenging to find them in America that I began to swap them out for figs whenever I shared the recipe. Over time, I've come to really love the parfait made with figs. The sweet dried figs and candied ginger are perfectly balanced by the tangy lime and yogurt. But if ever you come across dried Indian white apricots and want a taste of the original parfait that they inspired, just replace all the figs below with them.   **SERVES 6**

Juice and minced zest of 1 lime, plus more
    juice if needed and additional zest for
    garnish, if desired
1½ cups water
2 cups (10 ounces/283 grams) dried
    white figs, stems trimmed

1 cup (5 ounces/142 grams) dried Black
    Mission figs, stems trimmed
1 quart Greek yogurt
3 tablespoons diced candied ginger
Sugar (optional)

In a medium saucepan, bring the lime juice and water to a boil over medium-high heat. Add the figs, reduce the heat to medium-low, cover the pan, and simmer until the figs are soft, about 15 minutes. Transfer the figs and their liquid to a bowl and set aside until completely cool.

Place the figs and liquid in a blender or food processor and process until smooth. Transfer to a large bowl. Add the yogurt, candied ginger, and lime zest and mix well. Taste and add more lime juice and/or sugar if necessary.

Scoop the parfait into six small (about 6-ounce) cups. Cover and refrigerate until chilled, at least 2 hours, and up to 2 days.

Just before serving, if desired, use a Microplane grater to grate some lime zest on top of each serving (make sure to grate only the green and none of the bitter white pith from the lime).

COOKING TIME: ABOUT 30 MINUTES / INACTIVE TIME: ABOUT 30 MINUTES FOR COOLING THE FIGS AND 2 HOURS TO 2 DAYS FOR CHILLING

MASALA MARY

Whenever I have a Bloody Mary, I think of my dad, who liked his spicy and complex. When I opened Tabla, I knew we should offer a Bloody Mary, but I wanted it to be different from the standard fare you can order off a brunch menu just about everywhere. I set about deconstructing the Worcestershire sauce that is de rigueur in the standard mix to see where I could add some zing and spice. With my dad front and center in my mind, I came up with this version.

I know this looks like a lot of ingredients—it's definitely got more going on than the standard tomato juice–Worcestershire–horseradish mix—but you can make the base in advance and store it in the fridge for a couple of weeks. That means that you can easily be ready to mix up a batch of spicy and complex Masala Marys whenever the mood or event calls for it. That's how I do it, and I raise a glass to Dad each time that I do.

MAKES 8 TO 10 DRINKS

FOR THE MASALA MARY BASE

2 tablespoons cumin seeds

1 tablespoon coriander seeds

1 tablespoon black peppercorns

1 teaspoon fennel seeds, preferably Lucknow

1 teaspoon brown mustard seeds

Half a 3-inch cinnamon stick

1 whole clove

1 teaspoon canola oil

1 tablespoon diced celery

¼ cup thinly sliced shallots

2 garlic cloves, finely minced

1 teaspoon finely minced peeled fresh ginger

One ½-inch piece dried ginger, finely ground, or 1½ teaspoons ground ginger

2 tablespoons Tamarind Paste (page 340)

1 tablespoon brown sugar

½ cup water

Kosher salt

FOR THE DRINKS

Masala Mary Base (above)

Juice of 5 large limes

20 ounces tomato juice

Kosher salt

1 or 2 lime wedges

Ice cubes

12 to 15 fluid ounces good-quality vodka

A piece of peeled fresh horseradish for grating

8 to 10 light yellow celery sticks for garnish

To make the base, in a small heavy-bottomed skillet, toast the cumin seeds over medium-low heat, shaking the pan frequently, until fragrant and several shades darker, about 3 minutes. Transfer to a bowl to cool. Repeat with the coriander seeds, peppercorns, fennel seeds, mustard seeds, cinnamon stick, and clove, toasting each one separately.

Finely grind all the spices together in a spice/coffee grinder. Set aside.

Continued

Place a medium heavy-bottomed pot over medium heat. Add the oil, celery, shallots, garlic, and fresh and dried ginger and cook, stirring constantly, until the shallots are translucent. Add the tamarind paste, sugar, and water and bring to a boil. Reduce the heat and simmer for 10 minutes. Add the ground spices and salt to taste and simmer for 4 minutes. Remove from the heat and let cool slightly.

Transfer the base mixture to a blender and puree until smooth. Let cool completely, then transfer to an airtight container and refrigerate until cold, about 2 hours. (The base can be stored in the refrigerator for up to 2 weeks.)

When you are ready to make the drinks, taste the base and adjust the seasoning. (Do this even if you already tasted it and adjusted for seasoning before you refrigerated the base; foods taste different after they have been chilled.) Pour the base into a glass pitcher and add the lime juice and tomato juice. Stir until very well blended.

Pour some kosher salt onto a small plate. Have ready eight to ten 10- to 12-ounce glasses. Run a lime wedge around the rim of one of the glasses to moisten it. Holding the glass at an angle, roll the outer edge of the rim in the salt until fully coated. Repeat with the remaining glasses. Fill the glasses with ice.

Pour 1½ ounces vodka over the ice in each glass. Pour the Masala Mary mix into the glasses and stir to blend. Use a Microplane grater to grate fresh horseradish over each cocktail, and garnish each with a celery stick. Serve immediately.

COOKING TIME: ABOUT 55 MINUTES / INACTIVE TIME: ABOUT 2 HOURS FOR CHILLING THE BASE

MANGO LASSI SMOOTHIE

In India, any yogurt drink is a lassi, so I don't know when we began calling this a smoothie in my house. Maybe it was to get the boys to taste it the first few times. To me, this has always been and always will be a lassi, plain and simple, just like the ones I grew up with. Our boys have grown up with it too, since during mango season, Barkha makes sure there is always a big jug of this lassi smoothie in the fridge.

A small amount of rose water adds a lovely floral aroma to the lassi. You can find rose water in Indian and Middle Eastern grocery stores, or online.   **MAKES 6 DRINKS**

2½ to 3 cups sliced fresh or frozen
    mango
2 quarts plain yogurt
¼ cup agave syrup

1 cup ice
1 teaspoon rose water
Chopped pistachios for garnish

Place the fruit in a blender and blend until smooth; you should have 2 cups. Add one-quarter of the yogurt, the agave syrup, and ice and blend until smooth.

Transfer the mixture to a large bowl and add the remaining yogurt and the rose water. Whisk gently until well blended.

Pour into tall glasses and garnish with chopped pistachios. Store any leftovers in the refrigerator for up to 1 day.

COOKING TIME: ABOUT 10 MINUTES

CHANGING IT UP

This lassi is delicious with other seasonal fruit used in place of the mango. Replace the mango with an equal amount of fresh or frozen strawberries or sliced peeled peaches.

CHAPTER SEVEN

Summer Cooking

SALADS AND GRILLED VEGETABLES, MEAT,
AND FISH FOR WHEN THE WEATHER GETS HOT

New York City chefs have a funny kind of love-hate relationship with summer. On the one hand, we love the plethora of fresh ingredients that our local farmers bring us. On the other hand, we hate that just when we have at our fingertips the best, most flavorful ingredients of the whole year, most of our guests leave the city for the beaches and the mountains and suddenly our dining rooms slow way, *way* down.

Another big reason summer is not my favorite season is that I don't like the heat. But I always feel better when I have the opportunity to visit local farmers at the Union Square Greenmarket in Manhattan. In fact, it was the glorious abundance of the Greenmarket several years ago that inspired me (with a little extra push from chef Ben Pollinger; see page 99) to try out my green thumb in my own backyard. I started off with a very small patch; it was mostly herbs, really, which is the perfect way to begin. Most herbs are quite forgiving and will thrive in spite of the well-intentioned but often clumsy intrusions of novice gardeners. And nothing beats finishing a dish with freshly cut cilantro, mint, basil, thyme, or tarragon, nor inspires a new gardener to expand his plot "just a little more" the next season . . . and the next. As the years passed, I increased the number of plants I grew, until today, when I have had enough fun and success (sometimes too much success; see one way I've been "forced" to cope with my prolific harvests of mustard greens on page 166) that I truly and contentedly refer to myself as a "home farmer."

The experience of walking between the plants and cutting a cucumber from the vine or pulling a radish straight from the ground is incomparable—these are the moments that bring new meaning to the term "fresh produce." And then there's the actual cooking of the crops! Now it's no longer just as a chef in the city but also as a home farmer in the suburbs that I get especially excited when the first signs of spring sprout up in my garden in the form of garlic and asparagus. As spring turns to summer, I fire up my backyard grill every chance I get, just as I've always done—but now that I'm as dedicated to my crops as I am to my cooking, after I light the grill, I am as likely to be in the garden as in the kitchen looking for what to toss on it. This is actually funny to me, because I came of age thinking that only meat and seafood went on the fire. At first I was a little shocked by how incredibly good freshly grilled vegetables taste. Today I can safely say that I am an egalitarian griller, meaning that almost anything I grow will eventually find its way onto that hot grill grate at least once.

The recipes in this chapter are about turning the bounty of summer into great meals. It's easy to make a good dish at the height of summer when you can use fresh, perfectly ripe, in-season vegetables and fruit. But there are things you can do to make that dish truly great. Earlier in this book, I urged you to feel free to take poetic license with the recipes. Summer, in all of its abundance, is one of the very best times of year to let yourself riff on recipes. There's no shortage of alternatives to ingredients you can't find or don't favor. Change up the herbs in the Chimichurri Sauce (page 255), for instance, using whatever you have on hand. Summer Beans with Green Mango (page 226) are a blank slate when it comes to the beans. And the seasonings on the Grilled Asparagus with Lemon Zest and Mustard (page 229) will work equally well with grilled baby squash or young carrots. You can even toss some fresh garlic or spring onions on the grill too. Honestly, the one and only rule for summertime is to keep your grill hot and have fun!

HEIRLOOM TOMATO SALAD

Many people are turned off by heirloom tomatoes because they can be funny-looking and it's not easy to get perfect, round slices, but I consider that innate idiosyncrasy to be a major part of their appeal. Plus, I love to have any excuse to talk about my favorite farmer, Tim Stark of Eckerton Hill Farm in Hamburg, Pennsylvania. His heirloom tomatoes are just the excuse I need. Tim is one of the many passionate farmers I have the pleasure to work with, and he's one of the nicest guys I know. He has one golden rule for storing tomatoes: Don't ever put them in the refrigerator. You can't taste them when they're cold, and it also ruins the texture. On the other hand, if you really are awash in tomatoes, as can happen during the height of the season, freeze them whole to use later, such as in Stewed Chicken with Fresh Tomatoes (page 150).

You can slice and measure all the ingredients ahead, but toss them all together only at the last minute so that the salad doesn't get soggy. **SERVES 6**

1 tablespoon coriander seeds
¾ teaspoon black peppercorns
1½ pounds/680 grams mixed ripe heirloom tomatoes, cored and cut into even wedges
A pinch of chile flakes
½ cup thinly sliced red onion
1 teaspoon minced peeled fresh ginger
1½ teaspoons minced serrano chile
¼ cup mint leaves, torn just before use

¼ cup Thai basil leaves, torn just before use
2 tablespoons bush basil leaves (see below)
A small pinch of sugar
¼ cup extra-virgin olive oil
2 tablespoons aged balsamic vinegar
1 teaspoon fennel pollen (see Sources, page 345)

In a small dry skillet, toast the coriander seeds over medium-low heat, shaking the pan frequently, until fragrant and several shades darker, about 3 minutes. Transfer to a bowl to cool. Repeat to toast the peppercorns.

Finely grind the toasted spices together in a spice/coffee grinder.

Put the tomatoes in a large bowl and add the ground spice blend and chile flakes. Mix gently to distribute the spices evenly. Add the onion, ginger, chile, mint, Thai basil, bush basil, sugar, olive oil, and vinegar and stir gently to combine. Sprinkle the fennel pollen on top.

Serve the salad immediately, making sure to include some of the juices that have accumulated in the bowl with each serving.

COOKING TIME: ABOUT 15 MINUTES

BUSH BASIL

Bush basil grows as a small, round bush. It has leaves that are smaller than the more common sweet basil—as small as ¼ inch and usually not more than 1 inch long. If you can't find it, use torn sweet basil leaves.

SUMMER BEANS with GREEN MANGO

I didn't really and truly fall in love with beans until I met farmer and vendor Franca Tantillo at the Union Square Greenmarket. Franca grows many delicious things at her Berried Treasures Farm in Cooks Falls, New York, including all kinds of snap beans and shell beans, which she sells both fresh and dried. Her enthusiasm is infectious, as evidenced by all the smiles evoked by Franca herself and the handwritten "Tasting is believing—try some!" sign at her stand. Her beans inspired this recipe, which is a great way to serve any kind of snap bean. You can use the combination I suggest—long beans, haricots verts, and yellow wax beans—which provides a nice mix of texture and color. Or use whatever is abundant in your garden or at the market. Just make sure that you use about 1 pound of beans in all to keep in proportion with the other ingredients.

Green, or unripe, mango is often used in Asian cuisine but not much anywhere else. I like its acidity and fruitiness, which comes without any sweetness. In this preparation, the sweetness comes from the onions and beans. The mango adds the acid tartness that balances the sweet and cools the heat from the Thai chile. Together, these ingredients give that sweet-tart-spicy combination that I often seek to create in my food. You won't find a truly unripe mango at a regular grocery store. Go to a Mexican, Indian, or Asian store instead.   **SERVES 4**

Kosher salt

5 ounces/142 grams Chinese long beans, cut into 1-inch pieces (1½ cups)

1 tablespoon coriander seeds

1 tablespoon fennel seeds

3 tablespoons canola oil

1 tablespoon brown mustard seeds

1 dried Thai chile, broken into small pieces

2 cups sliced onions

5 ounces/142 grams haricots verts, cut in half (1½ cups)

5 ounces/142 grams wax beans, cut in half (1½ cups)

½ cup grated green (unripe) mango

Blanch, shock, and drain the Chinese long beans (see page 33). Set aside.

In a small dry skillet, toast the coriander seeds over medium-low heat, shaking the pan frequently, until fragrant and several shades darker, about 3 minutes. Transfer to a bowl to cool. Repeat to toast the fennel seeds.

In a spice/coffee grinder, grind the coriander seeds until medium-fine. Transfer to a small bowl. Repeat with the fennel seeds and add to the coriander. Set aside.

Heat a medium stew pot over medium heat. Add the oil, and when it starts to shimmer, add the mustard seeds. Cook until they begin to pop, 1 to 2 minutes. Add the chile and cook for 15 to 25 seconds. Stir in the onions and cook until translucent, about 8 minutes.

Add the haricots verts, wax beans, and reserved Chinese long beans to the pot and sauté until tender but still crisp, about 5 minutes. Reduce the heat and stir in the mango and the ground coriander and fennel. Cover and cook until tender, about 4 minutes. Season to taste with salt and serve hot.

COOKING TIME: 30 TO 40 MINUTES

GRILLED ASPARAGUS with LEMON ZEST and MUSTARD

I always preferred sautéing or roasting asparagus until I started growing it in my garden. I don't know if it was the proximity of garden to grill that provided a push in this direction, but from the first time I grilled asparagus, it has been my favorite way to cook it. I love the method here in particular because you can prepare everything several hours ahead of time so that it's ready to toss on the grill once it's hot. (Note that on a day when the grill isn't lit, you can go back to my old ways and sauté the asparagus in canola oil in a wide pan over high heat or roast it in a 425°F oven.)

If you don't grow your own, truly fresh asparagus can be hard to find. Choose asparagus bunches that are standing upright with their stems in water. The base of the stems should not be shriveled or dry. The tips should be stiff and tight, with no moist or mushy sections. Be sure to clean asparagus thoroughly. The shoots grow straight up out of the ground, and lots of dirt can hide in the tight leaves at the top of each spear. **SERVES 6 TO 8**

2 bunches pencil asparagus (about 2 pounds/107 grams), washed and dried (see page 103)
1 tablespoon canola oil
1 teaspoon brown mustard seeds
½ teaspoon chile flakes
Kosher salt

Freshly ground black pepper
3 tablespoons extra-virgin olive oil
Minced zest and juice of 1 lemon
¼ cup minced shallots
2 tablespoons minced peeled fresh ginger
1 teaspoon minced serrano chile

Prepare a hot grill. Place a grill basket on the grill to heat.

Trim the asparagus so that the spears are 4 to 6 inches long. Place the asparagus in a bowl.

Heat a small pot over medium heat. Add the canola oil, and when it starts to shimmer, add the mustard seeds. Cook, stirring and shaking the pan, until the mustard seeds pop, 1 to 2 minutes.

Pour the mustard seeds and oil over the asparagus. Add the chile flakes and season with salt and pepper. Pour over 1½ tablespoons of the olive oil and toss until well coated. Set aside.

In a small bowl, combine the remaining 1½ tablespoons olive oil with the lemon zest and juice, shallots, ginger, and chile. Set aside. (Everything can be done up until this point up to 2 hours in advance and set aside at room temperature.)

Place the asparagus in the hot grill basket and cook, shaking the basket occasionally, until crisp-tender, 8 to 10 minutes.

Transfer the asparagus to a serving dish. Pour the lemon–olive oil mixture over it and mix well. Serve.

COOKING TIME: ABOUT 20 MINUTES

THE SMASHED POTATOES with ROSEMARY and GARLIC THAT SAVED MY CHRISTMAS EVE

One Christmas Eve many years ago, soon after we'd moved into the house we still live in, I planned to make a prime rib for dinner. I confidently put it in the (new to us) oven and turned it on, and we left for church. Off we went, only to be greeted when we returned several hours later not by the succulent smell of roasting meat and herbs, but by a cold oven and raw meat. Clearly, I should have tested the oven.

I quickly lit the grill, then smashed parboiled potatoes with some fresh herbs and roasted garlic, and wrapped them in greased foil (a hobo pack). I tossed the package on the grill and then I cut that prime rib into rib-eye steaks and threw them on the grill too. An hour later, Christmas Eve dinner was saved!

I'm happy to say that I've never had to turn to this dish again to help me rescue a major holiday, but it has become a favorite dish at home, because we almost always have potatoes, rosemary, and garlic in the house. When the grill or oven is on, I often reach for them. I've since made this for my family in India and they absolutely loved it. It's an excellent recipe to have up your sleeve because it's so simple yet really delicious.

Incidentally, I call for russets here only because they are what I tend to have on hand, but you can use your favorite potato. **SERVES 6**

---

5 medium russet (baking) potatoes (about 2 pounds/907 grams), scrubbed and cut into 1½-inch cubes

Kosher salt

6 large Roasted Garlic cloves (recipe follows)

Leaves from one 6-inch rosemary sprig, roughly chopped

Freshly ground black pepper

¼ cup melted bacon fat or extra-virgin olive oil

Place the potatoes in a large pot, add cold water to cover by at least 1 inch and several generous pinches of salt, and bring to a boil over medium-high heat. Reduce the heat and simmer the potatoes until they are just tender but not completely cooked, 10 to 15 minutes. Drain thoroughly in a colander, then pat the potatoes dry with paper towels.

Prepare a medium-hot grill or heat the oven to 375°F.

Place the drained potatoes in a large bowl. Squeeze the garlic cloves from their skins into the bowl. Add the rosemary and salt and pepper to taste and toss until well combined.

Continued

Brush a large cast-iron skillet with some of the bacon fat. Place the potatoes in the skillet. Use a large wooden spoon or a potato masher to press and smash the potatoes in the skillet and press them together tightly; you want some texture, so don't mash them. Brush with the remaining bacon fat. Cover the pan with foil.

Place the skillet on the grill and cover the grill or place the skillet in the oven. Cook until the potatoes are tender and lightly browned on the bottom, 25 to 35 minutes. Serve hot.

COOKING TIME: ABOUT 1¼ HOURS

Note: Alternatively, make a hobo pack. After tossing the potatoes with the garlic and rosemary, use a large wooden spoon or a potato masher to press and smash the potatoes in the bowl. Brush a large piece of heavy-duty aluminum foil with bacon fat, leaving a couple of inches around the edges clean. Transfer the potatoes to the foil and drizzle with the remaining bacon fat. Fold up the edges of the foil and crimp them together to make a sealed pouch. Place the pouch on the grill and cook as directed. Be careful when opening the foil, as the steam that escapes will be very hot.

ROASTED GARLIC

Garlic is one of the many things I toss into the oven when I'm cooking something else. Roasting brings out garlic's natural sweetness and makes it melt-in-your-mouth tender. Plus, roasted garlic keeps well and there is no shortage of things you can do with it: You can simply spread the cloves on grilled slices of country bread, or smash a few into a bowl of drained hot pasta, or mix into salad dressing. Or add them to dishes like the smashed potatoes.

1 head garlic
Canola oil or extra-virgin olive oil

Preheat the oven to 350° to 425°F, depending on what else you are roasting.

Separate the garlic head into individual cloves (do not peel them). Place the cloves on one half of a large sheet of aluminum foil. Sprinkle with oil. Fold over the foil and crimp the edges to seal. Roast until tender, 25 to 30 minutes.

To use at once, open the foil, let the garlic stand until cool enough to handle, and then squeeze the garlic from the skin. Or let cool and store the unpeeled cloves in a sealed container in the refrigerator for up to 1 week.

COOKING TIME: 25 TO 30 MINUTES

CEDAR-PLANK GRILLED SALMON with ALEPPO PEPPER and LIME ZEST

I love smoked salmon and raw salmon, but I have an uneasy relationship with cooked salmon. I just can't abide the gamy fishiness that can develop if it is not extremely fresh wild salmon or if it ends up overcooked—a fate that seems to befall salmon with alarming regularity. When cooking salmon, always buy fish that is as fresh as possible (that's more than half the reason it tastes so good in restaurants). And choose wild salmon, because it is generally healthier, cleaner, and less ecologically harmful than farmed salmon. Plus, wild tastes so much better than farmed. This may be changing as salmon farms clean up their acts, but for my money, wild is the far better investment.

Once you have good, fresh salmon, avoid overcooking it. There are two ways to ensure perfectly cooked salmon: Either grill or roast it *just* until medium-rare, as in this recipe, or cook it in the oven at a very low temperature, as for Slow-Cooked Salmon with Fennel and Coriander (page 315). In fact, you can use the seasonings here and cook the salmon using that same technique.

Although the salmon can be grilled without them, cedar planks give the fish a really nice smoky flavor. I always pick up a pack when my local grocery store has them for a great price, which usually happens at least once right around the end of grilling season. They're not a huge investment and they can be used at least twice; they only get a bit charred on the bottom and sides. Just rinse them off—don't use soap, but do use a metal scrubber if necessary to scrape off any fishy bits—and dry thoroughly. You can also use them to cook the salmon in the oven; follow the recipe but roast in a 400°F oven for about the same amount of time as for grilling. **SERVES 6**

Six 5-ounce/142-gram skin-on salmon fillets

Sea salt

1 teaspoon Aleppo pepper

1 tablespoon sweet paprika

2 tablespoons extra-virgin olive oil

Minced zest and juice of 2 limes

2 tablespoons minced shallots

1 tablespoon minced peeled fresh ginger

Leaves from 2 thyme sprigs

Leaves from 1 tarragon sprig

Freshly ground black pepper

Canola oil for grilling

2 or 3 cedar planks

Soak the cedar planks in water for 4 to 6 hours.

Season the flesh side of the salmon lightly with salt and dust with the Aleppo pepper and paprika.

In a small bowl, stir together the olive oil, lime zest, shallots, ginger, thyme, tarragon, and black pepper to taste. Brush the mixture over the salmon flesh.

Continued

Put on a plate and let rest in the refrigerator for 1 hour.

Prepare a hot grill. If using a charcoal grill, once the coals are ashed over, cover the grill, making sure that all the vents are wide open so that it gets very hot. Meanwhile, remove the salmon from the refrigerator and let stand at room temperature for 10 minutes before grilling.

Brush the skin side of the salmon with canola oil. Place 2 or 3 pieces of fish skin side down on each cedar plank. Place the planks on the grill. Cover the grill and close the top and bottom vents to reduce the heat. Or, if using a gas grill, reduce the temperature to 350°F. Cook until the salmon is medium-rare, 10 to 12 minutes.

Remove the fish from the grill and sprinkle with the lime juice. Serve hot.

COOKING TIME: ABOUT 20 MINUTES / INACTIVE TIME: 4 TO 6 HOURS FOR SOAKING THE CEDAR PLANKS AND 1 HOUR FOR CHILLING

GRILLED SWORDFISH with CHERRY TOMATO SALAD

When grilling fish, you need to pick a variety with enough character and flavor to hold its own against the less-than-gentle environment of the grill. Swordfish and mahimahi are both great candidates for summer barbecues, as are sardines, mackerel, and bluefish. If using bluefish, make sure that it's very fresh. (As chef Dave Pasternack of Esca—who considers it the most underappreciated fish on the East Coast—once told me, when bluefish is fresh there is nothing like it. He's right. But it's lousy when it's not fresh.) Note that mackerel and bluefish should be skin-on, whereas swordfish and mahimahi should not.

Keep the vinaigrette and the salad separate until it's time to serve. If you toss it ahead, the tomatoes will get soggy and the fennel pollen will lose its fresh flavor. You can use other spicy greens in place of the mustard or arugula. **SERVES 4**

FOR THE VINAIGRETTE

¼ cup extra-virgin olive oil

4 garlic cloves, thinly sliced

3 anchovy fillets, chopped

1½ teaspoons chile flakes

3 tablespoons aged balsamic vinegar

2 tablespoons red wine vinegar

½ teaspoon sugar, or to taste

Sea salt

Freshly ground black pepper

FOR THE SALAD

4 cups halved cherry tomatoes

2 cups red mustard greens or arugula

¾ cup sliced sweet onion

1 tablespoon fennel pollen (see Sources, page 345)

FOR THE FISH

Four 6-ounce/170-gram skinless swordfish steaks, about 1 inch thick, or skin-on mackerel or bluefish fillets

Sea salt

Freshly ground black pepper

Canola oil

Juice of 1 lemon

Prepare a medium-hot grill. Remove the fish from the refrigerator.

While the grill is heating, prepare the vinaigrette: In a small saucepan, combine 3 tablespoons of the olive oil and the garlic. Place the pan over low heat and heat slowly until the garlic is aromatic, about 5 minutes.

Transfer the oil and garlic to a large bowl. Add the remaining 1 tablespoon olive oil, the anchovies, chile flakes, balsamic vinegar, red wine vinegar, sugar, and salt and pepper to taste. Gently whisk to blend and set aside.

In a large bowl, combine the tomatoes, greens, onion, and fennel pollen. Set aside.

Lightly season each fish steak with salt and pepper. Brush each with canola oil. Grill for 4 to 6 minutes on each side for medium, or to the desired doneness.

When the fish is ready, pour the vinaigrette over the salad, season with salt and pepper to taste, and mix lightly to coat. Divide the salad among four plates and place a fillet on top of each one. Sprinkle the fish with lemon juice to taste. Serve.

COOKING TIME: ABOUT 30 MINUTES

NEW YORK STRIP LOIN with MUSTARD, CORIANDER, and ROSEMARY CRUST

My dad loved—I mean *loved*—steak. Whenever I prepare strip steak, I try to make it so delicious that were Dad alive to eat it with me, it'd be the best steak he'd ever had. That is the inspiration that led to this dish. The secret is the coriander, mustard seed, and rosemary crust, which serves two distinct but harmonious purposes. First, those flavors beautifully complement the flavor of the meat, and second, the crust prevents the steak from charring. Charred meat can have a bitter taste; the crust allows a nice caramelization to happen without any burned char. Finish with good salt for a pleasing salty crunch. **SERVES 6**

1 tablespoon black peppercorns

2 tablespoons yellow mustard seeds

1 tablespoon coriander seeds

Leaves from three 6-inch rosemary sprigs

Four 8-ounce/227-gram boneless New York strip steaks, about 1 inch thick

Kosher salt

Canola oil

Finishing salt, such as Maldon, sel gris, fleur de sel, or Hawaiian sea salt

Extra-virgin olive oil for serving

In a spice/coffee grinder, coarsely grind the peppercorns. Add the mustard seeds, coriander seeds, and rosemary and grind until semi-fine, like grains of sand; don't grind to a powder.

Rub the spice mixture all over the steaks, pressing with your hands to make the rub adhere. Transfer to a plate and refrigerate for at least 1 hour, and up to 12 hours. Prepare a hot grill. Remove the steaks from the refrigerator and let stand at room temperature while the grill heats.

Sprinkle the steaks with kosher salt and brush them on both sides with canola oil. Grill to the desired doneness, 4 to 6 minutes per side for medium-rare. Transfer the steaks to a cooling rack to rest for 10 minutes.

Slice the steaks against the grain and place on a serving platter. Sprinkle with finishing salt and olive oil. Serve.

COOKING TIME: ABOUT 30 MINUTES / INACTIVE TIME: 1 TO 12 HOURS FOR CHILLING AND 10 MINUTES FOR RESTING

GRILLED SKIRT STEAK with POBLANO PEPPERS and ONIONS

Mexican food is a lot like Indian food: generally easy to prepare and based on very appealing flavors. Mexican cooking also boasts a pleasing alternative to the green pepper: poblano peppers. I don't like green bell peppers, and I love that I can get that grassy flavor from an ingredient that also lends interest and character, without any of the brassy underripe taste green bell peppers can have. I now use poblanos in many places where others might use green peppers. They are assertive but not overwhelming, so they lend themselves to lots of dishes. For instance, here you could use chicken thighs in place of the steak without having to worry that the pepper accompaniment will overpower the meat. And you can add great smoky flavor to ripe poblanos by fire-roasting them on the grill, as is done here.

You can grill the onion slices directly on the grill; they're thick enough that they can stand up to being flipped once. If you have a grill basket, though, it's a great tool for grilling onions and other small ingredients. I use mine all the time. Put it empty on the grill so it's piping hot and then you can "grill/stir-fry" all sorts of vegetables. I use it for beans, snap peas, sliced zucchini, and even corn cut off the cob. Finally, many recipes instruct to cut steak against the grain, but I prefer to slice skirt steak thin and with the grain because this brings out its wonderful texture. **SERVES 6**

FOR THE STEAK

⅓ cup water

3 ancho chiles, seeded

1 dried chipotle chile

2 tablespoons canola oil

8 garlic cloves

Juice of 3 limes

1 tablespoon black peppercorns, coarsely ground

1 teaspoon cumin seeds

1½ pounds/680 grams skirt steak

Kosher salt

FOR THE POBLANO PEPPERS AND ONIONS

3 poblano peppers

2 large white onions, cut into ¼-inch slices

Leaves from 2 thyme sprigs

Kosher salt

Freshly ground black pepper

2 tablespoons canola oil

1 cup cilantro leaves with tender stems, washed and dried (see page 39)

2 tablespoons freshly grated peeled horseradish

Juice of 1 small lime

3 ounces/85 grams red mustard greens, trimmed and washed

In a small saucepan, bring the water to a boil. Keep hot.

Heat a large cast-iron skillet over medium heat. Place the ancho and chipotle chiles in the pan and toast, turning once, until slightly colored on both sides,

5 to 10 minutes total. Remove from the heat and submerge the chiles in the hot water. Let stand for 10 minutes.

Transfer the chiles, with their soaking liquid, to a blender or food processor. Add the oil, garlic, lime juice, pepper, and cumin seeds and process until smooth.

Rub the mixture all over the steak and place it in a covered dish or ziplock bag. Marinate in the refrigerator for at least 4 hours, and up to 12 hours.

Prepare a hot grill. Have ready a grill basket, if you have one. Remove the steak from the refrigerator and let stand at room temperature while the grill heats.

Grill the poblano peppers, turning a few times, until charred on all sides. Place them in a bowl and cover with a napkin until cooled. Place the grill basket, if using, on the grill to heat. Sprinkle the onions with the thyme and season with salt and pepper. Brush on both sides with the oil. Grill the onions in the grill basket or directly on the grill, turning once, until tender and well marked on both sides, about 15 minutes. Remove from the grill.

Meanwhile, use a paper towel to rub off the charred skin from the poblano peppers. Remove and discard the cores and seeds. Slice the peppers into strips and transfer to a large bowl.

Add the onions to the bowl, separating them into rings if necessary. Add the cilantro, horseradish, and lime juice. Season to taste with salt and pepper. Keep warm.

Remove the steak from the marinade and season on both sides with salt. Grill the steak for 8 to 10 minutes, turning once, for medium-rare, or to the desired doneness. Transfer to a cooling rack and let rest for 10 minutes, then slice the steak thinly *with* the grain.

Place the mustard greens on a serving platter. Place the sliced steak on top of the mustard greens and arrange the peppers and onions around the steak. Serve.

COOKING TIME: ABOUT 1¼ HOURS / INACTIVE TIME: 10 MINUTES FOR SOAKING THE CHILES, 4 TO 12 HOURS FOR MARINATING THE STEAK, AND ABOUT 10 MINUTES FOR RESTING

GRILLED PORK LOIN with ORANGES and LEMONS

I have a strong preference for heritage-breed pork, such as Berkshire, Hampshire, or Mangalitsa. Thankfully, these days we can easily access this superior meat (see Sources, page 345). The beauty of this recipe, though, is that whether you use heritage breed or the leaner American pork you get at the grocery store, the citrus marinade suits both beautifully. If you're cooking the very lean standard pork, the marinade keeps it nice and moist; in fact, you really can't cook ordinary pork roasts without marinating them, or they'll dry right out. If you are working with heritage pork, this marinade complements its rich flavor.

If the only thing that's been keeping you from trying heritage pork is that you think it's fattier, please don't worry about that fat. The food these foraging pigs eat is very different from what is fed to conventionally raised pigs, and this means that the levels of HDL cholesterol (the "good" cholesterol) in their fat are higher than those in regular pork.

Finally, I'm surprised that some people still think that pork must be cooked well-done to avoid the danger of trichinosis, an infection that has long since been almost completely eradicated from the American food supply. It's true that if you're in another part of the world, you may want your pork more well-done, but if you're in the United States, please embrace the pink! **SERVES 6**

3 whole cloves

Half a 3-inch cinnamon stick

1 orange, thinly sliced

2 lemons, thinly sliced

2 tablespoons canola oil

4 garlic cloves, finely minced

One 2-inch piece fresh ginger, peeled and grated

Leaves from one 6-inch rosemary sprig, finely chopped

2 tablespoons sweet paprika

1 tablespoon black peppercorns, coarsely ground

1 tablespoon Colman's mustard powder, or yellow mustard seeds, finely ground

1½ tablespoons kosher salt

One 2-pound/907-gram pork loin roast

In a spice/coffee grinder, finely grind the cloves and cinnamon stick together. Set aside.

Squeeze the juice from the orange and lemon slices into a large ziplock bag and add the slices to the bag. Add the oil, garlic, ginger, rosemary, paprika, pepper, mustard powder, the reserved cloves and cinnamon, and the salt. Place the pork in the bag, seal the bag, and massage it to distribute the marinade all over the meat. Marinate in the refrigerator overnight.

Continued

Prepare a medium-hot charcoal grill for indirect heat, arranging the coals on one side of the grill. Or, if using a gas grill, turn one burner off after the grill has reached temperature. Remove the pork from the marinade and let stand while the grill heats.

Strain the marinade and reserve the solids; discard the liquid.

Place the pork loin on the cool side of the grill. Coat the loin with the reserved solid marinade ingredients. Cover the grill, with the vent in the lid directly over the meat if possible, and open the vent; you may have to adjust the vent in the bottom of the grill so that the smoke pulls properly through the top vent. Grill-roast until the pork is cooked to medium, about 30 minutes; it should still be pink and juicy. Transfer to a cooling rack and let rest, uncovered, for 8 minutes.

Slice the pork against the grain and serve.

COOKING TIME: ABOUT 40 MINUTES / INACTIVE TIME: OVERNIGHT FOR MARINATING AND 8 MINUTES FOR RESTING

BOMBAY GROUND LAMB KEBABS

The Indian *seekh kebab,* a delicious and aromatic caseless lamb "sausage" cooked on long skewers, is a very popular street food in Bombay and Old Delhi. This recipe will bring those flavors and aromas into your home, even if it doesn't come with the fun and noise of the streets.

Eat these just as is with the onion topping, or use them as the filling for a wrap or sandwich. If you do that, stuff it generously with a hearty spoonful or two of the onions, lots of crisp romaine leaves, and a cucumber and yogurt sauce. The only caveat is that the kebabs are best eaten as soon as possible; they are not so good if they start to dry out. Note that you do need a meat grinder to make these.

As for the onions, when I'm making this for kids, I use a sweet onion such as Vidalia, because kids don't tend to appreciate spicy onions. When it's for adults, I use something stronger, like a yellow onion. Soaking the onions in cold water before tossing them with salt and pepper mellows their flavor and keeps them crispy; you can soak them for anywhere from 30 minutes to 6 hours. But when I'm making these onions just for me, I don't soak them, because I like their spicy flavor, so I prepare them right before cooking the patties. **SERVES 6**

1 sweet or yellow onion (see headnote), thinly sliced

1½ teaspoons black peppercorns

2 black cardamom pods

3 green cardamom pods

1½ pounds/680 grams boneless leg of lamb, cut into 1-inch cubes

1 medium red onion, chopped (about 1½ cups)

1 serrano chile, chopped

1½ cups washed and dried cilantro leaves (see page 39) with tender stems, coarsely chopped

One 1-inch piece fresh ginger, peeled and sliced into thin coins

3 large garlic cloves, chopped

1 tablespoon kosher salt, plus more for the onions

¼ cup canola oil, or as needed for grilling

Freshly ground black pepper

Lime wedges for serving

If soaking the onions, place them in a medium bowl and add cold water to cover by several inches. Set aside in the refrigerator for at least 30 minutes and up to 6 hours.

Finely grind the peppercorns in a spice/coffee grinder. Transfer to a large bowl. Finely grind the black and green cardamom pods together. Transfer to the bowl with the pepper and stir to combine.

Add to the bowl, the lamb, red onion, chile, cilantro, ginger, garlic, and salt and use your hands to combine thoroughly.

Set up a meat grinder with the fine die. Push the mixture through the grinder into a clean bowl. Chill the mixture until cold, at least 1 hour, and up to 4 hours.

When ready to cook, form a small piece of the meat mixture into a small disk and microwave it for a few seconds so that you can taste for seasoning. Add salt to the mixture as necessary. Form the mixture into 6 large to 12 small patties.

Prepare a medium-hot grill or heat a heavy-bottomed skillet over medium heat.

Oil the grill grate or add the ¼ cup oil to the skillet and heat until it shimmers. Cook the patties until just a little pink on the inside, about 4 minutes per side for small patties and 6 minutes per side for large patties.

Meanwhile, drain the onions thoroughly if you soaked them. Add salt and pepper to taste to the onions and toss to combine.

Serve the kebabs with lime wedges and the onions.

COOKING TIME: ABOUT 45 MINUTES / INACTIVE TIME: 30 MINUTES TO 6 HOURS IF SOAKING THE ONIONS AND 1 TO 4 HOURS FOR CHILLING THE KEBAB MIXTURE

GRILLED LAMB SHANKS with SALSA VERDE

I always assumed that veal or lamb shanks could only be braised; I'd never seen any other sort of preparation. But then on a trip to Italy many years ago, Danny Meyer had grilled veal shanks, which tasted so good that he began to consider what else might work. When he returned to the United States, he wondered aloud to me what grilled lamb shanks would taste like. We both agreed that they're pretty fabulous—and I think you will too, once you try these.

They're cooked using a method often called grill-roasting, wherein you use your grill like an oven. It's a good way to cook thicker cuts of meat.

Check out Sources, page 345, for a good source for lamb. Try to get your hands on larger hind shanks, which are usually at least 1 pound each. If you use foreshanks, which are usually 10 to 12 ounces each, use 4 of them and grill-roast for about 20 minutes.

SERVES 4

FOR THE MARINADE

1 tablespoon black peppercorns,
    coarsely ground

3 black cardamom pods, finely ground

Leaves from two 6-inch rosemary sprigs,
    finely minced

4 garlic cloves, crushed

3 tablespoons canola oil

2 teaspoons kosher salt

2 lamb hind shanks (about 1 pound/
    454 grams each; see headnote)

FOR THE SALSA VERDE

1 lemon

¼ cup canola oil

3 tablespoons champagne vinegar
    or cider vinegar

1 tablespoon chopped parsley

1 tablespoon chopped dill

1 tablespoon thinly sliced mint leaves

1 tablespoon thinly sliced washed and
    dried cilantro leaves (see page 39)
    with tender stems

1 teaspoon minced garlic

1 tablespoon Aleppo pepper

1½ teaspoons minced shallot

Kosher salt

Freshly ground black pepper

To make the marinade, combine the pepper, cardamom, rosemary, garlic, oil, and salt in a small bowl. Place the lamb shanks in a shallow pan and rub the mixture all over them. Cover the pan with plastic wrap and place in the refrigerator for at least 12, and, preferably, up to 24 hours.

Prepare a medium-hot charcoal grill for indirect heat, arranging the coals on one side of the grill. Or, if using a gas grill, turn one burner off after the grill has reached temperature. Remove the lamb from the refrigerator and let stand while the grill heats.

Place the shanks on the cool side of the grill. Cover the grill, with the vent in the lid directly over the meat if possible, and open the vent; you may have to adjust the vent in the bottom of the grill so that the smoke pulls properly through the top vent. Grill-roast the shanks, giving them a quarter turn every 15 minutes, until the meat reaches 125°F for medium-rare, about 1 hour. Add more coals as necessary to maintain a medium-hot fire.

Meanwhile, make the salsa verde: Use a zester to remove the zest from the lemon and place the zest in a medium bowl. Juice the lemon and add the juice to the bowl with the zest, then add the oil, vinegar, parsley, dill, mint, cilantro, garlic, Aleppo pepper, shallots, and salt and pepper to taste. Whisk together and let stand for 10 minutes.

Remove the shanks from the grill and place on a cooling rack. Let rest, uncovered, for 10 minutes.

Slice the lamb shanks and arrange the slices on a warmed platter. Spoon over the salsa verde and serve.

COOKING TIME: 1½ TO 1¾ HOURS / INACTIVE TIME: 12 TO 24 HOURS FOR MARINATING, PLUS 10 MINUTES FOR RESTING

SMOKED and GRILLED PORK SPARERIBS

It's so common to be served pork ribs either Chinese style or BBQ style that a person could be forgiven for thinking that these are the only two ways to prepare spareribs. Not so. The flavorful meat and fat on ribs work extremely well with spices. For my ribs, mustard seed, black pepper, allspice, garlic, and fresh ginger are combined in a marinade base of dark rum and tamarind paste.

Smoking adds another layer of delicious flavor to the ribs. I'm not picky about what kind of wood chips I use. I tend to have hickory on hand, but use whatever you like or can get easily. If you don't have time to smoke the ribs, skip that and simply prepare a hot grill as instructed; you'll need to cook unsmoked ribs about 45 minutes longer. **SERVES 6**

1 tablespoon yellow mustard seeds

1 tablespoon black peppercorns

8 allspice berries

¼ cup dark rum

3 tablespoons red wine vinegar

2 tablespoons Tamarind Paste
  (page 340)

2 tablespoons sugar

6 garlic cloves

One 2-inch piece fresh ginger, peeled
  and sliced into thin coins

2 tablespoons sweet paprika

1 tablespoon turmeric

½ teaspoon cayenne

2 to 3 tablespoons kosher salt (see Note)

3 pounds/1.36 kilograms pork spareribs

Wood chips for smoking (optional)

Finely grind the mustard seeds, peppercorns, and allspice berries in a spice/coffee grinder. Set aside.

In a blender, combine the rum, vinegar, tamarind paste, sugar, garlic, and ginger and blend until pureed. Transfer to a bowl and add the reserved ground spices, the paprika, turmeric, cayenne, and salt. Stir until well blended.

Rub the ribs with the paste. Place them in a ziplock bag and marinate in the refrigerator overnight.

If smoking the ribs, soak 4 cups wood chips in water for at least 20 minutes. Meanwhile, build a small fire on one side of a charcoal grill or turn on just one burner of a gas grill to low heat. Remove the ribs from the refrigerator and let stand while the grill heats.

When the charcoal has ashed over, toss a handful of the soaked chips on top of it. Or, if using a gas grill, put the chips in a smoking box and place the box under the grate, next to the flame. Place the ribs bone side down on the cool side of the grill, cover the grill, and close all the vents. Smoke for 1½ hours, maintaining very low heat (around 200°F); add more lit charcoal as needed to maintain the temperature. To maintain a generous amount of smoke, add a handful of soaked chips to the charcoal or smoking box as needed, or every 30 minutes.

Continued

Uncover the grill, add enough charcoal to the pile to make a medium-sized fire, and let them burn to medium-high. Or, if using a gas grill, turn on all the burners and heat to 350°F. (If you did not smoke the ribs, remove them from the refrigerator now and let stand while the grill heats.)

Spread out the coals across the grate, if using a charcoal grill. Position the ribs so that they are directly over the fire (or place the unsmoked ribs bone side down on the grill). Cover the grill and partially open the upper and lower vents to bring the temperature down to medium-low. Or, if using a gas grill, bring the temperature down to around 275°F. Cook until the meat is tender, about 30 minutes if you smoked the ribs (or about 1 hour and 15 minutes if you did not smoke the ribs).

Remove the meat from the grill and cut into separate ribs. Place on a platter and serve.

COOKING TIME: 1½ TO 2¼ HOURS / INACTIVE TIME: OVERNIGHT FOR MARINATING AND 20 MINUTES FOR SOAKING THE WOOD CHIPS (IF SMOKING THE RIBS)

Note: If the ribs are very meaty, use the larger amount of salt.

CHIMICHURRI SAUCE for GRILLED BEEF, CHICKEN, or LAMB

The first time I had steak with chimichurri in Argentina, its country of origin, I was struck by how similar this herb-garlic-shallot combination is to the mint and coriander chutneys that I grew up eating in India. All of these are perfect to serve with grilled meat, because their bold flavor and moisture can even rescue dry meat. So if you are tempted to hold off on grilling that steak—or chicken or lamb—because you forgot to marinate it, just season it with some salt and pepper and whip up this chimichurri instead.

Chimichurri really is best if made the same day it's to be served. However, if you want to prepare it a day ahead, leave out the vinegar (it will discolor the herbs if stored for more than a few hours). Then stir in the vinegar 30 to 60 minutes before serving and let stand at room temperature. **MAKES 1 CUP**

1 teaspoon black peppercorns
1 teaspoon coriander seeds
½ cup extra-virgin olive oil
¼ cup red wine vinegar
1 teaspoon honey
3 tablespoons minced peeled fresh ginger
1 tablespoon minced shallot
1 large garlic clove, minced
½ teaspoon minced serrano chile

Leaves from 2 parsley sprigs, stacked a few at a time and thinly sliced
Leaves from 2 thyme sprigs, chopped
Leaves from 2 mint sprigs, stacked a few at a time and thinly sliced
Leaves from 1 tarragon sprig, stacked a few at a time and thinly sliced
Kosher salt

In a small dry skillet toast the peppercorns over medium-low heat, shaking the pan frequently, until fragrant and several shades darker, about 3 minutes. Transfer to a bowl to cool. Repeat to toast the coriander seeds.

Finely grind the peppercorns and coriander seeds together in a spice/coffee grinder.

In a small bowl, whisk together the olive oil, vinegar, honey, ginger, shallot, garlic, chile, parsley, thyme, mint, tarragon, the spice mix, and salt to taste. Let stand at room temperature for an hour. Taste and adjust the salt if necessary before serving.

COOKING TIME: 10 TO 15 MINUTES / INACTIVE TIME: 1 HOUR FOR RESTING

GRILLED PINEAPPLE with CRACKED BLACK PEPPER

My great-aunt had a pineapple field behind her house. When I was a kid, we would pick and eat pineapples right there in the field. I remember the luscious sweetness of a just-picked pineapple as distinctly as I recall the very unpleasant sensation of being poked by the pineapple's aggressive prickles. Whenever I taste a really ripe pineapple, I can't help but to be transported back to my great-aunt's backyard. For me, this is the defining characteristic of what I do: I am most successful when a lovely feeling or recollection is captured through the food I prepare, and perhaps even transports someone else to his or her own happy memory.

Try this just as is, with no accompaniment beyond the syrup. It is also delicious with vanilla ice cream or on top of pound cake. Or leave out the black pepper and serve this pineapple in place of the peaches for the Steel-Cut Oats with Grilled Peach Compote (page 210).   **SERVES 4 TO 6**

⅓ cup (2⅜ ounces/67 grams) sugar

⅓ cup water

1 vanilla bean, preferably Tahitian, split lengthwise in half

One 1-inch piece fresh ginger, peeled and sliced

1 ripe pineapple

½ cup Ghee (page 342), melted

1 tablespoon black peppercorns, coarsely ground

Combine the sugar and water in a medium saucepan, place over medium heat, and cook, stirring occasionally, until the sugar has dissolved. Remove the pan from the heat, add the split vanilla bean and sliced ginger, cover, and let stand for 30 minutes.

Remove the lid from the pan and let the syrup cool to room temperature.

Prepare a high-heat grill.

While the grill is heating, peel the pineapple. Slice into ½-inch-thick rounds and cut out the core from each slice. Alternatively, quarter the pineapple lengthwise, cut the core out of each quarter, and slice the pineapple lengthwise into ½-inch-thick wedges.

Brush the pineapple slices with the ghee. Grill until marked but still firm, about 5 minutes per side.

Transfer the slices to a large serving dish, arranging them in a single layer. Sprinkle over the pepper. Strain the syrup and pour it over the pineapple. Let stand at room temperature for at least 1 hour before serving. The pineapple can be stored in its syrup in the refrigerator for 2 to 3 days.

COOKING TIME: 30 TO 35 MINUTES / INACTIVE TIME: 30 MINUTES FOR STEEPING THE SYRUP AND 1 HOUR FOR RESTING THE GRILLED PINEAPPLE

CHAPTER EIGHT

Game Time

WHEN BOTH THE FOOD AND THE GAME MATTER

Anyone who knows me will confirm that I live and die by my favorite baseball and football teams. What not everyone may know is that my love for both began only when I came to the United States. I had never even watched baseball, let alone American football, before then. Cricket and soccer were the sports I knew and loved growing up. But soon after I moved to New York City, I learned that my brother Bryan had become a Giants fan. It didn't take much for me to get roped right in to football. My first apartment was not far from Shea Stadium, where the Mets used to play. In a bad season, it's easy to find cheap tickets. My first year in New York was one of those seasons (we Mets fans have had *many* of those seasons). For the very first Mets game I ever attended— or even watched, if memory serves—we secured field-level tickets for a measly $14! I may have had a fabulously clear view of the action, but I had absolutely *no* idea what was happening on the field. Know this: Being a lifelong cricket fan does not in any way help one understand the game of baseball.

The longer I lived in New York, the more my group of friends grew into people who were either Mets or Giants fans—or both—so, naturally, my days off were spent following whichever sport was in season. After many years, and many good and not-so-good seasons, my already deeply entrenched love for both sports blossomed into full-fanatical mode once my kids were born. Thankfully, both boys grew into enthusiastic partners in my obsession. I think it prudent to note how very grateful I am to my wife, Barkha, for indulging me in my vices and for not minding too much when I entice our sons to join me.

Over these years, one aspect of sports that really made an impression on me is how closely food and beverage are tied into the experience of watching a game. Since my first Mets game all that time ago, I have been lucky to be a regular at the stadiums of both of my teams, sometimes in truly excellent seats. It's too bad the quality of the view from those seats is rarely if ever matched by the quality of the food available. It's shocking to me that as soon as the game begins, we who are so discerning about all aspects of what is served to us in restaurants will readily stuff ourselves with unappetizing stadium food like terrible burgers; dry, stringy chicken; and overly salty snacks. Adding insult to injury, we pay a lot of money for this crap!

As the years have gone by, and I've attended as many Sunday Giants games as I possibly can, planning the menu for tailgating at the games has become a big part of the fun for me (and it allows us to avoid overpaying for badly prepared, awful-tasting food). During that tailgating, I have had the pleasure of meeting many fans who, like me, love food and drink and cook spreads that turn into the main attraction when our teams are having a poor year. I love preparing food in that setting that turns the cliché of "tailgating" and "game-time food" on its head. Made with good, fresh ingredients and combinations of spices, *my* game-time food is flavorful and appealing and as far from a stadium hot dog and greasy wings as you can get! In fact, I've become so invested that today I have a dedicated bag stocked with all the essentials I need for tailgating. It's also my go-to bag for camping and cookouts. If you like to cook outside as much as I do, check out the contents of my tailgating bag on page 265.

Of course, if I am not actually at the stadium for Sunday's games, I am almost always watching them at home. And these home-based game times eventually changed the way I cook at home—you see, when I watch games at home, I don't want to leave the room . . . for anything. A few years back, this began to mean that on Sunday, one of the few days of the week that Barkha had been relieved of tending to the family's nourishment, preparing all the food somehow became her responsibility again, a development she seemed not to wholeheartedly embrace. Clearly, change was in order. So I adapted strategies and recipes that allow me to cook the food before or during the game. If something has to be cooked during the game, it should be something that needs no watching over. No matter when the food is cooked, the degree of fussiness has to be minimal. And, naturally, the food has to be delicious. I believe I have gotten pretty successful at doing all of this, as I hope you'll agree when you see what's in this chapter.

At the end of the day this decades-long passion and learning curve has reinforced in my private life a tenet I hold dear in my professional kitchen: It doesn't matter whether you're tailgating, preparing a multicourse Sunday dinner for guests, or serving a dining room of two hundred—the success is all in the planning. And now, let's get ready for the game!

THE TAILGATING BAG

Tailgating is an art and a science, and to achieve success on both counts, you need the proper tools. Listed here are the contents of my tailgating bag, which is always packed and ready to go out the door to games, or to camping trips or cookouts.

Make it your after-game ritual to clean out the bag and everything you used. Wash and thoroughly dry all the tools and other supplies. Replenish the ingredients (except the oils; more on that in a moment) and put everything back into the bag.

You don't want to just keep topping off the oils, or you risk eventually having rancid oil on your hands. So, after every use, empty the oil bottles—I usually pour the oils into something temporary so that I can use them up the next time I cook. Wash and thoroughly dry the oil bottles and tuck them back into the bag. Then the only thing you have to do the next time you need the bag for tailgating or camping is to restock the oil bottles, and you're ready to go.

The grill is the only tool that I don't have in my bag, although it's obviously a necessity. But at tailgates, someone else always has one, and when we cook out while camping or at the beach, there are always grills there. If you're the one bringing the grill, make sure that you add it to your checklist, along with fuel—whether it's charcoal and a chimney or a full propane tank.

Prep and Serving Supplies
- BC multipurpose lighter
- Matchbook
- Newspaper
- Plastic wrap
- Reynolds heavy-duty aluminum foil (make sure that it's heavy-duty)
- Sturdy gallon-sized ziplock bags for leftovers
- Paper towels
- Linen kitchen towels
- Latex gloves (like those used in kitchens and hospitals)
- Metal or plastic serving spoons
- Foil containers for serving
- Paper plates
- Sturdy paper cups that can hold hot as well as cold beverages
- Plastic forks and knives
- Paper napkins
- Garbage bags: everyone forgets these!
- Corkscrew and bottle opener

Cooking Tools
Cutting board: sturdy plastic is best so that you can throw it in the dishwasher when you get home

- Paring knife
- Bread knife
- Sharp chef's knife
- Sharpening steel for knives
- Tongs
- Large metal spatula
- Metal grill brush
- Brush for oiling the grill (a wide pastry brush or food-safe paintbrush)

Food Supplies
- Kosher salt in a ziplock bag or plastic storage container
- Black pepper: grind it at home and put it in a ziplock bag or plastic storage container
- A bottle of extra-virgin olive oil and another of canola oil (these should be plastic or glass with squirt or just regular tops, not spray bottles)
- Bottle of balsamic vinegar
- Bottle of chile sauce
- Jar of good-quality prepared mustard
- Sugar in a ziplock bag or plastic storage container

SPICED PUMPKIN SOUP with CRABMEAT and PUMPKIN SEEDS

This longtime favorite at home served as my starting point for the more refined and very popular version we served at North End Grill. And at the other end of the elegance spectrum, I like to make a big batch of this for tailgates. I transfer the piping-hot soup to a thermos and as people arrive at the tailgate, I pour it over the crab in paper cups. It's always good to have something to feed people to warm their hands, stomach, and spirit while we all wait for the grill to get hot.

Make sure to buy fresh or high-quality canned crabmeat from the refrigerated fish and shellfish section of your store. Don't bother with the shelf-stable cans of crab sold alongside the canned tuna, which tastes more like the can it comes in than it does crab. **SERVES 8**

3 quarts White Fish Stock (page 338), Chicken Stock (page 337), or high-quality store-bought stock, plus more if needed

3 tablespoons canola oil

1½ tablespoons coriander seeds

3 whole cloves

One 2-inch piece pasilla de Oaxaca or dried chipotle chile, cut lengthwise into thin strips

2 cups sliced carrots

2 cups diced onions

2 cups sliced leeks (white and light green parts only)

1 cup diced peeled celery root

5 garlic cloves, smashed

One 1-inch piece fresh ginger, peeled and sliced into thin coins

Kosher salt

Freshly ground black pepper

4 cups cubed, peeled, and seeded pumpkin or other squash

Two 6-inch rosemary sprigs

Juice of 2 lemons, or as needed

1 tablespoon champagne vinegar, or as needed

¾ cup (about 8 ounces/227 grams) fresh or high-quality canned lump or jumbo lump crabmeat, picked over to remove shells

2 tablespoons mint leaves, stacked a few at a time and thinly sliced

2 tablespoons washed and dried cilantro leaves (see page 39), stacked a few at a time and thinly sliced

2 tablespoons snipped chives

¼ cup roasted pumpkin seeds for garnish

In a large saucepan, bring the stock to a simmer over medium heat. Keep warm over low heat.

Meanwhile, in a large stew pot or Dutch oven, heat the oil over medium heat until it shimmers. Add the coriander seeds, cloves, and chile and toast until fragrant and lightly colored, about 1 minute.

Add the carrots, onions, leeks, celery root, garlic, and ginger and cook, stirring occasionally, until lightly colored, 10 to 15 minutes. Season lightly with salt and pepper.

Continued

Add the cubed pumpkin and cook, stirring, until it is well coated with oil and beginning to soften, about 5 minutes. Season lightly with salt and pepper.

Add the warm stock and rosemary, bring to a simmer, and cook until the pumpkin is very tender and the flavors are well blended, 10 to 15 minutes. Remove and discard the rosemary sprigs.

Use a spider or large slotted spoon to scoop out the solid ingredients and transfer them to a blender or food processor. Puree until smooth, adding as much of the liquid from the pot as is necessary to keep the mixture moving (be careful—it's hot). Strain the puree and all of the remaining stock through a China cap or fine-mesh sieve into a clean pot, using a wooden spoon to push the soup through if necessary.

Heat the soup over low heat until hot; add more stock as necessary if the soup is too thick. Stir in the lemon juice and vinegar, then taste and stir in more lemon juice, vinegar, salt, and/or pepper as needed.

Put 1½ tablespoons crabmeat into each of eight warmed soup plates. Ladle the warm soup into the bowls. Garnish with the herbs and pumpkin seeds and serve.

COOKING TIME: ABOUT 1 HOUR

Note: You can use any good eating pumpkin or winter squash you want here. Good choices are sugar, butter, cheese, or buttercup pumpkins and kabocha, Hubbard, or acorn squash. That said, try to avoid using butternut, even though it is ubiquitous, because it is the least interesting option.

SUPER BOWL COCONUT CLAM CHOWDER

I made this chowder for the *Top Chef Masters* military challenge, in which each chef created a meal to celebrate the homecoming of a serviceman returning from overseas. I prepared a meal for U.S. Army captain Eric Palicia, who had recently come back from Afghanistan, and his family. In order to figure out what to prepare in Eric's honor, I spoke to his lovely wife, Jessica, to get a sense of what he liked to eat. To pretty much every ingredient I suggested, she sweetly replied with some variation of "no." She told me that he's a man of simple tastes. I thought, "*Damn,* how do *I* get the guy who hates spice?"

But Eric loves clam chowder, so I set about making what I intended to be a simple version, with many fewer spices than I usually add. In the end, though, I couldn't help but make it my own way. I'm honestly not sure whether he or I was more surprised by how much he loved the chowder. And my amazement turned to humility and gratitude when he presented me with his U.S. Army coin at the end of the meal. It was the only time during the filming of *Top Chef Masters*—a process that was always exhilarating but often grueling—that I actually cried on camera, so touched was I by his generous gesture.

Among the many times I've made this chowder since then was when the New England Patriots played my beloved New York Giants in the 2012 Super Bowl. This chowder is a big crowd-pleaser, so I was happy to make it, but the chowder was as close to New England as I wanted to get that day. I'm pleased to say that the New York Giants won. Again.

A few notes about the ingredients here. I like the ingredients in a dish to have a relationship to each other. Thus I use coconut vinegar here and elsewhere in dishes that contain coconut milk and also call for some acidity. Coconut vinegar is inexpensive and easier to find than you might think: Check out your local grocery store or an Asian market. You can use it anywhere you'd use cider vinegar. **SERVES 6**

36 littleneck clams (about
    3½ pounds/1.59 kilograms), well
    scrubbed (see page 54)
½ cup white wine
4 cups White Fish Stock (page 338),
    Chicken Stock (page 337), high-quality
    store-bought stock, or water
½ cup (2 ounces/57 grams) diced bacon,
    preferably smoky
1½ cups finely diced onions
1 cup finely diced celery
1 cup finely diced carrots
1½ teaspoons chopped garlic
½ pasilla de Oaxaca or dried chipotle
    chile

¼ cup rice grits or rice semolina
    (see Note)
2 cups diced Yukon Gold potatoes
1 cup finely diced leeks (white and light
    green parts only)
1 teaspoon freshly ground black pepper
    (use a peppermill)
Sea salt
1 tablespoon coriander seeds
2 green cardamom pods
One 13.5-fluid-ounce can Chaokoh-brand
    coconut milk (stir well before using)
1 cup milk
1 tablespoon coconut or cider vinegar
Thinly sliced chives and washed and dried
    cilantro (see page 39) for garnish

Place the clams and wine in a medium saucepan, cover the pan, and cook over medium heat until the clams just open. Discard any clams that have not opened. Pour the clams and liquid into a large strainer set over a bowl.

When they cool enough to handle, remove the clams from the shells. Discard the shells and set the clams aside.

Strain the clam juice through a strainer lined with cheesecloth or a paper coffee filter. Set aside.

In a small saucepan, heat the stock until hot. Keep hot.

Meanwhile, place the bacon in a large stew pot and cook over medium-low heat until the fat is rendered; do not let the bacon crisp. Use a slotted spoon to remove the bacon to a dish, leaving the fat in the pot.

Add the onions to the pot and cook until they begin to soften, 4 to 5 minutes. Add the celery and carrots and cook for 2 minutes. Add the garlic and chile and cook for just 1 minute; there should be no moisture from the vegetables in the pan. Add the rice grits and cook for 1 minute, stirring constantly to mix well.

Add the potatoes, leeks, and the reserved bacon and cook for 1 minute. Whisking constantly, slowly pour in the hot stock and continue whisking to thoroughly incorporate. Add the reserved clam juice, the pepper, and the salt to taste and cook until the potatoes are tender, 12 to 15 minutes.

While the soup is cooking, place a heavy-bottomed skillet over medium-low heat and lightly toast the coriander seeds, shaking the pan frequently, until fragrant and several shades darker, about 3 minutes. Transfer to a bowl and toast the cardamom in the same way. Set aside to cool.

Finely grind the spices in a spice/coffee grinder. When the potatoes are tender, stir the spices into the soup. Add the coconut milk, milk, and vinegar.

Taste and adjust the seasoning, then simmer for 5 minutes.

Remove the pot from the heat. Remove and discard the chile and stir in the clams. Garnish each serving with chives and cilantro and serve.

COOKING TIME: ABOUT 1 HOUR

Note: You can find rice grits at good markets and online (see Sources, page 345). You can use rice semolina in place of the rice grits, but don't substitute regular rice flour. Anything with a finer grind than semolina will just clump up.

CIDER-GLAZED SEARED SCALLOPS with CAULIFLOWER PUREE

This is a delicious marriage of the sweetness of seared sea scallops, the mild bitterness of pureed cauliflower, and the acidity of a cider glaze. When we served it at North End Grill, a *New York Times* writer who did a feature on me loved it so much that I gave her the recipe to run in the paper.

I like this dish because its preparation can be timed to match the game's rhythm. I prepare the puree and glaze before the game begins, then quickly sear the scallops during halftime and plate it all up in time for the second half.

The puree is an excellent way to use up the stems of cauliflower that ordinarily go to waste. Use the stems left from cauliflower florets you've used another way, or use a whole cauliflower and roast the florets to serve with this dish; they add nice texture to the plate.

Use two pans when cooking the scallops to avoid crowding them. Or, if you have a built-in griddle on your stovetop, use it. **SERVES 4**

FOR THE GLAZE

3 cups apple cider, preferably fresh
1 teaspoon minced shallot
1 teaspoon minced peeled fresh ginger
One ½-inch piece pasilla de Oaxaca or dried chipotle chile
3 tablespoons cider vinegar
Sea salt
Freshly ground black pepper

FOR THE CAULIFLOWER PUREE

2 tablespoons canola oil
½ teaspoon cumin seeds
2 tablespoons sliced shallots
1 teaspoon minced peeled fresh ginger
3 cups cauliflower stems
1½ cups Chicken Stock (page 337), Vegetable Stock (page 339), or high-quality store-bought stock
½ teaspoon Aleppo pepper or chile flakes
Sea salt
Freshly ground black pepper

FOR THE SCALLOPS

20 large sea scallops (1½ pounds/ 680 grams), tough side muscle removed
Sea salt
Freshly ground black pepper
6 tablespoons canola oil

To prepare the glaze, in a wide pan such as a chicken fryer or shallow Dutch oven, combine the apple cider, shallot, ginger, chile, and vinegar. Bring to a boil over high heat and boil until reduced to about ½ cup, about 15 minutes (this will take longer in a smaller pan). Remove from the heat and discard the chile. Season with salt and pepper. Set aside, covered to keep warm.

Meanwhile, prepare the puree: Place a large saucepan over medium heat, add the oil and cumin seeds, and heat until the oil shimmers. Add the shallots and ginger and cook for 1 minute. Add the cauliflower and stock and bring to a boil. Cover, reduce the heat to low, and simmer until the cauliflower is soft, about

10 minutes. Add the Aleppo pepper and season with salt and black pepper to taste.

Transfer the cauliflower, with the liquid, to a blender and blend, in batches if necessary, until smooth. Transfer the puree to a dish and keep warm in a very low oven or warming drawer.

Pat the scallops dry with a paper towel. Heat two skillets over high heat until very hot, about 3 minutes. While the pans are heating, season the scallops with salt and black pepper. Turn off the heat and add 3 tablespoons of the oil to each skillet; the oil should start smoking when it hits the pans. Divide the scallops between the pans and turn the heat back on to high (if the oil is smoking excessively, wait a few seconds before turning on the heat). Cook the scallops until well seared on both sides, 2 to 3 minutes per side.

Divide the scallops and puree among four warmed plates. Drizzle with the glaze and serve.

COOKING TIME: ABOUT 40 MINUTES

COD, COCKLES, and LINGUIÇA STEW

I love to surprise people with this unusual game-day dish, especially because it's so uncomplicated and easy to prepare. Plus, you can do just about everything in advance, right up until cooking the fish and clams. Then just warm the stew up, toss the fish and clams on top, and roast for about 15 minutes (during halftime, perhaps), then serve hot.

This is the kind of stew that I think people tend to consider a "restaurant dish," so they don't even try to make it. This is a shame, because it is, in fact, easy to make at home, and it allows you to use readily accessible ingredients and simple techniques to make a big impression. You can find good cockles at most fish markets these days, and if you can't get good cod, just use another fish—black cod, red snapper, hake, and swordfish are all good options. Whatever fish you use, be sure it is skin-on and use thick pieces; thin 4-ounce pieces will be too wide, won't fit in the pan neatly, and will overcook by the time the cockles are opened and ready.

I prefer to use a mortar and pestle to pound the spices for this dish because it preserves their coarse texture better than using a spice grinder. **SERVES 6**

¼ cup extra-virgin olive oil

3 ounces/85 grams linguiça, sliced

1½ tablespoons fennel seeds, pounded in a mortar with a pestle

1 tablespoon coriander seeds, pounded in a mortar with a pestle

One ¼-inch piece dried chipotle chile, very thinly sliced crosswise

6 garlic cloves, thinly sliced

1 cup thinly sliced onion

1 fennel bulb (fine fronds reserved), trimmed, cored, and cut into ¼-inch dice (about 2 cups)

3 cups White Fish Stock (page 338)

½ cup white wine

1 teaspoon turmeric

One 6-inch rosemary sprig

3 cups diced fresh tomatoes (about 1½ pounds/680 grams tomatoes) or one 28-ounce/794-gram can diced fire-roasted tomatoes, preferably Muir Glen brand, with their juice

Sea salt

Freshly ground black pepper

Six 4-ounce/113-gram pieces skin-on cod

1½ pounds/680 grams cockles, scrubbed (see page 54)

Leaves from 2 tarragon sprigs

Preheat the oven to 375°F.

In a 12-inch chicken fryer pan or shallow Dutch oven, heat the olive oil over medium heat until it shimmers. Add the linguiça and cook, stirring occasionally, until fragrant, about 2 minutes. Add the fennel seeds, coriander, chipotle, and garlic and cook, stirring occasionally, until the spices are fragrant and the garlic is golden, 2 to 3 minutes.

Stir in the onion and diced fennel and cook, stirring occasionally, until the onion is translucent, about 6 minutes. Add the stock, wine, turmeric, and rosemary, bring to a boil, and cook until slightly reduced, about 6 minutes.

Continued

Add the tomatoes, cover the pot, and cook until softened, about 4 minutes. Taste and add sea salt and pepper to taste; be careful not to oversalt, though, as the cockles will add brininess. (The dish can be prepared to this point up to a day in advance. Preheat the oven and reheat the stew in the same pot before continuing with the recipe.)

Season the pieces of fish with salt and pepper. Place the fish skin side down on top of the stew and the cockles on top of the fish. Transfer to the oven and cook until the fish is opaque throughout and the cockles are open, 13 to 15 minutes.

Place a piece of fish in each of six wide shallow bowls. Remove the rosemary sprig from the stew and gently stir in the tarragon. Ladle the stew and clams around the fish. Sprinkle each serving with some of the reserved fennel fronds. Serve.

GRILLED LIME-PEPPER CHICKEN

Everyone thinks of chicken wings as good finger food for the big game, but they're just no good on a grill that you don't have tight control over—and when you tailgate, you definitely don't have much control. Wings flame right up on a too-hot grill; there's nothing worse than burnt wings. So I came up with this, which is easy to transport to a tailgate—just bring the ziplock bag with the marinated chicken and grill it there—and not as prone to flare-ups as wings. Plus, this surprisingly simple recipe has amazing taste, in large part because it uses chicken thighs, which have so much more flavor than breasts.

You want thighs with the skin on to prevent them from drying out on the grill, but it's also ideal if the bones are removed. Removing the bones allows for faster cooking and easier eating—and both of these attributes are especially nice when you're feeding a big crowd. It can be hard to find skin-on boneless thighs, though, so you'll usually need to remove the bones yourself. Don't worry if you've never done it; it's a breeze to learn (see page 280). Just make sure that your knife is sharp, and by the time you've removed the bones from all the thighs, you'll be an expert. The bones freeze well and make great stock (see page 337). If you're really determined not to remove them, it's okay to leave the bones in, but you'll need to give the chicken extra time to cook.

Finally, here I'm presenting this for just eight for those times when you're serving a smaller crowd. If you want this to go a little further, cut each thigh in half after you grill them. But if you're serving a larger crowd, it is very easy to double or triple the recipe. And if you want to transport the finished dish—to a Super Bowl party, perhaps, as I have done on occasion—grill the chicken not long before you leave the house and transport it in a foil container. Then just pop the whole container in the oven to warm up a few minutes before putting the chicken out on the buffet table. The dark meat of thighs makes them very forgiving. **SERVES 8**

3½ pounds/1.59 kilograms whole chicken thighs (at least 8 thighs), boned (see page 280)
Kosher salt
6 tablespoons canola oil
Juice from 4 large limes (about 5 tablespoons)

12 garlic cloves, chopped
One 4-inch piece fresh ginger, peeled and chopped
2 tablespoons black peppercorns, finely ground

Season the chicken thighs with salt. Put on a plate and let stand in the refrigerator for 1 hour.

Pat the chicken dry and place in a large ziplock bag.

In a blender, combine the oil, lime juice, garlic, and ginger, and blend until smooth and creamy. Pour the marinade into the bag with the chicken, add the

pepper, and seal the bag. Massage the marinade and pepper into the chicken. Marinate in the refrigerator for at least 6 hours, and up to 24 hours.

Prepare a medium grill. Remove the bag of chicken from the refrigerator and let stand at room temperature while the grill is heating.

Remove the chicken from the bag and place it skin side down on the grill (discard the marinade). Grill until the chicken is nicely browned and releases easily from the grill, 9 to 12 minutes. Turn the thighs to the other side and cook until cooked through; the juices will run clear when pierced with a sharp knife. Serve hot right off the grill.

COOKING TIME: 20 TO 30 MINUTES / INACTIVE TIME: 1 HOUR FOR STANDING AND 6 TO 24 HOURS FOR MARINATING

DEBONING A CHICKEN THIGH

Boneless chicken thighs cook faster than bone-in, which is great when you're cooking for a crowd. But it's tough to find boneless thighs that still have their skin, which is a shame, because the skin adds flavor and protects the meat from drying out during cooking. So it's a good thing that removing the bones from the thighs is so easy! And you can always use a few more bones in your freezer bag of bones for stock (see page 337).

Lay a chicken thigh bone side up on a cutting board. Scrape the bone with the blade of the knife that is closest to the handle, starting at the knee joint, moving toward the hip joint, and pressing firmly on the bone as you move the knife. Then use the tip of the knife to slice the meat away from either side of the bone, cutting down its length on both sides but not piercing so deep that you cut through to the skin side. Finally, put the point of the knife under the bone just above the knee joint and slice the meat away from the bottom side of the bone. Now the bone will be free from the thigh at all points except the knee joint. Pull the bone up away from the thigh and cut the last bit away from the knee joint. Trim away any excess skin and fat from the chicken thigh and set it on a platter or baking sheet. Repeat with the remaining thighs.

ROSEMARY–BLACK PEPPER ROASTED SPATCHCOCKED CHICKEN

I have prepared this roasted chicken for pretty much every person I know who loves chicken. This recipe has spent time on the menus at both North End Grill and White Street. The brining and the rub really give the chicken wonderful flavor. And it's an ideal game-time dish. You can roast the chicken during the first half, quickly toss together a green salad such as the Romaine-Cucumber Salad with Lime and Thai Chile (page 39) and cut up the chicken for serving during halftime, and dinner will be ready just in time for the third quarter!

I like to remove the backbone and flatten the bird before roasting. This technique, called spatchcocking, allows the chicken to cook more evenly and quickly, and it makes fast work of cutting up the bird for serving. **SERVES 4 TO 6**

One 2½-pound/1.13-kilogram chicken
½ cup kosher salt
3 tablespoons sugar
1½ gallons water
3 tablespoons canola oil
3 garlic cloves, finely minced
1 tablespoon minced peeled fresh ginger

Leaves from three 6-inch rosemary sprigs, chopped
1½ tablespoons black peppercorns, coarsely ground
1 tablespoon coriander seeds, coarsely ground
Minced zest and juice of 2 lemons

Place the chicken breast side down on a cutting board. Starting at the neck end, use a sharp boning knife or poultry shears to cut down one side of the backbone toward the tail, stopping about two-thirds of the way down the backbone. Repeat on the other side of the backbone. Now cut down the last bit on either side to completely remove the backbone. (Add it to your freezer bag of chicken parts for stock; see page 337.)

Open out the chicken to reveal the breastbone and place it on the cutting board so that the legs are at the top. With the hilt of the knife (the part of the blade closest to the handle), cut straight down through the center of the arrow-shaped keel bone to crack it. Be careful not to cut into the breast. Then, to ensure that the meat closest to the thigh and leg bones cooks through, cut a roughly 1-inch-long slit down the length of the thigh bone and down the leg bone on both sides (four cuts in all). Flip the chicken over and press down hard on the center of the breast to flatten it. Tuck the wing tips under the wing bones.

In a large bowl or pot, combine the salt, sugar, and water and stir until the salt and sugar are dissolved. Add the chicken. Place in the refrigerator to brine for at least 12 hours, and up to 24 hours.

Remove the chicken from the brine. Discard the brine and pat the chicken dry with a paper towel. Place it in a baking dish.

In a small bowl, combine the oil, garlic, ginger, rosemary, pepper, coriander, and lemon zest and juice. Stir until well blended. Rub all over the chicken and marinate in the refrigerator for at least 2 hours, and up to 12 hours.

Remove the chicken from the marinade and discard the marinade. Pat the chicken dry, but do not wipe off the marinade. Place the chicken skin side up in a roasting pan. Let stand at room temperature for 30 to 45 minutes.

Preheat the oven to 450°F.

Roast the chicken for 15 minutes. Reduce the oven temperature to 425°F and roast, basting the chicken occasionally with the pan juices, for 30 minutes, or until the juices run clear when the thickest part of the thigh is pierced with a sharp knife. Remove from the oven and let stand on a cooling rack for 10 minutes.

Cut the chicken into 8 to 10 pieces and serve.

COOKING TIME: 45 MINUTES TO 1 HOUR / INACTIVE TIME: 14 TO 36 HOURS FOR BRINING, AND MARINATING, AND 40 TO 55 MINUTES FOR TEMPING AND RESTING

TABASCO CHIPOTLE–MARINATED PORK CHOPS

When I was a kid, my sister nicknamed me "Tabasco" because I added the spicy pepper sauce to everything, especially the European (i.e., spice-free) soups we ate. My love has not diminished with time. A few years ago, I was thrilled to be invited by the late Paul McIlhenny to visit Avery Island, Louisiana, where the McIlhenny Company still grows the seeds for the peppers that are turned into the tangy, piquant sauce (some of the peppers themselves are grown elsewhere). I felt like a kid in a candy store! I really enjoyed meeting Paul, whose passion for Tabasco sauce exceeded even my own. My taste for the original is as strong as ever, but the McIlhennys' growing collection of pepper sauces means there are many more flavors—and degrees of heat—to play with. Tabasco chipotle has a great smoky flavor that's enhanced by the grill, and it's a little less spicy-hot than the original Tabasco. That makes these chops great for kids of any age. I use this marinade for whole pork loin as well, then roast it.

To cook this dish while watching a football game at home, light the grill after the first quarter (or a little later if you're using a gas grill) and grill the chops during halftime. **SERVES 4**

1 tablespoon canola oil

½ cup orange juice, preferably fresh (from 1 to 2 oranges)

1 tablespoon fresh lemon juice

1 tablespoon fresh lime juice

1 to 2 tablespoons Tabasco Chipotle Pepper Sauce

½ cup thinly sliced onion

2 large garlic cloves, minced

½ tablespoon minced peeled fresh ginger

¼ teaspoon allspice berries, finely ground

Kosher salt

Freshly ground black pepper

Four 8-ounce/227-gram bone-in pork chops, trimmed of excess fat

In a large ziplock bag, combine the oil, orange juice, lemon juice, lime juice, Tabasco sauce, onion, garlic, ginger, allspice, and a generous pinch each of salt and pepper. Seal the bag and shake it to blend the marinade. Add the pork chops to the marinade and seal the bag. Let stand in the refrigerator for 2 to 4 hours.

When ready to cook, prepare a medium-hot grill. Remove the pork chops from the bag and set on a platter at room temperature while the grill heats.

Meanwhile, pour the marinade into a small saucepan and bring to a boil. Transfer the marinade to a glass measuring cup and set aside.

Grill the pork, brushing it occasionally with the marinade, for 5 to 7 minutes on each side for medium, depending on the thickness of the chops. Remove the pork chops from the grill and place on a cooling rack. Let rest, uncovered, for 4 minutes before serving.

COOKING TIME: ABOUT 45 MINUTES / INACTIVE TIME: 2 TO 4 HOURS FOR MARINATING AND ABOUT 4 MINUTES FOR RESTING

CHILE-RUBBED HANGER STEAK

When I was developing the menu for El Verano, I was exposed to all the nuances of the large variety of chiles used in Mexican cooking and how they are used to make ordinary ingredients taste so good. In this steak preparation, the ancho and guajillo chiles provide plummy notes and the chipotle brings heat and smokiness.

To serve it at a tailgate, bring the marinating steak in a ziplock bag and a stack of tortillas wrapped in aluminum foil. Grill the steak there, and after you pull it off the grill, pop the tortilla bundle on the fire for a few minutes to warm them up. Then slice the steak, roll it up in the tortillas, and serve. **SERVES 8 TO 12**

2 ancho chiles, seeds removed

4 guajillo chiles, seeds removed

4 dried chipotle chiles

1 cup boiling water

2 teaspoons dried Mexican oregano

1 teaspoon black peppercorns

½ teaspoon cumin seeds

4 whole cloves

8 garlic cloves

6 tablespoons cider vinegar

¼ cup canola oil

2 teaspoons sugar

3 pounds/1.36 kilograms trimmed hanger steak, cut into 5- to 6-ounce/142- to 170-gram pieces

Kosher salt

Finishing salt, such as Maldon

Heat a heavy-bottomed skillet over medium heat. Place the ancho, guajillo, and chipotle chiles in the pan and toast, turning once, until slightly colored on both sides, 5 to 7 minutes. Remove and submerge in the boiling water. Let soak for 10 minutes.

Meanwhile, in a spice/coffee grinder, finely grind the oregano, peppercorns, cumin seeds, and cloves. Transfer to a medium bowl and set aside.

Place the chiles and their soaking liquid in a blender. Add the garlic, vinegar, oil, and sugar and blend until smooth. Transfer to the bowl with the spices and stir until well combined. Rub the marinade over the steak and seal the steak in a ziplock bag. Place in the refrigerator to marinate for 24 hours.

Prepare a medium grill. Remove the steak from the marinade and season generously with salt. Let stand at room temperature while the grill heats.

Grill the steak for 5 to 7 minutes per side for medium-rare, or to the desired doneness. Transfer to a cooling rack and let rest for about 6 minutes. Slice the steak against the grain, sprinkle with finishing salt, and serve.

COOKING TIME: 35 TO 40 MINUTES / INACTIVE TIME: 24 HOURS FOR MARINATING AND 6 MINUTES FOR RESTING

CHANGING IT UP

Flank steak and skirt steak are both great options instead of hanger steak. You can even prepare flanken short ribs this way.

OXTAIL SOUP with DAIKON and DRIED SHIITAKE MUSHROOMS

Oxtails are by far my favorite cut of beef, and I can't understand why they and other such nontraditional cuts aren't more popular in American home kitchens. Oxtails often cost significantly less than the more "desirable" cuts, such as steaks and chops, and they become meltingly tender and delectable with slow, largely unattended, cooking. The cold months (that is, most of football season) are the best time to eat oxtails, not only because that's the best time to cook things slowly, but also because they are very gelatinous. Gelatin generates significant heat in the body; be sure to drink lots of water when you eat these, because that gelatin will not only warm you up, it'll also make you very thirsty.

I was first introduced to oxtails when I was growing up in Bombay, where we lived not far from a slaughterhouse. Oxtails were precious bounty to us, and being so close to the source meant that we had easy access to them. I can vividly recall how my siblings and I used our fingers to dig out every last morsel of succulent meat from the bones, and I still think eating oxtails with your hands is the most sensible approach. I'm happy to say that my boys love oxtails as much as I do, so we often have them at home. Here they are complemented by two of my pantry and kitchen standbys: dried shiitakes, which are among the most flavorful and least expensive dried mushrooms available, and daikon radish, a mild winter radish that has great body and flavor and stands up well in this sort of dish.

Note that you must use a wide pan here, such as a rondeau or Dutch oven. Don't use a tall stockpot, whose high sides are designed to minimize reduction of liquid and thus won't allow the broth to reduce properly. **SERVES 8 TO 10**

3 pounds/1.36 kilograms oxtails, trimmed of most fat

Kosher salt

Freshly ground black pepper

1⅛ ounces/32 grams dried shiitake mushrooms (2 cups)

4 cups boiling water

2 quarts cold water

1½ cups sliced onions

4 garlic cloves, smashed

One 2-inch piece fresh ginger, peeled and sliced into thin coins

1 serrano chile, split lengthwise in half

1 tablespoon black peppercorns

4 whole cloves

Half a 3-inch cinnamon stick

2 bay leaves

3 cups ½-inch-thick half-moons peeled daikon radish (about 1 pound/ 454 grams)

1 bunch cilantro, washed and dried (see page 39) and tied together with kitchen string

Steamed rice for serving

Season the oxtails generously with salt and pepper. Let stand at room temperature for 20 to 30 minutes.

Meanwhile, place the shiitakes in a medium bowl and cover with the boiling water. Set aside to soak until softened, about 20 minutes.

Lift the mushrooms out of the soaking liquid and drain them in a strainer; reserve the soaking liquid. Remove and discard the mushroom stems and cut the caps in half. Set aside. Strain the soaking liquid through a mesh strainer lined with several layers of cheesecloth. Set the liquid aside.

Place the oxtails and cold water in a large, wide stew pot and generously season the water with salt. Slowly bring to a boil over medium heat, skimming the surface.

Add the reserved mushroom liquid, along with the onions, garlic, ginger, serrano, peppercorns, cloves, cinnamon stick, and bay leaves (wrap the last three in a cheesecloth sachet if desired so that it is easy to find and discard after cooking) and return to a boil. Reduce the heat, cover, and simmer until the oxtails are tender, about 2 hours. (The dish can be prepared to this point up to a day in advance and refrigerated. Remove and discard the solidified fat on top of the broth and then reheat the oxtails and liquid in the same pot before continuing with the recipe.)

Add the reserved mushrooms, the daikon, and cilantro and cook until the daikon is tender, 35 to 40 minutes. Skim off any excess fat, and remove and discard the cilantro, cloves, cinnamon stick, and bay leaves. Taste and adjust the seasoning.

Serve the soup hot, with the steamed rice on the side.

COOKING TIME: 3¼ TO 3½ HOURS, OR 1¾ HOURS IN THE PRESSURE COOKER / INACTIVE TIME: 20 TO 30 MINUTES FOR TEMPING AND FOR SOFTENING THE MUSHROOMS

PRESSURE-COOKER FRIENDLY

To prepare the soup in a pressure cooker, follow the recipe as written in the uncovered pressure cooker (but add less water; do not go above the "fill to" line inside the pressure cooker). Then, once everything is in the cooker and brought to a simmer as instructed above, seal the pressure cooker. Follow the manufacturer's instructions to bring it up to pressure (it will begin to steam) and cook for 25 to 30 minutes, adjusting the heat as necessary to keep steady pressure. Remove the pressure cooker from the heat and let stand, covered, until the pressure releases.

Open the cooker and continue as directed above, adding the mushrooms, daikon, and cilantro and cooking, uncovered, until the daikon is tender. Serve as above.

BARKHA'S MANGO "MOUSSE"

The first few times Barkha made this, I teased her mercilessly (it's *not* a chef's dish). It's fair to say that I got my comeuppance, for among our friends' kids, this has become known as Auntie Barkha's specialty of the house. They love it so much that they beg her for it whenever they come over, which cracks us up. Of all the things the kids can eat when they come to our house, *this* is what they beg for? There's clearly something a little magical about it. In fact, it was the inspiration for the ambrosia I made that helped me stay on *Top Chef Masters* (see page 329).   **SERVES 6**

Two 3-ounce/85-gram packages
    orange-flavored Jell-O
1 cup boiling water
1 cup room-temperature water

2 to 2¼ cups diced ripe mango (or 1 cup
    defrosted frozen or canned mango
    puree)
1 quart vanilla ice cream, slightly softened

In a large bowl, combine the Jell-O and boiling water and stir until the Jell-O is dissolved. Add the room-temperature water and stir to combine. Set aside to cool completely. (Make sure that the Jell-O mixture is completely cool before adding the mango and ice cream, or the mousse will be dense. However, don't let it sit so long that it gels, or the mousse will be lumpy.)

Meanwhile, if using ripe mango, puree it in a food processor or blender. You should have 1 cup.

When the Jell-O mixture is cool, stir in the mango puree. Gently fold in the softened ice cream until well incorporated. Transfer to a serving bowl and refrigerate until set, 3 to 4 hours.

Spoon the mousse into cups to serve.

COOKING TIME: ABOUT 10 MINUTES / INACTIVE TIME: ABOUT 1 HOUR FOR COOLING AND 3 TO 4 HOURS TO SET

STICKY TOFFEE PUDDING with CANDIED GINGER

To me, sweet sticky toffee pudding laced with warm spices is the definition of comfort food. I have never encountered one that I didn't love. It is the one and only dessert that I will never skip if it's on the menu at a restaurant where I'm eating, and it's the only dessert that I sometimes actually crave. That is why I developed a home-kitchen version of the one I've made in my restaurants. I want to be able to have it whenever the craving hits (and making forty servings at a time is just not practical at home).

My spin on the traditional sticky pudding is a generous dose of dried ginger in the batter and some candied ginger sprinkled on top just before the puddings go into the oven—it sinks during baking and so reappears on the tops of the puddings when they are unmolded. Candied ginger is so good, a perfectly balanced combination of sweetness and the bracing kick of a little heat, I wonder why we don't see more of it in recipes. It's not expensive and it adds something special to savory dishes (see page 306) and desserts alike. The sauce and puddings both keep beautifully in the refrigerator for up to three days and are easy to reheat.   **SERVES 6**

FOR THE PUDDING
Nonstick baking spray
3 ounces/85 grams (⅔ cup) pitted
   dates, chopped
⅔ cup water
½ teaspoon baking soda
3⅜ ounces/96 grams (⅔ cup)
   all-purpose flour
1⅛ teaspoons baking powder
¾ teaspoon powdered ginger
2 tablespoons salted butter, softened

3 ounces/85 grams (⅓ cup plus
   1½ tablespoons) granulated sugar
2 large eggs
1 tablespoon finely diced candied ginger

FOR THE TOFFEE SAUCE
5⅝ ounces/159 grams (¾ cup) packed
   light brown sugar
6 tablespoons salted butter
½ vanilla bean, preferably Tahitian, split
   lengthwise in half
½ cup heavy cream

Preheat the oven to 325°F. Spray six 6-ounce ramekins or molds with nonstick spray. Place a folded kitchen towel in the bottom of a baking pan large enough to hold all the ramekins.

In a blender, combine the dates and water and blend until completely smooth. Add the baking soda and blend for a few seconds to thoroughly incorporate it. Set aside for 15 minutes.

Meanwhile, bring a large kettle of water to a boil.

In a medium bowl, whisk together the flour, baking powder, and ginger. Set aside.

Continued

In the bowl of a stand mixer fitted with the paddle attachment, or in a large mixing bowl, using a handheld mixer, cream the butter and granulated sugar together. Add one egg and beat until blended. Scrape down the sides of the bowl. Add the second egg and beat until well blended.

Scrape down the sides of the bowl. Add the dry ingredients and beat until combined. Add the date mixture and mix until smooth.

Divide the batter among the prepared ramekins (the batter should not come more than halfway up the sides of the ramekins). Place the ramekins on the kitchen towel in the baking pan. Pour enough boiling water into the baking pan to come halfway up the sides of the ramekins. Sprinkle the candied ginger over the puddings. Cover the pan with foil and bake until the puddings are set, 35 to 40 minutes.

Meanwhile, make the toffee sauce: Place the brown sugar and butter in a medium saucepan. Scrape the seeds from the vanilla bean and add them to the pan, along with the pod. Heat over medium heat until the butter has melted and then bring to a boil, whisking constantly.

Whisk in the cream and bring the mixture to a boil. Reduce the heat and simmer, stirring occasionally, until slightly thickened, about 5 minutes. Remove the pan from the heat and set aside, covered to keep warm. (The sauce can be made ahead and stored in a covered container in the refrigerator for up to 3 days. Reheat gently over low heat before serving.)

When the puddings are done, remove the ramekins to a rack to cool completely. (The puddings can be made ahead. Cover the cooled puddings and store in the refrigerator for up to 3 days. Reheat in a 300°F oven for 10 minutes before unmolding.)

When ready to serve, remove the vanilla bean halves from the sauce, and gently reheat the sauce. Unmold each pudding onto an individual plate. Pour some sauce on top of and around each pudding and serve.

COOKING TIME: ABOUT 1 HOUR

TAMARIND MARGARITA

This was the most requested cocktail at Tabla, hands down. In fact, it was so popular there that we put it on the menu at North End Grill, where it again became the highest-selling drink on the menu (by seven or eight times!). And now it's on my menu at Paowalla.

Fair warning: This cocktail goes down very smoothly. So to make sure that no one overdoes it, serve it in reasonably sized rocks glasses—not too big—and with generous amounts of ice. You want your guests to keep their focus on what's important: the game and the food!

This recipe presents a great opportunity to mention again that it's best to juice citrus fruit when it is at room temperature, so that it gives up maximum juice. **SERVES 10**

15 fluid ounces tequila

10 fluid ounces Triple Sec

2 fluid ounces Tamarind Paste (page 340)

20 fluid ounces fresh lime juice (from 20 to 30 limes)

4 fluid ounces fresh orange juice (from 1 to 2 oranges)

4 fluid ounces Simple Syrup (page 344)

FOR RIMMING THE GLASSES (OPTIONAL)

½ cup kosher salt

2 tablespoons grated orange zest

1 to 2 lime wedges

Ice

10 lime slices for garnish

Pour the tequila, Triple Sec, and tamarind paste into a 2- to 3-quart bottle with a lid. Cover and shake well until the tamarind paste is dissolved. Pour in the lime juice, orange juice, and simple syrup. Shake until very well combined.

If you want to rim the glasses with orange salt, on a small plate, combine the salt with the grated orange zest and stir well with a fork. Have ready ten rocks glasses. Run a lime wedge around the rim of one of the glasses to moisten it and, holding the glass at an angle, roll the outer edge of the rim in the salt until fully coated. Repeat with the remaining glasses.

Generously fill the rocks glasses with ice and pour over the tamarind margarita. Garnish each serving with a lime slice. Serve.

COOKING TIME: 10 TO 15 MINUTES

CHAPTER NINE

Special Dinners and Parties

RECIPES FOR HOLIDAYS, CELEBRATIONS, AND ENTERTAINING

I love throwing parties—a backyard barbecue, a cozy dinner for six, a game-viewing party for twenty, a holiday bash for forty, and pretty much anything in between. I thrive on cooking for many people, which probably explains my career choice, since I love it even when I'm working and can't sit down to eat with the people I'm cooking for. To be sure, this degree of passion has required a bit of acceptance on the part of our friends and family. I always bring food with us when we are invited to their houses. Since they know I'm going to bring something whether they ask me to or not, they're usually ready when I inquire about what they are cooking. I try to make sure that whatever I bring will complement what they are serving. I have a friend who teases that I'm a great guest because whenever he invites me over for dinner, I bring my own.

But it's entertaining at home that I love best, and my passion for it comes directly from the example set for me by my parents, Peter and Beryl (or Boodie, as most people know her). When I was growing up, we had people over for dinner at least three nights a week. We often had lavish dinner parties, which I would eagerly anticipate because the spread of dishes served was always amazing. Today, in addition to the smaller gatherings we have during the year, my wife, Barkha, and I try to host at least one major holiday dinner for our family and friends. The guest list for these dinners quickly grows to forty people, which makes us both very happy. But the planning for these parties can sometimes be a point of contention between Barkha and me. When I'm at the restaurant, working with a platoon of cooks, planning and scheduling are the only ways to guarantee success. However, when it comes to cooking at home, even when it's for a party of several dozen people, I rarely plan the menu beforehand, no matter if it's two weeks or two days away. I cook spontaneously, and I love letting the ingredients I find at my farmers' market, butcher, or produce aisle dictate what I am cooking. Sometimes on the morning of the party, I'll settle on a game plan—mostly to appease

Barkha. But it rarely sticks, and by the time I return from my shopping trip, the entire list and menu have changed. I know it drives Barkha nuts, but I find it invigorating. Spontaneity lets me cook from my heart, and that's when I most enjoy the process.

Since I've just confessed that my party menu planning is about as unstructured as my dear wife can stand, you might wonder how it is possible that I have a chapter's worth of recipes to share. The fact is that every recipe in this chapter is here only because someone asked me for the recipe the day of the party. If I do not write it down within a day, important details of a dish, including certain essentials such as ingredients and method, are soon forgotten. My friends have learned that if they want to replicate something I have made, they have to ask me for my notes as soon as we are finished eating. So now I want to thank all of them, for without their curiosity and persistence, this chapter would not exist (also, they're fantastic guests!).

Lest you think that my catch-as-catch-can approach to planning a menu for entertaining means that I do *everything* by the seat of my pants, there are a couple of things to think about ahead of time. First, always ask guests in advance if they have any dietary restrictions or allergies. There is nothing worse for host and guest alike than to have someone not be able to enjoy what everyone else is enjoying. While it might seem a hassle to impose one person's dietary restraints on an entire menu, it is a hassle well worth enduring so that everyone can enjoy your labor of love. Second, keep in mind that the best crowd-pleasing dishes are those that can be largely or entirely cooked in advance and don't require lots of last-minute attention. In short, the best dishes to cook for many are the dishes that let you *enjoy* the many!

SCRAMBLED EGGS with RAMPS and BACON

Each spring, ramps make their appearance on forest floors up and down the East Coast of the United States, their abundant greens obscuring slender, pink stems and pale bulbs nestled just below the surface of the earth. Ramps' aroma is unmistakable—some (not I) might say it is aggressively pungent. Their flavor falls somewhere between that of leeks and garlic; they are sometimes called wild leeks. When we buy ramps for the restaurant, we bring in fifty pounds at one time, 60 percent of which is the leaves. So when our main use for them involved just the bulb one spring a few years ago, you can imagine that I had a lot of greens on my hands! Naturally, there was no way I was tossing so much of something that only appears for a few weeks a year, and I immediately set to work figuring out how to use all those greens. Eggs are my most trusted go-to for this kind of "using up" in the kitchen, and bacon and ramps are really good together. So, I began there. In very little time, I had results that were even better than what I'd imagined.

Since that first time, this dish has become a standby at home, during the spring with ramps and during the rest of the year using spring onions or leeks. The flavor is less potent, but the dish is still pretty marvelous. This is a great quick lunch or dinner dish but I especially like to serve spoonfuls of the hot or warm eggs on top of thin baguette slices as an hors d'oeuvre at parties.   **SERVES 16 AS AN HORS D'OEUVRE**

8 extra-large eggs

¼ cup thinly sliced washed and dried cilantro leaves (see page 39) with tender stems (stack a few leaves at a time to slice)

Kosher salt

4 ounces/113 grams bacon, diced (1 cup)

Canola oil as needed

2 cups sliced ramps (white and green parts kept separate)

1 serrano chile, minced

Grilled or toasted sliced baguette for serving

Freshly ground black pepper

In a large bowl, beat the eggs with the cilantro and salt to taste.

Cook the bacon in a large sauté pan over medium heat until it has rendered its fat. Remove the bacon with a slotted spoon and set aside.

Add enough oil to the bacon fat in the pan to bring the total to ¼ cup. Increase the heat to high, add the whites of the ramps, and cook, stirring constantly, until they start to turn golden, 3 to 4 minutes.

Stir in the ramp greens, the chile, and the reserved bacon and reduce the heat to low. Add the eggs and cook, stirring constantly with a silicone spatula, until the eggs are softly scrambled and no longer runny, about 15 minutes.

Spoon the eggs over grilled or toasted bread and sprinkle with freshly ground pepper. Serve hot.

COOKING TIME: ABOUT 30 MINUTES

WHITE BEAN SALAD with POMEGRANATE PEARLS and CRUSHED PEANUTS

Too often there's not much texture in bean salads except for mushy beans. This is a shame, because salads with contrasting textures are far more interesting to eat, and I think that interest makes them actually taste better too. Every bite of this salad is punctuated by the pleasing crunch of lightly crushed salted peanuts and a burst of sweet-and-sour juice from pomegranate pearls. I also use my favorite spice blend, chaat masala, which enhances the smooth, buttery beans and crunchy extras. Chaat masala is the one commercial spice blend I use, making it the rare exception to my strict prohibition of preground spices in my cabinet. It adds just the right sweet-sour-salty-spicy flavor note. **SERVES 8 TO 12**

12 cups cooked white beans (see page 341) or canned beans, rinsed and drained
1 cup pomegranate pearls
1 cup salted peanuts, lightly crushed
1 cup finely minced shallots
2 tablespoons minced serrano chiles

FOR THE VINAIGRETTE
6 anchovy fillets, minced, or 2 tablespoons capers, coarsely chopped
2 cups very coarsely chopped washed and dried cilantro (see page 39) or parsley
Juice of 4 lemons
¼ cup maple syrup
½ teaspoon chaat masala
Kosher salt
Freshly ground black pepper

In a large bowl, combine the beans, pomegranate pearls, peanuts, shallots, and chiles and toss lightly.

To make the vinaigrette, in a jam jar or small Mason jar with a tight-fitting lid, combine the anchovies, cilantro, lemon juice, maple syrup, and chaat masala. Add salt and pepper to taste, close the jar tightly, and shake vigorously until well combined.

Pour the vinaigrette over the beans and toss gently until completely coated. Taste and adjust the seasoning. Serve cold or at room temperature.

COOKING TIME: ABOUT 10 MINUTES

GRILLED CAULIFLOWER with CANDIED GINGER, PINE NUTS, and RAISINS

I tip my hat to New Orleans–based chef Alon Shaya, who provided me with the inspiration for this recipe. On a trip down to NOLA, I found his simply grilled cauliflower so delicious and transforming that when I returned home, this dish was one of the first things I came up with. If you or someone you know thinks of cauliflower as bland and uninteresting, please try it prepared this way.

But don't just take my word for it. When I introduced this at White Street, it became one of our most ordered dishes. I've seen people eat it as an appetizer, as a side, and even as a main course, which I, dedicated meat eater that I am, definitely did not expect. It has been cool to see how many different people will accept and then embrace an unusual spin on a pretty ordinary ingredient. When you serve it for parties at home, leave the two halves intact and put them in a large shallow bowl. They look great with the dressing poured over them. Or, if you can find small cauliflower heads, you can prepare them as is as I often do, without halving them. A big spoon is all you need to pull florets off for serving.

Green raisins are easily found in Indian, Pakistani, and Afghani stores (and online; see Sources, page 345). They come from the Indian subcontinent, and I recommend trying to get them. They have a better acid-sweet balance than typical dried raisins, which tend to have a one-note sweetness. That acid component is important to the overall balance of the dish. It is true, however, that it's not crucial, so you can use the ubiquitous golden raisins in their place if you truly can't find green ones. **SERVES 8 TO 12**

Kosher salt

1 large head cauliflower (about
    3 pounds/1.36 kilograms)

¼ cup green or golden raisins

⅓ cup white wine, or as needed

¼ cup extra-virgin olive oil, plus more for
    brushing

2 tablespoons aged balsamic vinegar

1½ tablespoons maple syrup

Minced zest and juice of 1 lemon

1 teaspoon minced shallot

1½ teaspoons minced candied ginger

½ teaspoon minced peeled fresh ginger

2 tablespoons pine nuts, toasted (see
    page 76) and coarsely chopped

¼ teaspoon chile flakes

Freshly ground black pepper

Bring a large pot of generously salted water to a boil. Have ready a large bowl of ice water.

Meanwhile, cut the cauliflower straight through the stem to divide it in half. Cut several slits along the full length of the cauliflower stem on the cut side of each half; be careful not to cut so deep that you remove any florets or slice through to the other side.

Continued

Place the cauliflower in the boiling water and cook until it is just tender and a little translucent along the edges but still crisp, 3 to 4 minutes. After 2 minutes, check the cauliflower for doneness, and continue to check every minute so that it does not overcook; test doneness not with a knife but instead by looking at it and, if necessary, poking it with a spoon.

Immediately transfer the cauliflower to the ice bath and let stand until completely cool, 15 to 20 minutes. Drain the cauliflower and set aside in a colander for at least 1 hour, until thoroughly dry.

Meanwhile, place the raisins in a small saucepan and enough wine to cover the raisins. Bring to a boil over medium heat. Remove the pan from the heat and let stand until the raisins are softened and cool enough to handle, 10 to 15 minutes.

With a slotted spoon, transfer the raisins to a cutting board. Coarsely chop them and return them to the wine. Set aside.

In a jar with a tight-fitting lid, combine the olive oil, balsamic vinegar, maple syrup, lemon zest and juice, shallot, candied and fresh ginger, pine nuts, chile flakes, the reserved raisins and wine, and salt to taste. Cover and shake vigorously until well blended. Taste and adjust the seasoning. Set aside.

Prepare a high-heat grill, or preheat the oven to 450°F and line a baking sheet with parchment paper.

Lightly season the cauliflower with salt and pepper and brush with olive oil.

If grilling, place the cauliflower halves cut side down on the grill and cook until well marked. Flip them and cook until well marked on the rounded side. Continue to cook, turning the cauliflower as necessary, until tender and brown all over, about 20 minutes total.

If roasting, place the cauliflower cut side down on the baking sheet and roast until lightly browned and tender, 15 to 20 minutes.

Place the cauliflower halves in a large shallow bowl and pour over the topping. Serve hot.

COOKING TIME: ABOUT 1 HOUR / INACTIVE TIME: 1 HOUR AND 20 MINUTES FOR COOLING AND DRAINING THE CAULIFLOWER

GRILLED SHRIMP with FENNEL and RADISH SALAD

When I cooked at the Charleston Wine and Food Festival a few years ago, I asked the owner of the home where I was cooking to order local shrimp for the dinner I was preparing. Shrimp that fresh and local have more bite and sweetness than shrimp that have to travel a ways to get to the kitchen. It was the inspiration of those Charleston shrimp that led me to this dish.

I began by simmering the heads and shells in plain water. They have so much flavor, and it takes nothing more than simmering them for a little while to bring it all out. After straining the stock, I reduced it until it was thick and rich, with almost sticky bubbles on top. If you take the time to allow the shrimp stock to reduce, you will be rewarded with some of the best, most velvety shrimp "gravy" you've ever tasted. The reduction takes about 30 minutes, but you don't really have to keep an eye on it until the very end, when it can go from almost ready to almost *gone* in a flash.

You want to use Lucknow fennel seeds in this dish (see Sources, page 345). Lucknow fennel is more aromatic than regular fennel seed and here it highlights and enhances the sweetness of both the shrimp and the fennel salad.   **SERVES 10 TO 12**

FOR THE SHRIMP
1 tablespoon Lucknow fennel seeds

1½ teaspoons coriander seeds

1½ teaspoons black peppercorns

2½ pounds/1.13 kilograms (16–20 count) head-on shrimp, heads removed, shelled, and deveined, heads and shells reserved for Shrimp-Shell Stock

Sea salt

Extra-virgin olive oil for brushing

FOR THE SHRIMP VINAIGRETTE
Shrimp-Shell Stock (see page 311)

¼ cup extra-virgin olive oil

¼ cup canola oil

½ cup fresh lemon juice

Sea salt

Freshly ground black pepper

A pinch of cayenne

FOR THE FENNEL SALAD
1½ tablespoons Lucknow fennel seeds

1 large fennel bulb, trimmed, fronds reserved for garnish

12 to 15 red radishes

1 cup thinly sliced washed and dried cilantro leaves (see page 39) with tender stems (stack a few leaves at a time to slice)

¼ cup thinly sliced chives

1 tablespoon minced peeled fresh ginger

¼ teaspoon Thai chile oil

Sea salt

Freshly ground black pepper

2 limes, cut into wedges, for garnish (optional)

About 10 long metal or bamboo skewers

To marinate the shrimp, finely grind the fennel seeds, coriander seeds, and peppercorns in a spice/coffee grinder. Toss the shrimp with the spices and place in a ziplock bag. Refrigerate for at least 1 hour, and up to 24 hours.

Continued

To make the vinaigrette, place the shrimp stock in a large wide saucepan and bring to a boil. Boil until reduced to ¼ cup, about 30 minutes; keep an eye on it during the last few minutes, when it will reduce more quickly. Set aside to cool completely.

Transfer the cooled reduced shrimp stock to a clean jar and add the olive oil, canola oil, lemon juice, salt and black pepper to taste, and cayenne. Close the jar tightly and shake vigorously until well combined. Refrigerate until chilled, or for up to 1 day.

If using bamboo skewers, soak them in water for 40 minutes.

Prepare a high-heat grill.

While the grill is heating, remove the shrimp from the refrigerator and season with salt. Thread on the skewers. Set aside at room temperature until needed.

To prepare the fennel salad, in a small heavy-bottomed skillet, toast the fennel seeds over medium-low heat, shaking the pan frequently, until fragrant and several shades darker, about 3 minutes. Transfer to a bowl to cool completely.

Cut the fennel bulb in half and cut out the core. Thinly shave it using a mandoline. Transfer to a large bowl.

Thinly shave the radishes, using the mandoline. Add them to the bowl with the fennel. Set aside.

Finely grind the fennel seeds in a spice/coffee grinder and add to the fennel and radishes. Add the cilantro, chives, ginger, chile oil, and salt and pepper to taste to the bowl and toss to combine.

Just before grilling the shrimp, add enough vinaigrette to the salad to thoroughly coat it, tossing until well combined. Taste and adjust the seasoning. Arrange the salad in the center of a large platter. Set aside.

Brush the shrimp with olive oil. Grill, turning once, until the shrimp are firm and cooked through, about 4 minutes.

Remove the shrimp from the skewers and arrange them around the salad. Pour the remaining dressing around the shrimp. Garnish with the reserved fennel fronds and the lime wedges, if desired, and serve.

COOKING TIME: ABOUT 1¼ HOURS / INACTIVE TIME: 1 TO 24 HOURS FOR MARINATING

SHRIMP-SHELL STOCK

Place the reserved shrimp heads and shells from above in a large wide saucepan. Add 6 cups cold water and bring to a boil over high heat. Reduce the heat and simmer for 20 minutes. Strain, pressing on the shells with a spoon to extract all of the liquid. Discard the shells and heads.

COD EN PAPILLOTE with COCONUT BASMATI PILAF

For guaranteed tender results, great make-ahead potential, and minimal cleanup—all ideal party food characteristics—you can't beat cooking fish in individual packages, or *en papillote*. This recipe is based on a dish that I used to do at Tabla, but the first time I prepared it for a party outside of the restaurant, I wasn't at home—I was in a makeshift kitchen preparing dinner at the Cape Cod wedding reception of Shake Shack CEO Randy Garutti and Maria McGrath. The thing is, until I'd arrived at the breathtakingly beautiful location with all the makings for two hundred individual packages of aromatic rice and cod, I hadn't realized that I'd be preparing the food without the modest convenience of an actual oven. When I discovered that the only heat sources we had to work with were Sterno and plate warmers, I admit that I shared one or two colorful observations. But it turns out that Sterno and plate warmers can maintain a pretty constant temperature of 240°F, and that absolutely perfect, extremely tender results can be had by cooking cod en papillote for 45 minutes at this temperature. It's a trick I haven't felt compelled to repeat too often, thus the recipe below.

Another reason this is a good party dish is that the components are easy to prepare and can be done in advance. Then they are brought together to make something spectacular—both in flavor and appearance. This is especially true if you use banana leaves (available at Asian grocery stores), which impart a grassy, herbaceous quality that cannot be otherwise replicated. If you have a gas or electric flat-top stove, running the leaves through the flame or over the burner once or twice will soften them and keep them from tearing; if you have a different kind of stovetop, such as a traditional coil-burner electric stove, use parchment paper instead. Even in parchment, however, the dish is impressive, and always delicious. I also love the subtle but important role the salt cod plays. It is toasted so that it contributes a triple hit of aromatic goodness: saltiness, toastiness, and fishiness. When I was a kid in India, salt cod was a staple during monsoon season, when fresh fish was scarce. I like using it in a way that allows it to transcend its humble origins. **SERVES 12**

2 ounces/57 grams salt cod, thinly sliced

¼ cup canola oil

2 tablespoons minced shallots

One 1-inch piece fresh ginger, peeled and minced

2 whole cloves

1 bay leaf

1½ cups white basmati rice, rinsed, soaked, and drained (see page 136)

2½ cups Chaokoh-brand coconut milk, stirred well (or coconut milk and water; see Note)

Sea salt

Freshly ground black pepper

1½ cups shelled fresh peas (about 1½ pounds/680 grams in the pod)

1 pound (14 ounces/850 grams) cod fillet, cut into 12 equal pieces

12 large pieces (roughly letter-paper-sized) banana leaf or twelve 10- to 12-inch squares parchment paper

12 cilantro sprigs, washed and dried (see page 39)

Continued

In a cast-iron skillet, toast the salt cod over medium-low heat until it is lightly golden, about 10 minutes. Remove from the pan and set aside. If the pieces are large, shred slightly once cooled.

Heat a medium saucepan over medium heat. Add the oil, then add the shallots, ginger, cloves, and bay leaf and sauté, stirring often, until the shallots are translucent, 3 to 4 minutes.

Add the drained rice and stir with a silicone spatula to thoroughly coat it in oil. Cook, stirring frequently, for about 4 minutes. Add the coconut milk and salt cod, increase the heat to medium-high, and bring to a boil. Reduce the heat, season the rice with sea salt and pepper, cover the pan, and simmer until the rice is tender, about 15 minutes.

Remove and discard the cloves and bay leaf. Spread the rice on a rimmed baking sheet and let cool completely.

Meanwhile, blanch, shock, and drain the peas (see page 33). Both the rice and the peas can be made up to 1 day in advance. Refrigerate in two separate covered containers. Let stand at room temperature for 30 minutes before continuing with the recipe.

To make the papillotes, preheat the oven to 350°F. Have ready two rimmed baking sheets.

Season the cod with salt and a generous amount of pepper. Stir the peas into the rice and divide the mixture into 12 equal portions.

If using banana leaves, turn on a gas or electric flat-top burner to medium-high. Holding a leaf with tongs, pull it through the flame or across the burner once very quickly. Repeat on the other side. Repeat with the remaining leaves.

Place a banana leaf (or a sheet of parchment) on the work surface. Place one portion of rice and peas in the center of it, center a piece of fish on top of the rice, and top with a sprig of cilantro. Fold the two longer edges up over the fish and fold and crimp them together. Fold the two narrow ends under the package. If using banana leaves, you can tear a long thin piece from another leaf and tie it around the center to secure the package. Place the papillote on a baking sheet and assemble the remaining packages.

Place the papillotes in the oven and cook for 20 minutes. Transfer the papillotes to a large serving platter and serve immediately.

COOKING TIME: ABOUT 1 HOUR AND 40 MINUTES

Note: There's no need to open two cans of coconut milk and not use all the second can if you'd rather not. You can use just one can and make up the rest of the volume with water.

SLOW-COOKED SALMON with FENNEL and CORIANDER

Salmon is a good fish to serve to a large group, because it's pretty universally liked. However, there's not much that's worse than *overcooked* salmon, which is why this cooking method is great. The oven temperature is so low that there is practically no chance of overcooking it. I first prepared this for a Christmas dinner at home for about forty people, and it's become my favorite method for cooking salmon for a big group. It's also good for a party because it can go straight from the oven to the table, served directly from the baking dish. Thanks to the low, slow cooking, it'll be moist and delicious even if it sits for a bit.

Describing this method offers me a good opportunity to vent about something I often hear but know is categorically not true. There are those who will tell you that you can determine that a piece of fish or meat is done when it feels a certain way when you press it with your finger—for instance, firm means well-done and softer means less done, and so on. These people are full of shit. You can never tell if *anything* is done that way. The best way to tell when the salmon in this recipe is done is to set the timer and then look for the light mist on the plastic wrap. **SERVES 12**

1½ pounds/680 grams center-cut
    salmon, 1½ inches thick, cut into
    12 equal rectangles
Sea salt
Freshly ground black pepper
1 small fennel bulb
2 tablespoons salted butter, softened
Minced zest and juice of 1 orange
24 thin slices garlic

2 tablespoons minced shallots
1 tablespoon minced peeled fresh ginger
Leaves from 3 tarragon sprigs, thinly
    sliced
1 teaspoon coriander seeds, ground
    medium-fine
1 teaspoon fennel seeds, ground fine
12 thin slices serrano chile (about 1 chile)
3 tablespoons olive oil

Preheat the oven to 200°F.

Season the salmon with sea salt and pepper. Set aside.

Remove and discard the fronds and the tough tops of the fennel bulb. Thinly slice the bulb and the remaining tender stalks, keeping them separate. Set aside.

Brush the bottom of a large Pyrex or ceramic dish with the butter. Sprinkle the sliced fennel bulb over the bottom of the dish. Pour the orange juice over the fennel. Sprinkle with salt and pepper. Sprinkle with half of each of the following: the orange zest, garlic, shallots, ginger, tarragon, coriander, and fennel seed.

Arrange the salmon in a single layer in the dish. Place a slice of serrano and a slice of garlic on each piece of salmon. Sprinkle with the sliced fennel stalks

and the remaining orange zest, garlic, shallot, ginger, tarragon, coriander, and fennel seed. Drizzle the olive oil on top. Cover the dish tightly with plastic wrap. (The dish can be prepared to this point up to 1 day in advance and stored in the refrigerator. Before cooking, remove the dish from the refrigerator and, leaving the plastic in place, let stand at room temperature for 1 hour.)

Bake the salmon for 25 minutes. You don't want to cook it so long that it turns opaque throughout and the white albumin comes out. Usually, when the salmon is done, the plastic wrap is really tight and shiny and there is a light mist on the underside. But if you don't see the mist, just let the timer be your guide.

Remove the baking dish from the oven, remove and discard the plastic wrap, and serve.

COOKING TIME: ABOUT 35 MINUTES

GROUND CHICKEN KEBABS

To Americans, the word "kebab" evokes food that is cooked on a skewer, but in India, as in the Middle East, the term is used to refer to anything that is grilled, whether it's a piece of meat, a patty, or a sausage. These little ground chicken patties are so flavorful that they make a big impression, and no sauce or adornment beyond a squeeze of fresh lime juice is necessary. You can also roll bite-sized patties in panko (flaky Japanese bread crumbs) and deep-fry them to serve as a passed or plated hors d'oeuvre.

This goes well with the Romaine-Cucumber Salad with Lime and Thai Chile (page 39) or the seasoned onions from the Bombay Ground Lamb Kebabs (page 246).   **SERVES 8**

One 1-inch piece fresh ginger, peeled and
    cut into thin coins

2 large garlic cloves, coarsely chopped

½ serrano chile, chopped

2 tablespoons washed and dried cilantro
    leaves (see page 39)

2 tablespoons mint leaves

½ cup finely chopped white onion

1 pound/454 grams ground chicken,
    preferably dark meat

1 teaspoon kosher salt, or to taste

½ teaspoon black peppercorns, finely
    ground

½ teaspoon Garam Masala (page 23)

Canola oil

Juice of 1 lime

In the work bowl of a food processor, combine the ginger, garlic, and chile and process until finely chopped. Add the cilantro and mint and process until very finely chopped, about 45 seconds.

Transfer the mixture to a large bowl and add the onion, chicken, salt, pepper, and garam masala. Blend the mixture well with your hands. Form a small bit of the mixture into a small disk and microwave it for a few seconds so that you can taste for seasoning. Add salt to the mixture if necessary.

Form the mixture into 8 small patties, placing them on a baking sheet as you form them. Refrigerate while you heat the grill, or for up to 24 hours.

Prepare a medium-hot grill.

Brush the grill with oil. Place the kebabs on the grill and cook until well marked, about 3 minutes. Turn the kebabs 90 degrees and cook for another 2 to 3 minutes. Flip the kebabs over and repeat the process to cook the chicken through.

Remove the kebabs from the grill and sprinkle with the lime juice. Serve.

COOKING TIME: ABOUT 20 MINUTES

CHICKEN PILAF

This is a great meal for a crowd that can be pulled together quickly using pantry and freezer staples. Make sure that your liquid is hot before you add it to the rice, so that it will cook more evenly, and stir the rice very gently with a silicone spatula to keep the grains whole.   **SERVES 12**

Two 13.5-fluid-ounce cans Chaokoh-brand coconut milk (stir well before using)

About 6½ cups Chicken Stock (page 337), or high-quality store-bought stock

½ cup canola oil

2 teaspoons cumin seeds

One 2-inch piece cinnamon stick

6 whole cloves

4 cups finely chopped white onions

¼ cup minced peeled fresh ginger

6 garlic cloves, minced

2 tablespoons coriander seeds, finely ground

1 tablespoon black peppercorns (optional)

2 teaspoons turmeric

2 bay leaves

6 cups white basmati rice, rinsed, soaked, and drained (see page 136)

3 pounds/1.36 kilograms boneless, skinless chicken thighs, excess fat removed, quartered

Kosher salt

1 cup thinly sliced washed and dried cilantro leaves (see page 39) with tender stems (stack the leaves a few at a time to slice), plus more for garnish

Pour the coconut milk into a large glass measure. Add enough stock to make 2½ quarts. Heat the stock and coconut milk in a medium pot over medium-high heat until boiling. Reduce the heat and keep at a very low simmer.

In an 8-quart stew pot with a tight-fitting lid, heat the oil over medium heat until it shimmers. Add the cumin, cinnamon, and cloves and cook, stirring, until the spices are fragrant and little bubbles form around them, about 1 minute. Add the onions and cook, stirring, until softened but not at all colored, about 3 minutes.

Use a silicone spatula to stir in the ginger, garlic, coriander, black peppercorns, if using, turmeric, bay leaves, and the drained rice, then stir to coat the rice with the oil and spices. Stir in the chicken, tucking it into the rice, and stir over medium heat for 3 minutes.

Stir in the hot stock mixture and bring to a boil, stirring occasionally. Season to taste with salt. Cover and cook over medium heat until all the liquid is absorbed and the chicken is cooked, 15 to 20 minutes. Fold in the cilantro. Cover and let the rice rest for 15 to 20 minutes.

Fluff the rice with a fork; remove and discard the cinnamon stick, cloves, and bay leaves. Sprinkle with the chopped cilantro and serve.

COOKING TIME: ABOUT 55 MINUTES / INACTIVE TIME: 15 TO 20 MINUTES FOR RESTING

CHANGING IT UP

Add a bunch of fresh dill, roughly chopped, along with the cilantro.

RIB-EYE STEAK with PORCINI JUS

This is one of the most showstopping, elegant dishes that I serve to guests at home. I consider it a party dish for smaller gatherings when we have just two or three other couples over. The demi-glace and rib-eye are luxurious ingredients, and they can have price tags to match. For the wine in the sauce, it doesn't much matter what the grape is as long as it is a wine you'd be happy to drink on its own. Porcini powder is easily one of my favorite flavor-enhancing pantry ingredients. Instead of buying porcini powder, however, buy dried porcini—they keep indefinitely when stored in a dry, dark spot—and grind them yourself. The flavor of freshly ground dried porcini is miles better than the preground crap, which can have a comparably dusty flavor. **SERVES 8**

2 tablespoons canola oil

⅔ cup sliced shallots

4 garlic cloves, smashed

1 cup red wine, such as cabernet sauvignon or pinot noir

2 tablespoons red wine vinegar

One 6-inch rosemary sprig

Four 4-inch thyme sprigs

1½ teaspoons black peppercorns, ground medium-fine, plus more for the steaks

2 cups demi-glace (see Sources, page 345)

4 pounds/1.81 kilograms rib-eye steak (about 1½ inches thick)

Kosher salt

¼ cup porcini powder (from about ¾ ounce/11 grams dried porcini; see headnote)

In a medium saucepan, heat the oil over medium heat until it shimmers. Add the shallots and garlic and sauté until translucent, 5 to 8 minutes.

Add the wine and vinegar, bring to a simmer, and cook until the liquid is reduced by half. Add the rosemary, thyme, pepper, and demi-glace and simmer for 20 minutes.

Strain the sauce through a fine-mesh strainer and discard the solids. Clean the saucepan and return the strained sauce to it. (The sauce can be made ahead and set aside at room temperature for up to 4 hours.)

Prepare a high-heat grill. Season the steaks with salt and pepper and let stand at room temperature while the grill heats.

Cook the steaks for 5 to 6 minutes per side for medium-rare, or to the desired doneness. (Keep an eye out for the fat hitting the hot coals and flaming.) Remove the steaks from the grill, transfer to a cooling rack, and let rest for 10 minutes.

While the steak is resting, reheat the sauce over medium heat if necessary. Add the porcini powder to the sauce, season with salt to taste, and simmer for 4 minutes. Keep warm.

Slice the steak. Arrange the steak on a platter and pour the sauce over it. Serve.

COOKING TIME: ABOUT 1 HOUR

UBEROI-STYLE LEG OF LAMB

This tender, spicy, pretty much foolproof roasted lamb is named in honor of my good friends Angela and Hank Uberoi. We met at Tabla at a special wine dinner I prepared that Hank attended. We really hit it off and for many years now, Barkha and I have been blessed to count Angela and Hank among our close friends.

Of course, friendship with me means that I'll usually ignore you when you tell me not to bring any food to your dinner party. One year, Hank told me I could bring *one* item to their annual holiday celebration. So I turned up at their place the morning of the party with three legs of lamb marinating in a fragrant concoction I'd come up with the night before and a request to borrow their oven for a few hours. (Hank and Angela can confirm that friendship with me sometimes means that I'll take over your kitchen for a few hours when you are throwing a party for forty.) I'm pleased to report that any irritation I likely caused dissipated when the lamb turned out so beautifully that Hank's brother-in-law, Bill, requested the recipe that evening. Because the very first one was made in the Uberois' kitchen, it will forever more be my Uberoi-style leg of lamb.

A couple of ingredient notes are in order. First, I really do mean that you should have 8 ounces of trimmed cilantro, so make sure that you buy enough that you'll hit that target once it's trimmed. You can find big, inexpensive bags or jars of crispy fried shallots (sometimes called fried red onions) at any Asian or Indian grocery store. In the United States, the more processed and less delicious version is more familiar, especially since it appears atop thousands of green bean casseroles across the nation every Thanksgiving. Meanwhile, all across Asia and the Indian subcontinent, good fried shallots are a year-round pantry staple. **SERVES 8 TO 12**

One 7- to 8-pound/3.18- to 3.63-kilogram leg of lamb, leg bone left in, aitchbone and most of the external fat removed
Kosher salt
1½ dried chipotle chiles
1½ tablespoons coriander seeds
1½ tablespoons fennel seeds, preferably Lucknow
1½ teaspoons black peppercorns
Half a 3-inch cinnamon stick
4 green cardamom pods
3 black cardamom pods
4 whole cloves
1 tablespoon turmeric
⅓ plus ¼ cup water
8 large garlic cloves, peeled
One 2-inch piece fresh ginger, peeled and sliced into thin coins
1 cup plain low-fat yogurt
8 ounces/227 grams trimmed cilantro, including tender stems, washed and dried (see page 39) and coarsely chopped
¼ cup canola oil
2½ cups (6 ounces/170 grams) store-bought fried shallots

Season the lamb generously on all sides with salt. Let stand at room temperature while you make the rub.

Heat a small cast-iron skillet over medium heat. Add the chipotles and toast, turning once, until slightly colored on both sides, about 5 minutes. Remove from the pan and let cool.

Transfer the chipotles to a spice/coffee grinder. Add the coriander seeds, fennel seeds, peppercorns, cinnamon stick, green cardamom, black cardamom, and cloves and finely grind. Transfer to a small bowl. Add the turmeric and ⅓ cup of water and stir to make a smooth paste. Set aside.

In a blender, combine the garlic, ginger, and the ¼ cup water and blend to a smooth paste. Set aside.

Add the yogurt and cilantro to the blender and blend until pureed and uniformly green. Set aside.

In a Dutch oven or large stew pot, heat the oil over medium heat until it shimmers. Add the reserved ginger and garlic paste and cook, stirring, until very fragrant, 2 to 3 minutes. Add the reserved ground spice paste and cook, stirring constantly, until it is very fragrant and the oil begins to separate a little, 8 to 10 minutes.

Stir in the fried shallots and cook, stirring occasionally, until the flavors marry, about 10 minutes; add a little water if the paste begins to stick to the pan. Season to taste with salt. Remove from the heat and let cool completely.

Add the yogurt-cilantro mixture to the cooled spice paste and stir until well combined. Taste and add salt if necessary.

Place the lamb in a large baking dish and rub the paste all over it. Marinate in the refrigerator for at least 24 hours, and up to 36 hours.

Remove the lamb from the refrigerator and let stand at room temperature for 30 minutes. Preheat the oven to 350°F.

Place the lamb, with all the paste, in a turkey roaster or other large roasting pan. Add enough water to cover the bottom of the pan by about ¾ inch. Cover the roasting pan with foil, place in the oven, and roast for 1 hour.

Turn the lamb and baste with the liquid in the pan. Replace the foil and roast for 30 minutes.

Turn and baste the lamb, cover the pan with foil again, and roast for 30 minutes longer.

Remove the foil, turn and baste the lamb again, and cook until fork-tender, about 1½ hours. Transfer the lamb to a cooling rack and let stand for 10 minutes.

Meanwhile, place the roasting pan over two burners and bring the cooking liquid to a boil over medium heat, scraping the bottom of the pan to free any stuck-on bits. Pour into a bowl or a sauceboat. Slice the lamb. Serve with the sauce.

COOKING TIME: 4½ TO 5 HOURS / INACTIVE TIME: 24 TO 36 HOURS FOR MARINATING

CORN BREAD STUFFING for TWELVE

I made this stuffing for Thanksgiving one year using a collection of ingredients I dug out of our pantry. I'd just returned from a trip to New Orleans and I threw in some bell peppers and spicy sausage in an effort to re-create a little of that NOLA vibe. It was such a hit that the kids make me cook it often. We now eat it with some regularity, but somehow it's still no less special when we make it for Thanksgiving every year. This stuffing is so hearty and tasty that it's almost a meal in itself, but it's most delicious when served with roast turkey or chicken.

You can use store-bought or homemade corn bread. Both work beautifully. Be sure the bacon is nice and smoky and the sausage has a bit of heat so the stuffing has a little kick. Linguiça, chorizo, and andouille are all good choices. The amount of cayenne you use will depend on how spicy the sausage is. I use spicy sausage, so half a teaspoon of cayenne is plenty. Next, don't toss that small package of giblets tucked into the cavity of your chicken or turkey! The giblets are the bird's liver, kidneys, gizzard, and heart. No other ingredients can add such richness to the flavor of the stuffing. Lastly, don't wipe the pan clean after the first few steps, as you cook the bacon and then the beef. You want to save the accumulated bits and pieces from each stage to build the flavor of the stuffing. **SERVES 12**

4 ounces/113 grams thick-cut smoky bacon, sliced crosswise into ½-inch-wide pieces (about 1 cup)

2 tablespoons canola oil

1 pound/454 grams lean ground beef

Kosher salt

3 cups minced onions

6 garlic cloves, minced

1 cup sliced scallions (white and green parts)

⅓ pound/151 grams linguiça, chorizo, or andouille sausage, cut lengthwise into quarters and sliced crosswise (about 1¼ cups)

2 cups diced mixed green and red bell peppers

1 cup minced celery

1 cup diced carrots

½ cup finely minced turkey or chicken giblets (see following page)

2 to 3 cups Chicken Stock (page 337) or high-quality store-bought stock

Leaves from 5 thyme sprigs

½ teaspoon cayenne, or to taste

2 pounds/907 grams store-bought or homemade corn bread, crumbled

1 cup coarsely chopped parsley

Place the bacon in a large deep stainless steel skillet, set the pan over medium heat, and cook until the fat is rendered and the bacon is cooked but not crispy, about 8 minutes. Use a slotted spoon to transfer the bacon to a medium bowl. Pour the fat into a small bowl and reserve (do not wipe out the pan).

Pour the oil into the skillet. Add the ground beef, season with salt, and sauté until the beef is nicely caramelized, about 10 minutes. Use a slotted spoon to transfer the beef to the bowl with the bacon. Pour off and discard the fat.

Continued

Place the pan back over medium heat, add the reserved bacon fat, the onions, garlic, and scallions, and sauté until the onions are translucent, about 8 minutes. Add the sausage and cook until heated through, 3 to 5 minutes.

Add the peppers, celery, and carrots and cook until softened, 4 to 6 minutes. Add the giblets, along with the reserved ground beef and bacon, and cook until the giblets lose their pink color, about 4 minutes.

Add 2 cups stock, the thyme, and cayenne and bring to a boil. Season with salt. Add the crumbled corn bread. Reduce the heat, cover, and cook, stirring occasionally, until it all comes together and resembles a moist bread pudding. The longer it stands, the thicker it gets; you don't want it to be dry, so add more stock as needed.

Stir in the parsley and serve from the pan.

Or, if making the stuffing a day before you're going to serve it, transfer it to a glass baking dish, flatten the top surface, cover the dish, and refrigerate it. The following day, uncover the dish and put it in the oven toward the end of the roasting time for the chicken or turkey. Leave the stuffing in the oven while the bird rests and you carve it, then serve hot from the oven.

COOKING TIME: ABOUT 1 HOUR

GIBLETS

Whenever I prepare a whole chicken or turkey at home, I transfer the giblets to a ziplock bag and store them in the freezer for occasions like this recipe or My Dog Shadow's Favorite Dinner (page 161)—just make sure to first remove them from the paper bag they usually come packed in. Before using the gizzard, peel off the silvery membrane.

TOP CHEF AMBROSIA

When I competed on *Top Chef Masters,* most episodes ended with an elimination challenge. On the second episode, the theme for the challenge was iconic 1960s food. My task was to create both a traditional and an updated version of ambrosia salad. Seeing as how I am not a fan of supersweet desserts, nor was I a child in America in the 1960s, I hadn't a clue as to what ambrosia was.

When the first waves of panic had subsided, I looked at the picture they had provided me and began asking anyone who would talk to me what ambrosia tastes like. In case you're as in the dark as I was, traditional ambrosia salad is a concoction of canned fruit, miniature marshmallows, shredded coconut, and a copious amount of whipped "topping" that can be whipped cream but is more typically one of those chemical-laden alternatives. It reminded me in principle of Barkha's much better mango "mousse" (see page 292). Long story short, I prepared a traditional version (which has the advantage, I suppose, of taking less than five minutes to assemble), and for the modern version, I created a sort of deconstructed ambrosia, borrowing from Barkha the tasty trick of stirring some fresh fruit into the cream. Then I began to mentally pack my bags, so sure was I that I'd be kicked off the show at the end of the challenge. In fact, my ambrosia not only didn't lose, it was voted one of the top three, guaranteeing my "safety" that week! I'm glad that I learned what ambrosia salad is—this modern ambrosia is now part of my special-occasion menus. **SERVES 8 TO 10**

FOR THE COCONUT-MANGO ANGLAISE

1¼ cups heavy (whipping) cream

1¼ cups Chaokoh-brand coconut milk (stir well before using)

½ cup whole milk

1 vanilla bean, preferably Tahitian, split lengthwise in half

9 large egg yolks

½ cup (3½ ounces/100 grams) sugar

½ cup canned or frozen mango puree

1 cup orange segments (from about 2 oranges; see following page)

FOR THE WHIPPED CREAM

1½ cups heavy (whipping) cream, well chilled

2 tablespoons sugar

FOR SERVING

Grilled Pineapple with Cracked Black Pepper (page 258), drained

6 peaches, grilled as in the recipe on page 210, peeled and sliced into wide wedges (omit the syrup and ginger)

1 pound/454 grams fresh cherries (about 4 cups), pitted

¼ cup pecans, toasted (see page 76) and chopped

18 to 24 6-inch bamboo skewers

To make the anglaise, in a medium heavy-bottomed saucepan, combine the cream, coconut milk, and milk. Use a paring knife to scrape the seeds from the vanilla bean and add the seeds and the pod to the pan. Bring the mixture to a simmer over medium-low heat, then remove from the heat.

Continued

Meanwhile, whisk the egg yolks and sugar in a medium bowl to blend. Gradually whisk the hot milk mixture into the yolk mixture. Return the custard to the saucepan, place over low heat, and cook, stirring, until the custard thickens and coats the back of the spoon, 5 to 8 minutes; when you run your finger across the back of the spoon, the trail your finger makes should remain. Do not allow the custard to boil.

Remove from the heat and stir in the mango puree. Strain the sauce through a fine-mesh strainer or chinois into a bowl. Cover and chill until very cold. (The anglaise can be made up to 1 day in advance.)

No more than 1 hour before serving, prepare the whipped cream: Place the cream in a large bowl and beat with a handheld mixer until frothy and beginning to thicken. Add the sugar and continue to beat until soft peaks form when the beaters are lifted. Cover and refrigerate until needed.

Slice each pineapple ring into 6 pieces (or, if you grilled wedges, slice into 1½-inch pieces). Thread the pineapple, peaches, and cherries onto the skewers.

Just before serving, stir the orange segments into the anglaise. Pour the anglaise into a serving bowl and sprinkle with the pecans. Place the whipped cream in another serving bowl. Arrange the skewers on a platter and serve.

COOKING TIME: ABOUT 1 HOUR / INACTIVE TIME: ABOUT 4 HOURS CHILLING TIME

PREPARING CITRUS SEGMENTS

When you cut away the membrane that surrounds each delicate segment of citrus fruits (called *suprêmes* by chefs), you get a big burst of citrus flavor with every bite.

Use a sharp thin-bladed knife to cut off just enough of the top and bottom of the citrus to expose the flesh. Set the fruit cut side down on a cutting board and slice off the peel and bitter white pith, following the curve of the fruit with the knife. Holding the fruit over a bowl to catch the segments, cut the segments away from the thin membranes holding them together, letting them fall into the bowl. If the recipe instructs you to save the juice as well as the segments, when all of the segments are cut away from the membranes, squeeze the membranes over the bowl, then discard them.

COCONUT LAYER CAKE (BIBINCA)

This classic Goan Portuguese cake, known as *bibinca*, is a real showstopper. This recipe comes from my great-grandmother, and my lovely wife still makes it for me every Christmas. My great-grandmother made it often when I was a kid, and to this day I remember her technique vividly. She had only a wood-fired oven, so she'd cook the first layer of cake by placing the pan directly on top of the stove. For the subsequent layers, she basically rigged up a semi-portable broiler: She'd pour in more batter, cover the pan, and then cover the lid with live hot coals. I can never eat this cake without remembering her.

Traditionally the cake is made up of seven coconut-flavored, caramel-colored layers; the batter for each one is ladled on top of the one before and broiled. Achieving the most delicious results depends on a couple of ingredients. First, the ghee: It's absolutely critical to the flavor of this cake. I don't recommend store-bought, because in my experience it's not as flavorful as what I make myself. And making ghee is really quite simple (see page 342). It can be done anywhere from an hour to many months in advance, and once you have ghee in your refrigerator, you'll soon find many other ways to use it. The other crucial ingredient here is the coconut milk, which has to be Chaokoh brand (see page 27). **MAKES ONE 8-INCH CAKE; SERVES 12 TO 16**

¾ cup plus 1½ tablespoons (4 ounces/ 113 grams) all-purpose flour
2¼ cups (1 pound/454 grams) sugar
½ teaspoon freshly grated nutmeg

One 13.5-fluid-ounce can Chaokoh-brand coconut milk (stir well before using)
10 large egg yolks, lightly beaten
¾ cup Ghee (page 342), melted

Place the flour in a large bowl. Add the sugar and nutmeg and whisk to combine. Add the coconut milk and stir with a wooden spoon or spatula until the sugar has dissolved and the mixture is smooth. Add the egg yolks and stir until the batter is thoroughly blended and has no lumps. Let rest at room temperature for 20 minutes.

Set an oven rack 6 to 8 inches away from the heat source and preheat the broiler to low.

Heat a heavy-bottomed nonstick 8-inch round cake pan over low heat. Add 2 tablespoons ghee and turn the pan to coat the bottom and sides completely. Remove the pan from the heat and ladle in enough batter to form an even layer (about ⅛ inch deep) that completely covers the bottom of the pan. Place the pan over low heat again and cook until the batter begins to set and the edges get a little color, 4 to 7 minutes. As the batter cooks, gently move the pan in a circular motion over the burner so that the entire bottom of the pan is heated evenly.

(Alternatively, you can place a cast-iron skillet big enough to hold the cake pan over medium heat and place the cake pan in it to diffuse the heat evenly.)

Transfer the pan to the broiler and cook until the batter is golden on top, 3 to 5 minutes.

Remove the pan from the oven and brush the top of the layer with ghee, making sure to completely coat it right up to the edges of the pan. Use a ladle to add just enough batter to completely cover the first cake layer with a thin layer, gently tilting the pan so that the batter spreads evenly (this is a little like making crepes). Place the pan under the broiler and cook until the batter sets and is golden brown, 4 to 6 minutes.

Remove the pan from the oven and repeat to form a third layer. Repeat 4 more times to make 6 or 7 cake layers in all, using all the remaining batter and most or all of the ghee. After the last layer has browned, remove the cake from the oven and set on a cooling rack (do not coat the final layer with ghee).

If you're serving the cake right away, let it cool for about 10 minutes, then run a thin knife around the outside of the cake and unmold it onto a serving plate. Slice and serve. This cake is best served unadorned.

Or, to serve later, as I always do, let the cake cool completely in the pan, cover the pan, and store in the refrigerator for up to 2 days. A little while before you're ready to serve it, place the pan in a low oven to warm up a bit. (I like to put it in the cooling oven after I've pulled out the roast I'm serving for dinner and have turned the oven off). Do not try to unmold the cake before it is warm, or it will stick and possibly tear. When the cake is warm, unmold and serve.

COOKING TIME: ABOUT 1¼ HOURS / INACTIVE TIME: 30 MINUTES FOR RESTING AND COOLING

KACHUMBER KOOLER

This great summer drink was inspired by the ubiquitous North Indian chopped salad of cucumbers, chiles, onions, tomatoes, cilantro, and lime called *kachumber*. One day when I was preparing a version of it at Tabla, it occurred to me that with a little tweaking and a lot of gin, it'd be a pretty fantastic warm-weather cocktail. At the restaurant we usually use a juicer to achieve a really smooth and elegant result, but for backyard barbecues at home, I just pull out the blender. The only thing you really want to think about is the chiles. First, make sure to use green chiles—red ones will mess with the color of the drink. And, as ever, if you want a spicier drink, as I almost always do, leave in the chile seeds; for less of a kick, remove some or all of the seeds. **MAKES 10 DRINKS**

½ hothouse English cucumber or 2 Persian cucumbers, coarsely chopped, plus 10 cucumber slices for garnish

1 moderately hot chile, such as Calistan or serrano, coarsely chopped

1 cup ice cubes, plus more for serving

1 large bunch cilantro, trimmed, washed and dried (see page 39), and coarsely chopped

20 fluid ounces Bombay gin

5 fluid ounces fresh lime juice (from 7 to 8 limes)

5 fluid ounces Simple Syrup (page 344)

10 lime slices for garnish

Place the chopped cucumber and chile in a blender, add the ice, and pulse just until the ice is broken up. Add the cilantro and pulse until it is crushed well and slightly mashed; you want some texture, so don't let the mixture get too smooth.

Transfer the mixture to a large bottle with a lid. Add the gin, lime juice, and simple syrup, cover, and shake vigorously until very well blended.

Fill ten double rocks glasses with ice and use a cocktail strainer to strain over the cocktail. Garnish each with a slice of cucumber and a lime slice. Serve.

COOKING TIME: ABOUT 10 MINUTES

CHANGING IT UP

For a smoother, less rustic result, use a juicer to juice the cucumber with the cilantro and the chile, then blend everything as instructed.

Basics

CHICKEN STOCK

Use chicken wings, backs, necks, and skin. Yes, skin! It is rich in gelatin, which will add significant body to the stock. **MAKES ABOUT 4 QUARTS**

2¼ pounds/1 kilogram chicken bones and
   parts
6 quarts water
3 cups chopped white onions
2 cups chopped celery
1 carrot, cut crosswise in half
1 medium leek, coarsely chopped and
   washed well

1 garlic head, loose skin removed and
   (unpeeled) cloves coarsely chopped
½ cup thickly sliced unpeeled fresh ginger
2 bay leaves
4 whole cloves
1 tablespoon black peppercorns

Put the chicken bones and parts and water in a large stockpot and slowly bring to a boil, uncovered, over medium-high heat. Skim the froth from the surface. Put the onions, celery, carrot, leek, garlic, ginger, bay leaves, cloves, and peppercorns in the pot and return to a boil. Reduce the heat and simmer, uncovered, for 3 hours.

Strain the stock through a mesh strainer into a large bowl, pressing on the solids with the back of a spoon; discard the solids. Cool completely.

Store in an airtight container in the refrigerator for up to 2 days or in the freezer for up to 1 month.

COOKING TIME: ABOUT 4 HOURS

BEEF STOCK

To make beef stock, use 2¼ pounds/1 kilogram beef or veal bones in place of the chicken bones and simmer for about 6 hours.

Alternatively, use a pressure cooker: Follow the recipe as written, taking care to not go above the "fill to" line inside the pressure cooker. Once the stock is at a simmer, seal the pressure cooker. Follow the manufacturer's instructions to bring it up to pressure (it will begin to steam) and cook for 1 hour, adjusting the heat as necessary to keep steady pressure. Remove the pressure cooker from the heat and let stand, covered, until the pressure releases.

Open the cooker and continue as directed above.

WHITE FISH STOCK

I learned this method for making fish stock from a Japanese chef I met a few years ago. The water is brought very slowly to a gentle simmer and kept there for 45 minutes. The result is an amazing stock that is clear and has a clean, fresh flavor. I'll never go back to the bad old days when I would bring a fish stock to a boil as quickly as possible. The key is the just-below-boiling temperature—you never want this to come above 199°F (93°C)—so be sure to stick around the kitchen while making this. You'll be glad you did.   **MAKES ABOUT 3½ QUARTS**

2 pounds/907 grams bones and heads from white fish such as snapper, bass, cod, flounder, fluke, and/or turbot, gills and bloody spots removed, cut into pieces

3 tablespoons canola oil

2 cups chopped white onions

4 celery stalks, including leaves, chopped

1 large leek, coarsely chopped and washed well

4 large unpeeled garlic cloves, halved

2 bay leaves

3 whole cloves

4 quarts water

2 cups white wine

Two 6-inch rosemary sprigs

Four 4-inch thyme sprigs

Twelve 3-inch cilantro stems

Place the fish bones and heads in a large bowl, add cold water to cover by 2 inches, and set aside to soak for 1 hour. Drain thoroughly.

Heat the oil in an 8- to 9-quart heavy-bottomed stockpot over medium-high heat until it shimmers. Add the onions and cook, stirring, until softened but not colored, about 3 minutes. Stir in the celery, leek, and garlic and cook until softened, about 5 minutes.

Add the bay leaves, cloves, and the reserved fish bones and heads and stir well to coat. Add the water, wine, rosemary, thyme, and cilantro, reduce the heat to medium, and heat very slowly until the liquid reaches 199°F on an instant-read thermometer. As soon as the liquid reaches temperature (you'll see wisps of steam rising from the pot), reduce the heat to low and cook for 45 minutes. Don't let the stock come to a simmer at any time. Skim the foam from the surface frequently.

Ladle the stock through a mesh strainer lined with several layers of cheesecloth or a coffee filter into a large bowl (do not pour the stock and bones out into the strainer, or the stock will become cloudy.) Discard the solids. Cool completely.

Store in an airtight container in the refrigerator for up to 2 days or in the freezer for up to 1 month.

COOKING TIME: ABOUT 1½ HOURS / INACTIVE TIME: 1 HOUR FOR SOAKING THE FISH BONES

VEGETABLE STOCK

MAKES 3 QUARTS

2 pounds/907 grams white onions, coarsely chopped (about 5 cups)

1 bunch celery, including leaves, coarsely chopped

3 large carrots, halved lengthwise and sliced ½ inch thick

½ garlic head, roots and excess papery skin discarded, cut horizontally in half

1 large fennel bulb, with stalks and fronds, coarsely chopped

1 large leek, coarsely chopped and washed well

2 whole cloves

1½ teaspoons black peppercorns

One 6-inch rosemary sprig

Two 4-inch thyme sprigs

4 parsley sprigs

½ cup white wine

1 tablespoon kosher salt

2 bay leaves

4 quarts water

Place all of the ingredients in an 8-quart stockpot and bring to a boil over medium-high heat. Reduce the heat and simmer, uncovered, for 45 minutes.

Strain the stock through a mesh strainer into a large bowl, pressing on the solids with the back of a spoon; discard the solids. Cool completely.

Store in an airtight container in the refrigerator for up to 2 days or in the freezer for up to 1 month.

COOKING TIME: ABOUT 1¼ HOURS

TAMARIND
PASTE

MAKES ABOUT 4 CUPS

One 14-ounce/397-gram block tamarind   5 cups water

Tear the tamarind block into several chunks and put them in a small saucepan. Add 3 cups of the water, bring to a simmer over medium heat, and simmer until the tamarind is soft, 30 to 35 minutes, occasionally mashing the pulp against the side of the pan with a wooden spoon.

Remove the pan from the heat and let stand for 30 minutes.

Use your fingers to work the pulp free of the seeds and fibers. Strain the mixture through a ricer or sieve into a bowl, adding the remaining 2 cups water a little at a time and pressing hard on the solids with the back of the wooden spoon to extract all of the pulp.

Transfer the strained pulp back to the pan, making sure to scrape the pulp from the underside of the ricer or sieve, and bring the mixture to a vigorous boil. Remove from the heat and let cool completely.

Transfer the paste to a glass or plastic container with a tight-fitting lid. Store in the refrigerator for up to 1 month or in the freezer for up to 3 months.

COOKING TIME: ABOUT 1½ HOURS

COOKED BEANS or CHICKPEAS

The cooking time for all dried beans and legumes, and especially for long-cooking ones like chickpeas, can vary tremendously depending on the age of the beans. The older they are, the longer they take to cook. When possible, buy them from a busy store with lots of turnover; that's where you'll have the best chance of getting beans that haven't been sitting around for months. **MAKES 5 TO 6 CUPS**

1 pound/454 grams dried beans, such as Great Northern or other white beans, or chickpeas

1 small onion, quartered

1 bay leaf

Kosher salt

Place the beans in a stew pot or large saucepan and cover with cold water by 3 inches. Bring to a boil over medium heat and boil gently for 1 minute. Remove the pot from the heat, cover, and set aside for 1 hour.

Drain the beans and return them to the pot. Add the onion, bay leaf, and water to cover by 1½ inches. Bring to a boil over medium heat. Skim the foam from the surface. Reduce the heat and simmer until the beans are tender, 50 minutes to 1 hour for white beans and 1 to 1½ hours for chickpeas, adding water if necessary to keep the beans submerged. Remove the pan from the heat, stir in salt to taste, and set aside, uncovered, until cool.

Store the beans in their liquid in an airtight container in the refrigerator for up to 4 days or in the freezer for up to 1 month.

COOKING TIME: 1 HOUR TO 1¼ HOURS FOR WHITE BEANS, 1¼ TO 1¾ HOURS FOR CHICKPEAS, OR 20 TO 25 MINUTES IN THE PRESSURE COOKER FOR WHITE BEANS AND 45 TO 50 MINUTES FOR CHICKPEAS / INACTIVE TIME: 1 HOUR FOR SOAKING (IF NOT USING THE PRESSURE COOKER)

PRESSURE-COOKER FRIENDLY

Beans and chickpeas can be cooked in a fraction of the time in a pressure cooker, and there is no need to soak them (if you do soak them, however, note that they'll take even less time to cook). Place the dried beans or chickpeas in the pressure cooker, add the onion, bay leaf, and water to cover (do not fill the cooker more than halfway). Bring to a simmer. Seal the pressure cooker.

Follow the manufacturer's instructions to bring it up to pressure (it will begin to steam) and cook for 4 to 6 minutes for navy beans; 6 to 8 minutes for Great Northern beans or cannellini beans, and 30 to 35 minutes for chickpeas, adjusting the heat as necessary to keep steady pressure. Remove the pressure cooker from the heat and let stand, covered, until the pressure releases.

Open the cooker and continue as directed above.

GHEE

Making ghee is one of the easiest techniques in the world. Ghee is basically the Indian version of clarified butter, but it offers so much more than its milder cousin. Longer cooking—until the water in the butter evaporates and the milk solids separate from the remaining liquid and turn golden—gives it an intensely buttery, almost nutty flavor. That specific taste is critical in recipes like the Coconut Layer Cake (page 331), and ghee can be used in place of butter or oil in any type of cooking. Because it doesn't contain any milk solids, which burn at high temperatures, ghee can be heated just like you would vegetable oil. Because of its flavor, versatility, and shelf life—it'll keep for up to 6 months in the refrigerator—ghee is a staple in my home kitchen.

For best results, use a pan that is large enough that when the butter melts, it won't fill the pan more than halfway. Don't skim the butter while it cooks, because the toasted milk solids are what give the ghee its flavor. And do not stir the butter—at all!—during cooking. The milk solids will separate from the liquid and form a sort of a crust on top. Their color will tell you when the ghee is done, so keep an eye on the pan, but resist the urge to touch it. Cook the ghee until the solids are lightly colored and the ghee itself is golden blond. You can certainly keep cooking it until the crust is chestnut colored; the ghee will be browner and the flavor will be deeper. It's hard to estimate exactly how long it'll take you to cook the ghee because so much depends on the size and weight of the pan you use, but it typically takes about 30 minutes from beginning to end to get to the point described below using a wide medium saucepan.   **MAKES ABOUT 1½ CUPS**

**1 pound/454 grams salted butter, cut into
  1-inch cubes**

Place the butter in a wide medium saucepan and heat over medium heat, without stirring, until the butter melts. There will be foam on the surface; do not touch it. Bring the butter to a boil and boil until the foam on the top forms a thin crust. Then continue to boil until the crust turns a blond color.

Remove the pan from the heat and strain the ghee through a mesh sieve lined with 2 or 3 layers of cheesecloth or a coffee filter into a heatproof jar or glass measuring cup. Let cool to room temperature, then cover and store in the refrigerator for up to 6 months.

COOKING TIME: ABOUT 30 MINUTES

SIMPLE
SYRUP

MAKES 1 CUP

1 cup (7 ounces/198 grams) sugar   1 cup water

Put the sugar and water in a small saucepan and stir to combine. Bring to a simmer over medium-high heat, then reduce the heat and simmer until the sugar is completely dissolved and the syrup is slightly thickened, about 3 minutes. Remove from the heat and let cool completely.

Transfer the syrup to a glass or plastic container with a tight-fitting lid. Store in the refrigerator for up to 2 months.

COOKING TIME: ABOUT 10 MINUTES

Sources

Listed below are my favorite retailers and resources for information and ingredients. If you can't find what you're looking for from any of these, do an online search and you'll surely find a good source. Note as well that most of the less-familiar ingredients I use are staples in most local Asian and Indian grocery stores.

Anson Mills
ansonmills.com
803-467-4122
Rice and grains, including rice grits

The Chile Guy
thechileguy.com
800-869-9218; 505-867-4251
Dried chiles

The Chile Shop
thechileshop.com
505-983-6080
Dried chiles

Costco
costco.com
800-774-2678
Black pepper, chile flakes, cloves, paprika, and cayenne

DeBragga
debragga.com
212-924-1311
Heritage pork, beef, veal, and lamb; demi-glace

Heritage Foods USA
heritagefoodsusa.com
718-389-0985
Heritage pork, beef, poultry, lamb, and goat

Niman Ranch
nimanranch.com
510-808-0330
Beef, pork, and lamb

Patel Brothers
patelbros.com
630-213-2222
Green raisins, wet kokum, dals, Indian bay leaves, and Lucknow fennel and other spices; fresh curry leaves in stores

Pat LaFrieda Meat Purveyors
lafrieda.com
800-876-0898
Beef, veal, lamb, and pork

Penzeys
penzeys.com
800-741-7787
Spices and dried chiles

Pierless Fish Corp.
pierlessfish.com
855-203-8596; 718-222-4441
Fish and shellfish

Pure Bred Lamb by Elysian Fields Farm
purebredlamb.com
724-852-2535
Lamb

Seafood Watch from the Monterey Bay Aquarium
seafoodwatch.org
This website and the smartphone app from the Monterey Bay Aquarium provide up-to-date information on the best, sustainable choices for fish and shellfish.

SOS Chefs
sos-chefs.com
212-505-5813
Lucknow fennel, fennel pollen, green raisins, and dried chiles

The Spice House
thespicehouse.com
847-328-3711
Spices, dried chiles, and demi-glace

Acknowledgments

Writing a book is definitely not a one-person endeavor. First and foremost, I owe so much to Barkha, my wife and best friend, whose support for my vice of cooking and food helps give me the freedom to create delicious dishes for our family, friends, and even strangers at tailgates. Thank you for letting me be the chef and cook I am. My sons, Peter and Justin, are two amazing young men whose love for food and eating make my life a joy and who have inspired many of the dishes in this book.

I also want to thank the following artisans who contributed to making this book possible and for making it better.

Judy Pray, for your insights, dedication, and support. You delivered everything you promised and more to make the writing of this book an amazing experience. Michelle Ishay-Cohen, you and your artistic vision were a pleasure to work with. Judith Craig Sutton, whose meticulous copyediting made me see things differently. Lia Ronnen, for your support, vision, and guidance. Also at Artisan, Sibylle Kazeroid, Nancy Murray, and Allison McGeehon.

The very talented Lauren Volo, whose work blew me away and whose keen photographer's eye and suggestions for the pictures made the food even more appetizing. Kristine Trevino, amazing understated prop stylist, thank you for understanding my quirkiness.

Ty Kotz, a true buddy, chef de cuisine, and a huge asset to me in the kitchen always, especially while cooking the Upma and Rendang on *Top Chef Masters*.

David Black, friend, agent, and "good people," who convinced me I should do this book and who is always there when I need him.

Zia Sheikh, an asset on every team I have had, thanks for your help during the photo shoot, prepping and weighing out everything I needed for the recipes. Quincy Garner, for coming in on your own time to assist with cooking the food for the photo shoot. Sam Lesser, my go-to guy for ingredients, prep, and support during the shoot. The entire team at White Street, especially Christine Cole, Jason Lawless, Dan Abrams, and Dave Zinczenko, for your support. My sous-chefs at North End Grill, Adam Harvey, James Kim, Chris Robertson, Matthew McCarthy, and Jay Lakhwani.

Sameer Seth and Yash Bhanage, my partners at the Bombay Canteen, for enjoying and supporting my cooking.

Danny Meyer, for giving me the opportunity to play with charcoal and wood fire, which have influenced my cooking.

I want to thank a few wonderful people and organizations that made the production of this book a lot easier, and help to make every day in my kitchen a little more joyful.

Le Creuset, for providing some of the cookware used in the shoot; Lisa Callaghan and All-Clad, for providing me with my favorite home and restaurant pots and pans to cook with and for your generous donations of pots for the shoot; Libeco-Lagae, for the beautiful Belgian linens used in the photographs; GIR, the producer of my favorite silicone spatulas and spice grinder that make cooking so much easier; Bobby Demasco at Pierless Fish, for always supplying me with the freshest possible fish; Mark Pastore and Pat LaFreida Jr. from Pat LaFreida Meat Purveyors for always providing me with the best meat products; and all the friends, farmers, family, and acquaintances who have inspired the dishes in this book.

Marah Stets, I never would have thought it possible to write a book with someone in a different city, let alone state. Your meticulous love for detail and passion for writing has made this a much better book than I would have thought it could be.

Index

Note: Page numbers in *italics* refer to illustrations.

Conversions

WEIGHTS		VOLUME		
US/UK	METRIC	AMERICAN	IMPERIAL	METRIC
¼ oz	7 g	¼ tsp		1.25 ml
½ oz	15 g	½ tsp		2.5 ml
1 oz	30 g	1 tsp		5 ml
2 oz	55 g	½ tbsp (1½ tsp)		7.5 ml
3 oz	85 g	1 tbsp (3 tsp)		15 ml
4 oz	115 g	¼ cup (4 tbsp)	2 fl oz	60 ml
5 oz	140 g	⅓ cup (5 tbsp)	2½ fl oz	75 ml
6 oz	170 g	½ cup (8 tbsp)	4 fl oz	125 ml
7 oz	200 g	⅔ cup (10 tbsp)	5 fl oz	150 ml
8 oz (½ lb)	225 g	¾ cup (12 tbsp)	6 fl oz	175 ml
9 oz	255 g	1 cup (16 tbsp)	8 fl oz	250 ml
10 oz	285 g	1¼ cups	10 fl oz	300 ml
11 oz	310 g	1½ cups	12 fl oz	350 ml
12 oz	340 g	1 pint (2 cups)	16 fl oz	500 ml
13 oz	370 g	2½ cups	20 fl oz (1 pint)	625 ml
14 oz	400 g	5 cups	40 fl oz (1 qt)	1.25 l
15 oz	425 g			
16 oz (1 lb)	450 g			

OVEN TEMPERATURE

	°F	°C	GAS MARK
VERY COOL	250–275	130–140	½–1
COOL	300	148	2
WARM	325	163	3
MEDIUM	350	177	4
MEDIUM HOT	375–400	190–204	5–6
HOT	425	218	7
VERY HOT	450–475	232–245	8–9